How to Use Computers to Improve Your Chess

Christian Kongsted

First published in the UK by Gambit Publications Ltd 2003

ISBN 1 904600 02 6

DISTRIBUTION:
Worldwide (except USA): Central Books Ltd, 99 Wallis Rd, London E9 5LN.
Tel +44 (0)20 8986 4854 Fax +44 (0)20 8533 5821.
E-mail: orders@Centralbooks.com
USA: BHB International, Inc., 302 West North 2nd Street, Seneca, SC 29678, USA.

For all other enquiries (including a full list of all Gambit Chess titles) please contact the publishers, Gambit Publications Ltd, P.O. Box 32640, London W14 0JN.
E-mail: info@gambitbooks.com
Or visit the GAMBIT web site at http://www.gambitbooks.com

Edited by Graham Burgess
Typeset by John Nunn
Printed in Great Britain by The Cromwell Press, Trowbridge, Wilts.
Front cover image by Wolff Morrow

10 9 8 7 6 5 4 3 2 1

Gambit Publications Ltd
Managing Director: GM Murray Chandler
Chess Director: GM John Nunn
Editorial Director: FM Graham Burgess
German Editor: WFM Petra Nunn

Contents

Part 2: Improving with the Computer

Symbols

+	check
++	double check
#	checkmate
!!	brilliant move
!	good move
!?	interesting move
?!	dubious move
?	bad move
??	blunder
+−	White is winning
±	White is much better
⩲	White is slightly better
=	equal position
⩱	Black is slightly better
∓	Black is much better
−+	Black is winning
Wch	world championship
Ch	championship
Cht	team championship
1-0	the game ends in a win for White
½-½	the game ends in a draw
0-1	the game ends in a win for Black
(D)	see next diagram

Introduction

This book is aimed at players who are interested in improving their chess and want to get some advice on how to use a computer to achieve this aim. Personally, I have been interested in computer chess since 1982, when I was ten years old and my father gave me my first chess computer. It was a Fidelity Chess Challenger about the size of a pocket chess board, and it had two diodes, one for 'Check' and one for 'I lose'. While it was thinking, the light switched between these two diodes until it finally made a move, and I remember being fascinated by looking at the diodes. One move before being checkmated the computer would usually realize that it was losing and light up the 'I lose' diode.

By modern standards the Chess Challenger was laughably weak, and within a year it had stopped being a challenging opponent for a 10-year-old boy. Fortunately, the development of the computers seemed to fit my own development as a child. Some years later I got a Novag Super Constellation chess computer, which was much stronger than the Chess Challenger and allegedly played at an Elo level around 1600-1700. I battled with it for some years, and later, in 1992 my father bought a Mephisto Amsterdam, which

was probably 300-400 Elo points stronger again. In those ten years the computers had improved by nearly 1000 points and the development was still going on. Chess computers were getting stronger and stronger.

During the 1990s, I had a long pause from tournament chess, and when I came back to the chess world around 1999, everything had changed. In the 1980s and early 1990s, I believe people were mostly using computer programs for playing some occasional games, and at that time the fight between club players and computers was still more or less equal.

Now computers can be used for a lot of things apart from just playing. Databases have made it a lot easier to prepare for a game and study openings. Internet chess clubs have popped up, and chess programs have achieved a strength comparable to that of a grandmaster.

I became interested in the many possibilities and started to search for some books about how to get the best out of the new tools. To my surprise, I found no literature that covered the question in a satisfying way. Only a few books included a chapter about this subject.

Just then I felt like I had stumbled upon a gap in chess literature, which I have now attempted to fill. I believe the issue of chess and computers deserves more than a chapter in a book. For the serious chess-player, the computer is currently the most important companion (maybe except for board and pieces!). Only a very small number of players in the world elite get by without making use of the new possibilities.

My own serious experiments with computer analysis started when I took part in some correspondence chess tournaments. During games in the ICCF (International Correspondence Chess Federation) Master Class I realized that most players seemed to be very 'inspired' by the computer. Often it looked like they would just play the move Fritz suggested, even in positions where the program was of no use. In correspondence chess circles these players are called 'postmen', because their main function is to send the move that some program has calculated for them.

After playing in some correspondence chess tournaments, I felt that there was a serious need for a discussion about how to use a computer program as a partner in analysis. During this period I gradually developed a better understanding of the strengths and weaknesses of computer play, and I have now used my knowledge in writing this book.

The main problem when using computer programs for playing or analysis is that they do not explain anything to

you. They just take your pieces if you put them *en prise*. Even though their strength is impressive, it is not at all obvious how the average chess-player can use them for improvement. Thus, I seek to answer exactly this question on these pages.

I have divided the book into two main parts. Part 1 is mainly about how computer programs work. After a brief historical overview in Chapter 1, the second and third chapters give some insights into how computers 'think'. The information in this chapter will be useful later. For instance, when performing computer-assisted analysis, it is of great importance to have some knowledge of the processes that lead a computer to recommend a certain move. Especially Chapter 3, about the weaknesses of the computers, will give a better idea of when to trust computer analysis and when to rely more on one's own intuition. Finally in Chapter 4, I have included a discussion of how to beat computer programs. Knowledge of the computer's weaknesses described in Chapter 3 is clearly an essential basis for having any chance of beating a modern computer program.

In Part 2, I concentrate on how to improve various aspects of one's own play with the help of the computer. First of all, in Chapter 5 I present an overview of some of the software available, and in Chapter 6 there is a discussion of how to use the combined forces of the human brain and a chess program for performing computer-assisted analysis. Chapters 7-9 focus on how to improve various areas of one's play by using databases and by means of playing out positions against the computer. Chapter 10 is about Internet chess and how to integrate this in chess training, and finally in Chapter 11, a few words about chess and computers in the future.

For ease of reference, I have used ChessBase programs for the examples throughout the book. This does in no way mean that alternative programs are inferior. Other companies like Convekta (Chess Assistant), Lokasoft (Chess Tiger) and Ubisoft (Chessmaster) have products which are of similar quality. The reason why I have included these examples is that I would like this book to be a useful and concrete guide, and I did not want to leave the reader without any clue as to how to perform specific operations with a chess program. Most modern computer programs come without a really good manual, and this leaves the user to explore things for himself by using the help files in the program. I believe that there is a need for better guidance than that. However, a detailed explanation of all programs and their functions would have been too space-consuming, and it is also most unlikely that the book would have been very interesting if I had done

that. Thus, I hope the reader will understand and appreciate this arrangement.

I would like to thank my family and my girlfriend Michela Tenze for supporting me during my work with this book, helping me reading the proofs and commenting on the manuscript. During my work I have also had the pleasure of meeting the Danish programmer Steen Suurballe and to play and analyse with his excellent program Gandalf. Our discussions about computer chess have been going on for months and they have given me a lot of insight into the possibilities and limitations that exist in the fascinating world of computer chess. I am sure that this has made the book a much more interesting read. Moreover, I would like to thank my editor Graham Burgess for giving me the possibility of writing this book and for a productive dialogue about which topics to include in this book and how to deal with them.

Finally, I should mention that I have used a computer with an AMD 850 MHz processor and 640 Mb RAM, with 256 Mb RAM used for hash tables for all computer test examples in this book.

Christian Kongsted
Copenhagen, March 2003

1 The History of Computer Chess

Chess masters used to come to computer chess tournaments to laugh. Now they come to watch. Soon they will come to learn.
MONTY NEWBORN, computer scientist, 1977

Since the middle ages, man has been obsessed with the idea of creating a being that could take simple decisions on its own and perform certain operations independently. These endeavours have the same fascination as the attempts to create gold from metals, to find the elixir of life, which would guarantee eternal life, or to construct a *'perpetuum mobile'* – a machine that would produce energy out of nothing.

While the early attempts were mainly focused on modelling simple human processes like constructing a machine that was able to write some simple sentences, attention soon shifted to creating a 'thinking' machine. The first machines that performed simple tasks had been a big success, and thus there was reason to believe that a 'living robot' would create a big sensation.

The actual idea of a chess-playing machine predated the technological possibilities by nearly 200 years. In 1769 Baron Wolfgang von Kempelen created the first chess automaton, which he called 'the Turk'. The construction looked like a large desk with a chessboard on its top. The Turk was a human-like figure dressed as a Turk with a turban on his head and a very long pipe in his hand. Before each game von Kempelen would open the two doors of the machine and a long drawer in the bottom so that everyone could make sure that it was a purely mechanical construction and that no person could be hiding in there. After this presentation the doors were closed and the Turk made the first move with its free arm, accompanied by a lot of noise and clattering of machinery. Every tenth move von Kempelen would wind the machine – so as to make sure it did not suddenly stop playing.

The whole construction was, of course, a hoax. Inside the machine a strong player of small stature was concealed, and he was playing from within his hiding place. The Turk became a great success and was exhibited in several European cities. In 1809 it played a game against Napoleon I, which it won. After the game the French Emperor got so angry and felt so humiliated that he knocked the pieces off the board. Being a mediocre chess-player himself, Napoleon was no match for the well-known Austrian master Allgaier who operated the machine at the time.

Other famous people were fascinated by the mysterious Turk. Edgar Allan Poe tried to solve the mystery, and he wrote an essay about the Turk. The American writer did not get completely to the bottom of the issue. He wrongly thought that there was a man placed inside the Turk itself and this man would move the pieces by putting his arm into the arm of the Turk. However, Poe found out that during that period the machine was operated by a man called Schlumberger, who was a strong chess-player and at the same time a man of small stature. Schlumberger was always there before and after the exhibition, but never during a game. Moreover, during a period when Schlumberger was suffering from illness, all exhibitions and games of the Turk was cancelled.

The First Mechanical Machine

The simple principle of putting a man inside a box was employed in several later 'chess machines', but in 1890 the Spanish scientist Torres y Quevedo created the first real mechanical machine, which was able to play some simple endgame positions with king and rook against king. However, it could sometimes take more than 50 moves to mate the opponent's king,

and thus the machine was mainly a curiosity. It can still be seen in the *Universidad Politécnica* in Madrid.

The real breakthrough in teaching a machine to play chess came with the development of the electronic digital machine. The first computers were invented with particular purposes in mind, and mainly to solve mathematical problems. During the Second World War one of the first computers, Colossus, helped to break the German 'Enigma' codes. This was done by a group of cryptoanalysts and computer scientists in Great Britain; the group included several strong chess-players and scientists with an interest in machine intelligence. One of them was the British mathematician, Alan Turing who has become famous for devising a test for intelligence in computers, whereby a human is allowed to interrogate a computer program via a teletype. If the human cannot tell that he is communicating with a program, then the behaviour of the machine can be said to be intelligent.

Turing also constructed his own chess-playing program, but he did so without a computer, making all the necessary calculations on paper. He designed a simple evaluation function for chess in which material was the dominant factor. If material was even, then a few simple positional factors were used to decide which move to make. These were: mobility, piece safety, king safety, castling possibilities, and pluses for each rank a pawn advanced, and a bonus for check or mate threats. All lines were examined to a depth of two plies (i.e. half-moves), but the search was extended if there were 'considerable' moves in the final position. Only when a 'dead' position was reached would the analysis stop. A 'dead' position was defined as a position where there was no possibility of capturing an undefended piece, recapturing a piece, capturing a defended piece with one of lesser value, or giving mate.

As all calculations were made by Turing himself, it would usually take around 10 minutes to decide upon a move. The following game is an example of how the program performed against Alick Glennie, a weak chessplayer.

Turing's machine (simulation) – A. Glennie

Manchester 1952

1 e4 e5 2 ♘c3 ♘f6 3 d4 ♗b4 4 ♘f3 d6 5 ♗d2 ♘c6 6 d5 ♘d4 7 h4 ♗g4 8 a4 ♘xf3+ 9 gxf3 ♗h5 10 ♗b5+ c6 11 dxc6 0-0 12 cxb7 ♖b8 13 ♗a6 ♕a5 14 ♕e2 ♘d7 15 ♖g1 ♘c5 16 ♖g5 ♗g6 17 ♗b5 ♘xb7 18 0-0-0 ♘c5 19 ♗c6 ♖fc8 20 ♗d5 ♗xc3 21 ♗xc3 ♕xa4 22 ♔d2 ♘e6 23 ♖g4 ♘d4 24 ♕d3 ♘b5 25 ♗b3 ♕a6 26 ♗c4 ♗h5 27 ♖g3 ♕a4 28 ♗xb5 ♕xb5 29 ♕xd6 ♖d8 0-1

Although the quality of the play in Turing's simulation was not impressive, Turing's ideas paved the way for

later experiments with programs running on a computer. With the birth of computer technology it became clear that the machines could perform mathematical calculations with a blinding speed. Even some of the first computers could perform in a few hours calculations that would take a whole lifetime for several people dedicated to the task. Hence chess programs running on a computer could be expected to play much better than Turing's simulation.

A few years before Turing's experiments in the beginning of the 1950s, Claude Shannon, a scientist at Bell Telephone Laboratories, had published a paper entitled *Programming a Computer for Playing Chess*. Shannon, who is generally regarded as the father of computer chess, never actually wrote a chess program himself. Nevertheless, his work became of crucial importance for the development of computer chess, and his techniques are employed in nearly all of today's chess programs. Shannon described two approaches for programming a chess computer. One was the brute force-solution (i.e. examining all possibilities in the position to a certain depth), while the second was a selective search, in which the program should look at fewer variations to a greater depth. Most of today's programs combine these two elements, but are generally based on a bruteforce search.

In the years after Second World War and until the 1970s it was difficult to get access to computer time, and hence the development of chess-playing computer programs was slow. Today thousands of chess programs have been written on personal computers, but the fathers of computer chess did not have the possibilities of writing computer programs themselves.

Early Developments

In the late 1950s several groups of scientists tested the ideas put forward by Turing and Shannon. In 1957 a simple playing program was made in the Los Alamos Scientific Laboratory. The laboratory in the New Mexico desert was originally built during the Second World War with the purpose of developing atomic weapons. It hosted a giant computer called MANIAC 1 that was filled with thousands of vacuum tubes and switches and could execute 11,000 instructions per second. The computer was programmable and the scientists started experimenting with creating a chess-playing program. The result was a program that could play a simple form of chess on a 6x6 board – without the bishops and with only 6 pawns on each side.

The Los Alamos program lost a game against a strong chess-player despite being given the odds of a queen. In another game, the program had to play a beginner, a young woman who had just been taught the game with the purpose of measuring how the program would do against a beginner. The program won the game in 23 moves, and although its level of play was still unimpressive, it became apparent that it would be possible to teach a computer program to play chess within some years.

In the 1960s chess programming became more popular in the United States and in the Soviet Union. While the two superpowers were competing in many areas in the years of the Cold War, the field of computer chess saw some kind of cooperation. A friendly computer match was arranged between a program from the American MIT (Massachusetts Institute of Technology) and one from the Soviet ITEP (Institute for Theoretical and Experimental Physics). The games would be adjudicated a draw if they lasted more than 40 moves, as neither the American nor the Soviet programmers wanted to show the embarrassingly low level of endgame play that their programs would display. The match was won by the Moscow-based group, and in general the Soviet programs did best in the early years. Eight years after the match, the first World Computer Championship in 1974 was won by the Soviet chess program Kaissa, named after the goddess of chess.

Former World Champion Mikhail Botvinnik also started to show interest in computer chess after losing the World Championship in 1963. With his program Pioneer he experimented with very selective searching, modelled on the way that a human master thinks. Botvinnik believed that we should create chess machines 'in our own image', but the actual paths that programmers have pursued since that time have been of a completely different nature. No games from Botvinnik's program have been published and it never took part in any official tournaments. In most of the period when Botvinnik was researching into computer chess, access to computer time in the Soviet Union was very limited. Consequently he never got very far with the project.

Haunted by 'Bugs'

Since 1970 the United States Computer Chess Championship has been held annually and in the early years it was an amusing spectacle for chess-players. The following situation arose in a game between two programs in the second US Championship, in 1971:

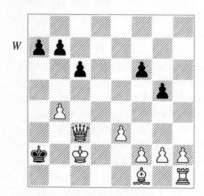

COKO III – Genie
US Computer Ch, Chicago 1971

The program COKO III was obviously winning in this position, but the program suddenly displayed an odd indecisiveness. It was not able to choose between the various mating possibilities it had. 38 ♗c4# and 38 ♕b2# are mate in one and there are several possibilities of mate in two, three, four and so on.

38 ♔c1?

The program was not 'told' to prefer a mate in one to a mate in two or more moves, so this move was as good as any.

38...f5 39 ♔c2

White is still not in a hurry to deliver mate.

39...f4 40 ♔c1 g4 41 ♔c2 f3 42 ♔c1 fxg2 43 ♔c2 gxh1♕ 44 ♔c1??

Amazing. Because of a 'bug', the program could still not decide to mate the black king and so it chose a line that does not lead to mate at all. COKO III's programmers were quite depressed at this point.

44...♕xf1+ 45 ♔d2 ♕xf2+ 46 ♔c1 ♕g1+ 47 ♔c2 ♕xh2+ 48 ♔c1 ♕h1+ 49 ♔c2 ♕b1+ 50 ♔d2 g3 51 ♕c4+ ♕b3 52 ♕xb3+ ♔xb3 53 e4 ♔xb4 54 e5 g2 0-1

The programmers resigned on behalf of COKO III.

A Computer Program Becomes a Master

In accordance with the quote from computer scientist Monty Newborn at the beginning of this chapter, chess masters had a good many laughs during those early years. However, the second and third parts of his prophecy were to come true as well.

International Master David Levy had made a bet with several computer programmers that he could beat any program in a match up to the end of 1978. Levy won an exhibition match against the program CHESS 4.7 in 1978, but lost one game in the process, and thus the human monopoly on playing chess at master level seemed to have ended. Levy played most of the match in an anti-computer style, being aware of and exploiting the weaknesses of the computer. In the one game he lost, he decided to battle the computer in a tactical struggle, and this strategy turned out to be too risky.

In the late 1970s Ken Thompson, a computer scientist at Bell Laboratories, built a special-purpose high-speed circuitry for chess. The chess machine was called Belle and had the shape and dimensions of a medium-sized fridge. It could search through 180,000 positions a second and was able to analyse eight to nine plies in a tournament game. In 1983 it had reached a USCF rating of 2203 in human chess tournaments, and with this result it was the first program to qualify officially for the title of US Master.

Several other special purpose chess machines were built, and in 1985 some students at the Carnegie Mellon University in Pittsburgh initiated a project with the clear purpose of being able to challenge the human chess world champion some day. Originally their program was called Chiptest, but it later changed name to Deep Thought and afterwards to Deep Blue. Even in its first few years, the program was much faster than any other program at the time, searching 300,000 positions a second, and the machine soon showed its powers. In 1988 it took part in the Software Toolworks Championship that was held in Long Beach, California and finished in a first-place tie with Grandmaster Tony Miles, scoring 6½/8 points. It finished ahead of former World Champion Mikhail Tal, and Grandmasters Walter Browne, Samuel Reshevsky, and Bent Larsen, whom it defeated in round 3. Larsen was very unhappy that he had to play the machine, and this may have affected his performance. Nevertheless, history was written. For the first time a grandmaster was defeated by a chess-playing machine – but it was not going to be the last time.

Playing the World Champ

The students from Carnegie Mellon continued improving their program. They joined IBM, and in 1996 they had created a machine capable of calculating 100 million positions a second. Although the chess knowledge the machine possessed could not be compared to a human grandmaster, its incredible calculation speed seemed able to pose a threat even to the human world champion.

A match with Garry Kasparov was set up. On Saturday the 10th of February, World Champion Garry Kasparov arrived shortly before 3.00 p.m. at the Philadelphia Convention Center to play a six-game match with Deep Blue. The first game was a shock for the champion:

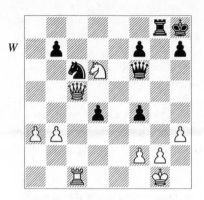

Deep Blue – G. Kasparov
Match (1), Philadelphia 1996

1 e4 c5 2 c3 d5 3 exd5 ♕xd5 4 d4 ♘f6 5 ♘f3 ♗g4 6 ♗e2 e6 7 h3 ♗h5 8 0-0 ♘c6 9 ♗e3 cxd4 10 cxd4 ♗b4 11 a3 ♗a5 12 ♘c3 ♕d6 13 ♘b5 ♕e7 14 ♘e5 ♗xe2 15 ♕xe2 0-0 16 ♖ac1 ♖ac8 17 ♗g5 ♗b6 18 ♗xf6 gxf6 19 ♘c4 ♖fd8 20 ♘xb6 axb6 21 ♖fd1 f5 22 ♕e3 ♕f6 23 d5 ♖xd5 24 ♖xd5 exd5 25 b3! ♔h8

Kasparov is launching a dangerous attack against White's king but Deep Blue has everything under control.

26 ♕xb6 ♖g8 27 ♕c5 d4 28 ♘d6 f4 *(D)*

29 ♘xb7!?

The machine picks up pawns while its king is under heavy fire. It is not very likely that any human player would dare to play like this against Garry Kasparov, but the machine just calculates. If it does not see any danger, it will continue eating pawns and, unlike most humans, it is not disturbed by the fact that it is playing the world champion.

29...♘e5 30 ♕d5 f3 31 g3 ♘d3 32 ♖c7 ♖e8 33 ♘d6!

A very precise move. The computer goes for the kill instead of defending its own king. It has now become more than evident that the word 'fear' is not a part of its vocabulary.

33...♖e1+ 34 ♔h2 ♘xf2

Black is threatening mate in one, but the machine has calculated everything.

35 ♘xf7+ ♔g7 36 ♘g5+ ♔h6 37 ♖xh7+ 1-0

The black attack comes to an end after 37...♔g6 38 ♕g8+ ♔f5 39 ♘xf3.

Mount Everest Grows

The game created a worldwide sensation, and Garry Kasparov started to worry whether the machine would be beatable at all. However, in the rest of the match the world champion showed that he was more than up to the task, and he was able to learn and to adjust his style slightly to play optimally against the machine. Kasparov won three of the following games and drew two, and thus won the match convincingly by a score of 4-2.

Feng-Hsiung Hsu – one of the creators of Deep Blue – remarks that the task, which had been compared to a mountaineer climbing Mount Everest, was actually quite different. The world champion in chess is a living being and thus the programmers of Deep Blue felt that they were climbing a 'Mount Everest that grows'. In the first part of the match the creators of Deep Blue caught a glimpse of the top of the mountain. However, the mountain all of a sudden started growing in front of the whole world, and the programmers had to go back to the drawing board again.

A little more than a year later a rematch was set up. This time the speed of the machine had been doubled so that it could analyse a terrifying 200 million positions a second. Moreover, and probably more importantly, the American grandmaster Joel Benjamin had been taking Deep Blue into 'chess school', and the result was a markedly better understanding of many positional factors in chess. Garry Kasparov won the first game, but lost the match with 3½-2½ as the machine was able to win two of the following games, while three were drawn. The match result created headlines all over the world, and during and after the match discussions between Kasparov, IBM and the programmers were raging. Kasparov indirectly accused the Deep Blue team

of cheating, and appeared to imply that there had been human intervention in at least one game. In game 2 Deep Blue made some unusual moves for a computer, and this prompted a demand from Kasparov to receive printouts of the machine's thought-processes. Deep Blue was not located in the playing room, but in another room in the same building, and Kasparov wanted to verify that it was actually Deep Blue playing, and not a team of grandmasters.

Some time after the match IBM published some printouts which were difficult to understand for anyone but computer scientists and people involved in the development of Deep Blue. Personally, I find it hard to understand why IBM did not just make a public demonstration with Deep Blue to show that the machine was actually able to replay some of the controversial moves.

The Legend of Deep Blue

To the surprise of many chess enthusiasts, IBM did not offer a rematch after winning the second match. Instead the machine was disassembled, before the world was actually able to see what it could do. 'They killed the only independent witness', said Garry Kasparov, and I believe that he expressed the feelings of many chess and computer enthusiasts that would have liked to see the latest version of Deep Blue play more than six games before retiring. However, IBM had nothing to win by pitting the machine against the world champion once again, especially in view of Kasparov's allegations. After all, Kasparov had won the first match, and if the two matches were put together, he would have been the overall winner with 6½-5½. In the public eye, however, machine had now finally defeated man, and some people seemed to have the feeling that this would make the game of chess less interesting.

Deep Blue became a legend, like a rock star or movie star dying too early. Even today, six years later, the moves of the 1997 match are discussed in computer chess newsgroups and the strength of the machine is being compared to the current programs. However, the six games of the 1997 match are simply too little information for accurately assessing its playing strength.

After the 'death' of Deep Blue, the baton has been carried by commercial programs running on PCs, and these are the main subject of this book. On good hardware they can calculate 2-3 million positions a second, which is much less than Deep Blue. Nevertheless, chess programming has advanced a great deal since 1997 and I believe that the best programs have a positional evaluation which is superior to that of Deep Blue in 1997. This may compensate for some of the speed difference, but probably not all.

Three matches between the best humans and computers were played in 2002-3, and all ended in draws. These were Kramnik-Fritz, Kasparov-Junior and Bareev-Hiarcs.

For some reason I got the feeling that the humans could have won in these matches if they had wanted to. In the match between Kramnik and Deep Fritz in October 2002, the human world champion started very convincingly with a clear 3-1 lead, only to lose two games in a row. In game five he blundered away a knight in an admittedly very difficult ending, and in game six he made an unclear sacrifice, after which a tactical and complicated position arose. Both of these games were rather bizarre incidents and very unlike the excellent anti-computer play displayed by Kramnik in the first half of the match.

Some more matches are needed to determine the level of the best programs. Despite the results, I do not feel convinced that the programs are level with the absolute world's best. After a lot of experimenting with the programs, I believe their level to be comparable to a strong human grandmaster, but no more than that.

However, there is no doubt that sooner or later the programs will surpass the achievements of Deep Blue and hopefully give us some new insights in the fascinating world of chess.

2 Inside the Machine

Chess is not mathematics.
GARRY KASPAROV, World Champion
1985-2000

The human attempts to build a chess-playing machine have often been compared to our efforts to learn to fly. In the beginning, humans endeavoured to fly like birds do, taping wings to their back and flapping their arms frantically. As we all know, these attempts failed.

Today we have aeroplanes that can take us anywhere in the world and spaceships capable of going to the moon. However, the planes and spaceships are not built in the same way birds are, and similarly, the 'thinking' of chess computers cannot be compared to the way that humans think either.

Researchers have studied the way humans analyse and perceive the game, but to describe human thoughts in detail has turned out to be a very complicated matter. The chess master recognizes the shape and size of the pieces, and he is acquainted with patterns and formations. When analysing, he usually selects a few moves to look at, and these are chosen intuitively, drawing upon many years of experience and knowledge of principles and exceptions to these principles.

The computer perceives the game in a quite different way. Having no brain, no common sense, no actual intelligence, and very limited possibilities of learning from past experience, it does not seem to possess any important skills when it comes to learning and playing a game like chess. It understands nothing but combinations of 1's and 0's, and it usually starts all over again every time the 'New game' button is pushed, having learned next to nothing from the previous game.

Yet modern computer programs have achieved a strength comparable to a human grandmaster, without possessing the skills that were considered crucial by humans.

Some of the early research in the field of computer chess, such as Botvinnik's investigations, focused on the idea of creating chess machines 'in our own image', trying to model the way a human master thinks. However, computers have completely different abilities from humans, and thus the most successful approach has been to let the computers do what they do best, namely to calculate. All modern programs are based on the general concept of a brute-force search, i.e. that all moves are examined to a certain depth. In some more 'interesting' lines the programs are able to extend the search, and some lines are cut off earlier than others. I shall return to this later.

The computer's capabilities in the field of mathematical calculations are well-known, and if we can change the game of chess completely into mathematics, then the computer can carry out the calculations and, after that, change it into an output that we are able to understand. This is the way that all computer programs work.

The first step is to tell the computer what the board looks like. We create 64 cells and assign each of them with numbers from 1 to 64. Each of these cells will carry a piece of information, a number, corresponding to a piece or an empty square. The initial position could look like this:

W	-4	-2	-3	-5	-6	-3	-2	-4
	-1	-1	-1	-1	-1	-1	-1	-1
	0	0	0	0	0	0	0	0
	0	0	0	0	0	0	0	0
	0	0	0	0	0	0	0	0
	0	0	0	0	0	0	0	0
	1	1	1	1	1	1	1	1
	4	2	3	5	6	3	2	4

Or: 4, 2, 3, 5, 6, 3, 2, 4, 1, 1, 1, 1, 1, 1, 1, 1, 0, 0, 0, 0, 0, 0, 0, 0, 0, 0, 0, 0, 0, 0, 0, 0, 0, 0, 0, 0, 0, 0, 0, 0, 0, 0, 0, -1, -1, -1, -1, -1, -1, -1, -1, -4, -2, -3, -5, -6, -3, -2, -4

0 is an empty square, 1 represents a pawn, 2 a knight, 3 a bishop, 4 a rook, 5 a queen and 6 a king. Positive values correspond to white pieces, negative values are black pieces.

The next step is to tell the computer how the pieces move. Let us take a look at the chess board:

57	58	59	60	61	62	63	64
49	50	51	52	53	54	55	56
41	42	43	44	45	46	47	48
33	34	35	36	37	38	39	40
25	26	27	28	29	30	31	32
17	18	19	20	21	22	23	24
9	10	11	12	13	14	15	16
1	2	3	4	5	6	7	8

Suppose we have a knight posted at the square x. Assuming that the board is empty, we tell the program that it can move the knight to x−17, x−15, x−10, x−6, x+6, x+10, x+15 and x+17. A knight on 22 (f3) can go to 5, 7, 12, 16, 28, 32, 37 and 39.

Further complications arise when one of these squares are occupied by a piece of the same colour of the knight or a piece of the opposite colour. Moreover, not all of these numbers will apply to a knight close to the rim, and the program will have to know about these exceptions as well.

Every piece has simple calculations like this attached to it. To know if a rook on c1 is standing on an open file the program has to look into each of the cells 11, 19, 27, 35, 43 and 51 to see if any of these contain a 1 (white pawn) or a -1 (black pawn). A human being will see the open files on the board at a glance.

As you can easily understand from this short description, the computer is not actually playing chess, it is merely crunching numbers, making nothing else than mathematical calculations. Not very difficult mathematics, but a huge amount of simple operations in a very short time.

The Search Tree

Given the enormous speed of today's computers, some people may expect that you could simply put the initial position into a computer program and let it calculate all the way through the game. However, as all chess-players know, this is not the case.

In the initial position White has 20 different possibilities, and Black has 20 possible answers. This adds up to $20 \times 20 = 400$ possible positions after the first full move. As the game develops, the pieces' mobility increases and it is not unusual that somewhere in the middlegame the number of possibilities on each move will exceed 40 or even 50. If we set the average number of possible moves to 35, there will be 1,225 positions to consider after 2 plies ('ply' is a technical term for half-move). After two full moves, or 4 plies, we pass 1.5 million positions, and 6 plies

later we have reached 1,838,265,625 positions, or close to 2 billion positions. The number of positions to analyse increases exponentially with depth.

The number of possible different chess games has been assessed to be somewhere around 10^{120} – an astronomical number which exceeds the number of atoms in the known universe. Watching these numbers, it becomes clear that computers have to find other ways to play good chess than trying to calculate everything. Both humans and computers have to look at a small part of this gigantic variation tree.

To know which moves are good, and which are not, we introduce an evaluation function. Let us assume that this function only considers material and gives the following values for the various pieces, with positive values for white pieces, negative for black pieces:

Pawn   =   100
Knight =   300
Bishop =   300
Rook   =   500
Queen =   900
King   =   100,000

The computer does not like to calculate with decimals – that is why the programmers say that a pawn is worth 100, not 1. In the end, the program will have to divide the result by 100 to give the right output to the user.

The king must have a value greater than all other factors combined, so that we can make sure that the program does not suddenly sacrifice its king.

Fig. 1

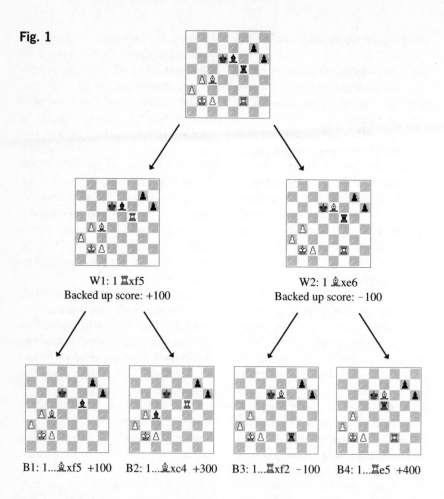

W1: 1 ♖xf5
Backed up score: +100

W2: 1 ♗xe6
Backed up score: −100

B1: 1...♗xf5 +100   B2: 1...♗xc4 +300   B3: 1...♖xf2 −100   B4: 1...♖e5 +400

In the first diagram we have an endgame position in which we can try to use our simple evaluation function. The position contains 26 possible moves for White, and thus the variation tree would normally be much wider than the tree in fig. 1.

In this example, however, we will only examine the two captures 1 ♖xf5 and 1 ♗xe6 and assume that our program searches only 2 plies deep. After 2 plies the evaluation function gives us the following values: +100, +300, −100, and +400. Line B4 (1 ♗xe6 ♖e5) returned the highest evaluation, so should White choose 1 ♗xe6 here to reach a score of +400? No, of course not, a chess-player would say, because

Black can just take the f2-rook, as in line B3.

Consequently, something is wrong with our program. We have to construct the search in such a way that the program assumes that both White and Black will make the best move possible on each turn. This process of searching the tree is called the **minimax** procedure. White tries to **maximize** the value of the evaluation of the position on his turn, while Black tries to **minimize** the value.

Following this procedure, the program would choose B3 over B4 when analysing Black's reply. Black wants to minimize the value and therefore chooses −100 rather than +400. Between B1 and B2, Black would choose B1 (+100) over B2 (+300). Black's best choices (B1 and B3) can now be backed up to the position 1 ply earlier, giving White a choice of a line which is worth +100 (W1) or −100 (W2). As White wants to maximize, he chooses W1 with the backed up score +100, leading us to the conclusion that in our very simple search tree, the best move for White is 1 ♖xf5 and the best line of play 1 ♖xf5 ♗xf5 with an expected advantage of +100, according to our evaluation function.

The Alpha-Beta Algorithm and Extensions

As we have previously experienced, the number of positions to be evaluated explodes as the number of plies increases. For this reason, programmers have attempted to limit the number of branches that the program has to search through. If, for instance, we could limit the number of moves to be searched in each position to 5, the program would be able to get much deeper into these lines. Going 6 plies down each line, the program would 'only' have to search through, and evaluate, a total of 15,625 positions – a number considerably lower than the 2 billion positions mentioned earlier where the average number of moves is 35 in each position.

One way of limiting the possibilities to be analysed is the alpha-beta algorithm. Looking at our example in Fig. 1, we can actually cut off the possibility B4. The program, playing White, has analysed B1 and B2 and found out that by optimal play by Black it will reach +100 after the first possibility analysed for White (W1). When it goes to 1 ♗xe6 (W2), it finds the line 1...♖xf2 (B3) with a score of −100. This is a refutation of 1 ♗xe6 (W2), because the score −100 is lower than the backed up score of White's first move (+100). Consequently, 1...♖xf2 (B3) refutes White's second try, and the program does not need to analyse B4 or any other black move, as 1 ♗xe6 has already been refuted.

This means that only one line is cut off in our example. When we know, however, that the real search tree would contain 26 branches instead of two, we can imagine that cut-offs like this can eventually help get rid of large chunks of the search tree.

Another technique to avoid calculating unimportant lines is 'killer moves'. The following diagram shows a simple example of this.

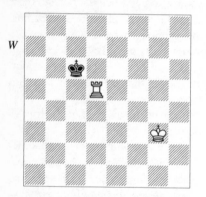

The program analyses 1 ♔f4, but reaches the conclusion that this loses a rook to 1...♔xd5. Now 1...♔xd5 will be characterized as a 'killer move', and this means that on all other white moves, the program will start by analysing the reply 1...♔xd5, if it is possible, instead of a move like 1...♔b7. This means that precious time is saved, as it is easily established that 1...♔xd5 is the refutation of the 8 different king moves in this position. Because of this, other moves do not need to be considered.

While the alpha-beta algorithm and killer moves are making the search tree slimmer, we also need to go more into depth with some lines in order to improve the analytical ability of the

engine. In the beginning of the computer chess era many programs would search to a fixed depth, e.g. 4 plies, and everything beyond that was darkness. In most modern programs, you can still set the depth to a fixed value, but this will seriously worsen the quality of the play.

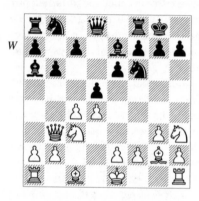

Here we have a position where it is obvious to analyse the consequences of exchanging on d5. A 4-ply program analyses 1 cxd5 exd5 2 ♘xd5 ♘xd5 and gives a score of −200, not realizing that one move later White will play 3 ♕xd5 and regain the knight with a score of +100. The program should also analyse that 3...♕xd5 4 ♗xd5 does not disturb the material balance further. All of this adds up to a total of 7 plies.

Most of today's programs get well beyond 7 plies in many lines if they are running on normal hardware, but if we suppose that the program analyses a line 14 plies deep, and a sequence of captures is initiated on ply 11 and ends on ply 18, then the program can miss something very important if it stops at ply 14. For this reason all modern programs extend the search when a capture is made, while in some programs the extension only takes place when there is a capture of equal material or a capture winning material, called 'healthy captures'. Modern programs will also extend the search after a check and in a few other situations which can be defined accurately; e.g., when a passed pawn is close to the promotion square. The extension after a check is one of the reasons why computers can often find mates much faster than humans.

The technical explanation of how the search works is as follows:

Let us assume that the program is analysing a position. It has finished analysing ply 13 and goes to ply 14. The depth is set to 14. Internally in the program, it makes a countdown to search 14 plies ahead. After each move, the depth is lowered by 1, except when there is an extension. In that case the depth is not lowered. After 14 plies without any extensions, the depth is 0. At depth 0 the so-called quiescence-search starts. This means that the program starts searching for a position that is stable. In the quiescence-search only 'healthy captures' are allowed, nothing else. The reason for this is that the evaluation of the final position will almost certainly be wrong if pieces are hanging on one or both sides. So the program makes all the 'healthy

captures' and after this it evaluates the position.

I believe it will be obvious for most chess-players that extensions and a quiescence search are of great significance for the quality of play, because of the more variable search depth. In situations with a lot of tactical possibilities, with checks and captures, the program will reach better conclusions much faster when these features are included.

'Gimme Your Best Shot!' – the Null-Move

At the beginning of the 1990s a new and very effective way of pruning the search tree came up. Given that a large percentage of the moves that computers search through are junk, programmers have been working on how to get rid of the lines that make no sense. The most absurd sacrifices can take a lot of time to go through. For the computer, any sacrifice could prove valuable at a later time, while humans often have an intuitive feeling about a sacrifice that the computer does not possess. Take a look at the diagram overleaf.

Imagine that we have a program with no opening book analysing this well-known position in the Ruy Lopez. The computer takes a look at the sacrifice 4 ♗xa6 and analyses the move 8 plies deep.

Even a beginner will see that this move leads to nothing but the loss of a

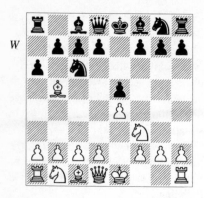

bishop for a pawn. The computer program, however, has to go down 8 plies of this line with around 25-35 ramifications at each ply to find out that the move is a bad one, and essentially losing. This is a serious time-waster, and analysing these 'junk lines' will keep the computer from looking at more relevant lines. For this reason the null-move was invented. Null-move actually means 'not moving' or 'pass' – something that is not normally possible in chess. Basically, it can be compared to a very confident boxer allowing his opponent to take an extra shot or two.

Imagine that a computer program is analysing the first three plies 4 ♗xa6 bxa6 5 ♘c3 (or another fifth move) and then makes an evaluation. A program based on material evaluation alone will give the value −200 – a two-pawn plus for Black. Now it is time for the null-move. The program, playing Black, believes that Black's position is so superior that it 'passes' and gives White another shot. White seems to have nothing special here. The best

moves are probably 0-0 or d4. Despite the fact that White gets an extra move, Black will still have his two-pawn plus.

Now the computer concludes that White cannot do anything special **even** with an extra move, and therefore all lines containing 4 ♗xa6 are not analysed any further. In the diagram position White could play a lot of other moves (such as, for instance, 4 0-0) that leave the bishop *en prise*, but most of these lines will be cut off quickly by a null-move procedure.

Programmers are still experimenting and testing if there are positions where one side needs to make two or more null-moves to find the hidden dangers in the position. No matter what, the result is a dramatic reduction of the branching factor of the search tree, and this can lead to an improvement in search depth.

Naturally, this kind of pruning also has its dangers. First of all, by cutting off a lot of useless junk, it also becomes less likely that the program will find the good sacrificial lines, as some of those will be pruned off. The speed of modern computers compensates for this to a certain degree. However, when analysing with a computer – or playing against a computer – the human player should be alert about this weakness of the programs. When performing computer-assisted analysis it is very important always to execute the actual sacrifice and perhaps a few more moves, especially if they are nearly forced. Taking the computer a little way down a sacrificial line will help it a lot.

When playing against a computer, a long-term positional pawn sacrifice or an unclear piece sacrifice that leads to an attack are strong weapons. However, when it comes to short-term tactics and sacrifices, the programs are second to none. They never make short-term mistakes.

Let us look at an example from the match between Vladimir Kramnik and Deep Fritz in October 2002, in which Kramnik made an unclear knight sacrifice which I have already mentioned in chapter one.

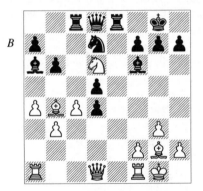

V. Kramnik – Deep Fritz
Match (6), Bahrain 2002

In this position from game 6, we have nearly reached the critical moment. Deep Fritz is analysing 18...dxc4, and at this point it has to analyse 46 different answers to this move, one of them is the sacrifice 19 ♘xf7. I would like to use this example to illustrate some of the points that I have discussed so far, so we shall imagine, for a moment, that we are a computer program trying to analyse this position. First of all, we shall look at the main line as played in the game, counting plies and extending when there are checks or captures. Let us assume that our program only extends the search when there is a 'healthy capture', a capture of equal material or a capture winning material.

18...dxc4
Ply 1.
19 ♘xf7
Ply 2. This is not a straight exchange, so the search is not extended.
19...♔xf7
Ply 3.
20 ♗d5+
Ply 3. The line is extended one ply because of the check.
20...♔g6
Ply 4.
21 ♕g4+
Ply 4. The line is extended another ply because of the check.
21...♗g5
Ply 5.
22 ♗e4+
Ply 5. The line is extended another ply because of the check.
22...♖xe4
Ply 6. This is not a straight exchange, so the search is not extended.
23 ♕xe4+
Ply 6. The line is extended because of check.
23...♔h6

Ply 7.
24 h4 *(D)*
Ply 8.

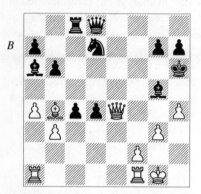

This is the first time since the knight sacrifice on move 19 that the black king has not been in check. Most programs should get to this point fairly quickly. Normally we would have reached 12 plies here, but because of all the checks it is only counted as 8 plies. Consequently, the program will go deeper in this line than in quieter lines without checks and captures.

Counting material, Black is the equivalent of two pawns up, i.e. he has a knight, a bishop and a pawn for a rook. At this point the program throws in a null-move, as if it is saying: 'My position is superior when it comes to material. Would White have anything if it were his turn to move?' If he does not, then the program (playing Black), will throw away the whole line.

However, the computer soon discovers that White can use his extra move to take the bishop with 25 hxg5+,

so the line cannot be thrown out yet. In the continuation, White keeps checking, and this extends the search.
   24...♗f6
   Ply 9.
   25 ♗d2+
   Ply 9, search extended.
   25...g5
   Ply 10.
   26 hxg5+
   Ply 10, search extended.
   26...♗xg5
   Ply 10, search extended, as this is an exchange of equal material. In the game, Vladimir Kramnik now played 27 ♕h4+, but let us continue a while down the line which is critical for the assessment of the sacrifice on move 19.
   27 ♕e6+
   Ply 10, search extended.
   27...♘f6
   Ply 11.
   28 f4
   Ply 12.
   28...♗h4!
   Ply 13.
   29 gxh4
   Ply 14.
   29...♕g8+
   Ply 14, search extended.
   30 ♕xg8
   Ply 15.
   30...♖xg8+
   Ply 15, search extended.
   31 ♔h2
   Ply 16.
   31...♘g4+
   Ply 16, search extended.

32 ♔g3

Ply 17.

32...♘e3+

Ply 17, search extended.

33 ♔f3

Ply 18.

33...♘xf1

Ply 19.

34 ♖xf1

Ply 20.

34...c3

Ply 21.

The program would have to reach approximately this point to make a correct assessment of the refutation move 28...♗h4!, which appears to be the only saving resource. At move 34 the position is not even stable yet, as White will lose further material because both the rook and the bishop are threatened, and the pawns on c3 and d4 are a dangerous force. Anyway, at move 34 the material evaluation will be that Black is a pawn up, and this essentially refutes White's sacrifice. This line is only one of the main lines in the analysis of the sacrifice, but giving a thorough analysis is not the point here.

I have included this example to show how the engine analyses a complicated position. In the game the machine was searching 2.5 million positions per second, and it is of course not possible to reproduce the program's 'thoughts'. However, the example shows how extensions and null-moves operate. At move 24 the program tried to throw out the whole line with a null-move

procedure, but it had to continue the search, since White's threats were too strong (unlike the example with the 4 ♗xa6 sacrifice in the Ruy Lopez).

The analysis above show that computers are capable of going quite deep into the critical lines, but it also tells us that some sacrifices may be beyond the computer's horizon. I set up the initial position (before Black's 18th move) on an AMD 850 MHz processor with 432 Mb set for hash tables. With Fritz 8 it took the machine 5½ hours to reach ply 18 in the main line, extending the search up to 56 plies in some lines (yet we do not know if these are relevant positions). To go 1 ply deeper, the program usually needs 3 times more time, so it would probably need about 17 hours to reach ply 19, and approximately 51 hours to get to ply 20. Obviously, the multi-processor machine that played this game was much faster, so it is not easy to say how much of the refutation of the sacrifice Deep Fritz actually saw. However, the example above should give some idea about it.

Unfortunately for the programs, there are positions where the null-move does not work. In the endgame in particular, the null move is of little use, as it leads to trouble in zugzwang positions. Here is one simple example of this (*see diagram overleaf*):

White does not actually have a threat here. He is waiting for Black to make the move ...♔g7, so he can play ♔e7 and queen his pawn. For obvious

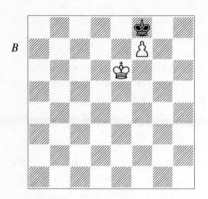

reasons, a null-move does not work in these situations, as making a pass in this case will result in Black drawing the game, instead of losing it. Thus, the null-move algorithm is normally not used in endgames.

Razoring

Programmers have found other methods to refine the search and make it more selective. Another method of pruning the search tree is called razoring, and it works by cutting off more lines when the search is getting closer to the maximum depth analysed. Let us imagine that we have a program analysing 15 plies deep in the middlegame. With the razoring procedure the program evaluates all positions three plies before the end, in this case before ply 12, and if the evaluation function shows that the computer is a queen or more down, it will immediately throw out the whole line. The reason is that it is unlikely that the 3 last plies in the search will change

anything significantly – although of course this does happen! However, the most important thing is that the program will get rid of some junk lines, which will save time for focusing on more important variations.

Like the null-move procedure, this is of course a risky method. However, in practice it seems to work well, and according to the programmers of the program Dark Thought this method shrinks the search tree by 5-15% on average when the search depth is more than 10 plies.

The Evaluation Function

So far, we have only been speaking about material evaluation when discussing the evaluation function. Most chess computer users will know, however, that chess programs do not merely count the material and nothing else. How, for instance, do we tell a computer program that a knight is often better placed in the centre than on the rim, or in the corner of the board?

-10	-5	0	0	0	0	-5	-10
-5	5	10	10	10	10	5	-5
-5	5	15	15	15	15	5	-5
-5	5	15	15	15	15	5	-5
-5	0	10	10	10	10	5	-5
-5	0	5	10	10	5	0	-5
-10	0	0	0	0	0	0	-10
-20	-5	-5	-5	-5	-5	-5	-20

The above diagram shows a possible piece-placement table for a white knight.

By assigning a number to each of the 64 cells, i.e. the 64 squares of the board, the computer will get a bonus for centralizing the knight. The distribution of points in the diagram can, of course, be discussed.

Following this table the program will be encouraged to develop a knight from g1 to f3 for instance, gaining 10 points, as the value goes from −5 to +5. Note that these values are not necessarily strictly comparable to our material evaluation earlier in this chapter, as programmers assign different values for putting a knight on d5 for example. In our example it would be worth '15 points', but the actual value will differ from program to program. Each piece has a table like this, and the positive thing about the tables are that they do not 'cost' much for the program in time. When Fritz won the World Computer Chess Championship and beat Deep Blue in Hong Kong in 1995, the program had nothing but this kind of piece-placement tables and a well-tuned search function. This tells us that the piece-placement tables are effective, but of course modern programs have many more factors included in their evaluation.

Many factors are important when analysing where the pieces will be well placed. One of them is where the opponent's king is placed. To get an aggressive and attacking program you

can give a bonus for putting the pieces close to the opponent's king. This is done by counting the number of king moves from the square to the opponent's king. The piece placement is illustrated in the following example.

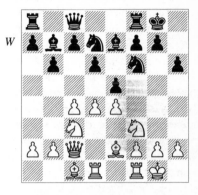

V. Korchnoi – O. Romanishin
Leonid Stein memorial, Lvov 2000

Black has castled kingside, and White has a knight on f3 that he would like to transfer to f5 via h4. From the f3-square there are 5 king moves to g8 (e.g. f3-f4-f5-f6-f7-g8), but on f5 the knight is only 3 king moves from the opponent's king (f5-f6-f7-g8), and this gives a bonus. Moreover, the knight will get a +10 bonus for making this manoeuvre according to our piece-placement table, and for this reason it is possible that White will try this – provided that there is no tactical drawback and that nothing else returns a higher score.

The next step is to expand the positional evaluation by looking at the pawn-structure. The program will award a further bonus if no pawn can threaten it on f5 (i.e. the e- and g-pawns have been exchanged or are too far advanced), or if the knight is covered by one of its own pawns. In this situation the knight is covered by e4, but it can actually be threatened later by the g-pawn, although this is unlikely to happen in the following moves, as the black h-pawn hangs.

Computer programs contain various kinds of positional evaluations. One of these is a rook on an open file. Some programs may want to play 12 dxe5 in this position to underline the white rook's position on an open file, even though its position would probably soon be challenged by a black rook. Anyway, this move seems to be no worse than 12 ♘h4 and perhaps the two plans can be combined.

To mention all the values that a modern program considers is the same as giving a list of most of the rules of thumb that human chess-players use. Some of these would be: pluses for the bishop-pair, knight outposts, a rook on an open or semi-open file, passed pawns, connected passed pawns, good king safety; and minuses for doubled pawns, isolated pawns, doubled isolated pawns, backward pawns, a bad bishop, etc. All of the computer's positional evaluation is, of course, borrowed from human knowledge of chess positions, and this is the reason why they can sometimes play very reasonable and almost human-like chess.

Essentially, when your chess program displays, e.g., '1.09' this evaluation consists of hundreds of pluses and minuses calculated by the computer.

In a few cases it seems that programmers have actually expanded the existing theory a bit. One example is that many programs work with as many as ten phases of the game, instead of the three well-known ones (i.e. opening, middlegame and endgame). Perceiving the game as three phases is too simplistic to understand what is going on in many games. These ten phases probably do not have fixed names, but they correspond to different phases of the opening, middlegame and endgame, such as 'early middlegame', 'late middlegame', 'early endgame', 'late endgame' and so on. These phases are essential for understanding the value of a bishop vs knight, the centralization of the king, and so on. In the 'late endgame', such as a pawn endgame, king activity and opposition are important factors, while other values may be more important in an 'early endgame'. To determine which phase the game is in, the computer will count the number of pieces and work out which pieces have been exchanged. The queens are especially important in determining the phase of the game.

The values of positional pluses and minuses are quite easy to explain in computer language. 'If Black has a set of doubled pawns, then -30', for example. However, most chess-players may imagine some of the problems arising with the evaluation function. Sometimes a rook has nothing to do on an open file, sometimes the knight-pair is stronger than the bishop-pair, sometimes doubled pawns can be good because they result in the opening of a file which can be used for attacking purposes, and so on. How can we 'tell' the program about these issues?

When 'teaching' a program to play better positionally, we have to set everything up as simple rules. One example of a rule could be that the bishop is bad if there are two or more pawns on the c-, d-, e-, and f-files that are on the same colour as the bishop. These rules may seem somewhat simplistic to humans, and they can often lead to wrong evaluations. For a chess programmer, however, there is no other way. The programmer has a difficult task. He has to invent the rules that can be explained to a program and give them the right values. All of these have to be weighted against each other and the result is the evaluation displayed on the screen. The problem is that in chess there are numerous exceptions for any rule you may create. This is one of the reasons why chess is so fascinating and difficult. Most chess-players will probably say that you cannot express chess as a formula, but this is essentially what the programmers have to do. Arguably, chess programs are the most dogmatic of all players!

Much will depend on the chess insight of the programmers, which may vary. Actually, there are many examples of programs having, for instance, no code for a bad bishop or opposite-coloured bishop endgames. All of this leads me to the conclusion that you should not trust the computer evaluation blindly, even though the strongest of today's programs have well-tuned evaluation functions. Take a good look at the position yourself, and your own intuition may surprise you!

One last point to consider is the mobility of the pieces. The simple way of measuring mobility is to count the number of legal moves for Black and White, and then calculate the difference between the two numbers. In the diagram on page 31, White has 36 legal moves, while Black has 31. This gives White a lead in mobility of 5 – a number which can then be multiplied by a factor chosen by the programmer to fit into the evaluation function. If we choose to multiply it by 10, we will give White a mobility advantage worth 50 points, or ½ pawn. Some programs work with a more sophisticated mobility evaluation, which gives a better picture of the actual scope of the various pieces. Let us imagine we have a position with a knight trapped on h8. It has the possibility of going to f7 or g6, but it will be captured immediately if it does so. A simple mobility evaluation will tell us that the knight has a mobility of 2, while the more sophisticated mobility evaluation will give a score of 0. The advanced evaluation is more 'expensive' in time, and thus it is not included in many programs. One would expect the programs that analyse the fewest positions per second to have elaborate functions like this, and these probably include Hiarcs and Gandalf.

The Engine Output

During the analysis of a position, the engine displays information about the lines that it is currently analysing. Let us take a look at the output of one of the strongest positional engines, starting from the diagram position.

12 ♘h4 exd4 13 ♘f5 ♖e8 14 ♖xd4 ♘c5 15 ♘d5 ♗d8 16 f3 ± (0.75) Depth: 9/20 00:00:06 526kN

Hiarcs 8 suggests the move 12 ♘h4, played by Korchnoi, quite quickly. It gives this move as the best in less than one second. After this it displays a main line with the moves it currently considers best for White and Black to a depth of 9 plies. On the screen the program will also give information about which move it is currently analysing. Furthermore, it shows how many positions it is analysing per second. In this example it was analysing 85 kN/s, which means approximately 85,000 positions a second.

The evaluation of the position is given in brackets. At this point it is 0.75, which means a '0.75 pawn plus for White'. This evaluation refers not only to the current position, but also of the potential in the position. In reality,

it is an evaluation of the position arising if the moves in the main line were played out. In the main line the program displays the line which it considers the best – it assumes that both Black and White make the best moves on each turn. Obviously, the program's evaluation of the position 9 plies later can change if the program is set to analyse at that point.

In the variation window Hiarcs gives a main line of 9 plies. It displays Depth = 9/20, in which the first number corresponds to the number of plies in the main line displayed by the program, and the second refers to the deepest line it has found, which is 20 plies long. This line includes extensions and 'healthy captures' at the end of the search. '526 kN' means that after six seconds the program has examined approximately 526,000 positions in total. This may sound like a lot, but actually Hiarcs is a slow-searcher compared to other modern programs. However, it has a lot of knowledge built in to compensate for this. Some other programs could search half a million positions per second starting from this position (with the same hardware), but this does not mean that these fast-searching programs are necessarily stronger. Actually, it is difficult to say exactly how the user can use the information that a program is searching x kN/s. The only thing you can say for sure is that if this value if relatively low, you are dealing with a more 'knowledgeable' program, which may know more rules about positional play and the endgame. With all this knowledge of chess rules and of positional play, some may ask why the computer programs still have problems with positional chess, and we will get back to this in Chapter 3, when discussing the weaknesses of the computer.

Information about which programs are more knowledge-based can be of help when choosing a program to analyse with. The 'slow' programs are not necessarily the ones that do worst when calculating tactical strokes, as we shall see in the following example.

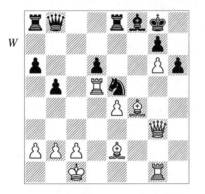

The main line here is the spectacular sequence 1 ♗xh6! gxh6 2 g7 ♗e7 3

♖xe5! dxe5 4 ♕b3+ ♔h7 5 ♕f7, mating. I tested some programs, and the results for finding the first move of the solution were:

Nimzo 8: 2 sec. (625 kN/s)
Shredder 7: 4 sec. (143 kN/s)
Gandalf 5 beta: 5 sec. (112 kN/s)
Chessmaster 9000: 5 sec. (119 kN/s)
Hiarcs 8: 37 sec. (73 kN/s)
Junior 7: 37 sec. (700 kN/s)
Crafty 19.03: 58 sec. (355 kN/s)
Fritz 8: 109 sec. (396 kN/s)
Chess Tiger 15: 342 sec. (209 kN/s)
Gambit Tiger 2: 726 sec. (238 kN/s)

This result shows that programs such as Shredder, Gandalf and Chessmaster find this combination quite quickly despite the fact that they calculate fewer nodes (or positions) per second than, for example, Junior or Fritz. Both Hiarcs and Junior find the solution after 37 seconds, even though the latter calculates 10 times more nodes per second! Thus, variations in the way of searching and knowledge have a great impact on the output. Note, however, that the best time of all is achieved by a fast-searcher, and another fast-searcher, Goliath, also finds the solution extremely quickly.

3 The Blind Spots of the Computer

Man is still the most extraordinary computer of all.
JOHN F. KENNEDY (1917-1963), President of the United States

Having analysed the 'thought-processes' of a program in the previous chapter, we have a good basis for understanding the limitations of modern chess programs. Every program has its own 'personality' and different weaknesses, and these may change over time. I will mention some of the individual weaknesses in Chapter 5, when discussing the various engines, while this chapter addresses the general weaknesses. Knowledge of computer weaknesses will prove useful later when discussing how to perform computer-assisted analysis.

Formerly, computer scientists used to speak about the 'horizon effect' as one of the most critical weaknesses of chess computers. This problem is still haunting the programs, but in a different way from before. The horizon effect relates to the fact that there are limitations to the depth to which a computer can analyse a position.

In the following diagram it is quite obvious that the black bishop will be

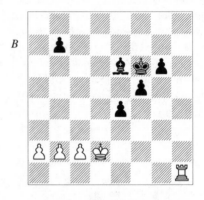

B

trapped after 1...♗xa2 2 b3. 10-15 years ago, many programs could have taken the a-pawn, not realizing the danger that would arise. The reason for this is that the capture of the bishop can be postponed by checks so that it will occur beyond the computer's horizon. One possible line is 2...f4 3 ♖a1 e3+ 4 ♔e2 f3+ 5 ♔xe3 ♗xb3 6 cxb3, postponing the capture of the bishop until ply 10. This sequence would have caused problems for most programs ten years ago, but with the speed of modern computers and with search extensions, those days are over. Naturally, extending the horizon further has led to an increase in the playing strength of the computer programs.

Positional Problems Deriving from the 'Horizon Effect'

Nowadays the problems with the horizon effect can, of course, still be tactical, but the consequences of not looking deeply enough into the position are more visible in positions of a quiet positional nature, where planning is required. Under tournament time conditions the programs may look ahead 10 to 18 plies in a middlegame position, depending, of course, on the program and the position. Within this horizon they may make moves which actually look like they are part of a plan, even if they are just moves (or numbers) for the computer. If a computer has to use five moves to get a strong knight outpost, it is still within its horizon. But suppose that the program is distracted and has to make some moves to fend off an attack. Then the planned knight manoeuvre is pushed beyond the horizon. Long-term planning is not currently within the reach of the programs, and this is especially felt in quiet and closed positions where there are fewer search extensions because tactical clashes occur less often. If the goal of a certain plan is beyond the horizon, the computer will never play it. The computer is ignorant in the build-up phase of an attack, when the tactical clashes are still far ahead. Let us take an example from a theoretical position of the King's Indian, where most programs show a lack of 'understanding'.

1 d4 ♘f6 2 c4 g6 3 ♘c3 ♗g7 4 e4 d6 5 ♘f3 0-0 6 ♗e2 e5 7 0-0 ♘c6 8 d5 ♘e7 9 ♘e1 ♘d7 10 f3 f5 11 ♗e3 f4 12 ♗f2 *(D)*

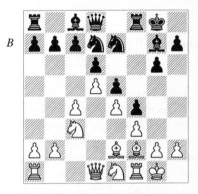

The most frequently played moves in this position (by humans) are, according to the ChessBase Megabase 2002, 12...g5 (926 times), 12...h5 (74 times) and 12...♘f6 (36 times). All of those are a part of the same plan: pushing the h- and g-pawns to start a kingside attack (though 12...♘f6 is a poor implementation). The plan is quite clear for human beings, yet the consequences of this attack will occur well beyond 20 plies. Unless the program awards a special bonus for pushing the kingside pawns in positions with a closed centre, it will never play this plan. The programs probably do not like the idea of pushing the pawns, as this will destroy the king's pawn shield, and they will penalize such moves due to the reduced king safety.

The answers of the best programs are, after 1 minute of analysis (without opening book):

Chessmaster 9000:   12...b6
Hiarcs 8:   12...b6
Fritz 8:   12...b6
Junior 7:   12...b6
Nimzo 8:   12...a6
Crafty 19.03:   12...♘f6
Shredder 7.04:   12...b6
Gandalf 5 beta: 12...b6
Chess Tiger 15:   12...b6
Gambit Tiger 2.0:   12...g5

All of the programs (except Gambit Tiger and Crafty) prefer a move that bolsters the queenside and in their main lines none of them show any intention of pushing the kingside pawns.

In the build-up phase of an attack the programs' suggestions are far from optimal and the reason is that the actual tactical consequences are beyond their horizon. Even in simpler positions where the kings have castled on opposite wings, it is not 'natural' for the programs to push their pawns to attack the opponent's king. Some programs will, however, award an evaluation bonus for pushing these pawns, just to get the attack started.

In the following diagram, there is no reason for White to postpone an attack on the kingside with the g- and h-pawns. The only obstacle for the white attack is his g5-bishop, which has to be moved, and then the kingside pawns can advance.

Anand pushed the g- and h-pawns at once, and the game concluded:

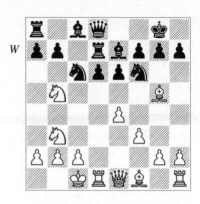

V. Anand – M. Tissir
FIDE World Cup, Shenyang 2000

13 g4 b6 14 h4 ♗b7 15 ♘5d4 ♘xd4 16 ♘xd4 ♖c8 17 ♔b1 a6 18 ♗c1 ♖dc7 19 g5 ♘d7 20 ♖h2 d5 21 e5 ♗c5 22 h5 ♗xd4 23 ♖xd4 ♘f8 24 ♗d3 ♖d7 25 g6 1-0

A very logical and simple plan, flawlessly executed by Anand. The general idea is not difficult to understand for humans, yet this kind of strategic build-up is still beyond the reach of many modern programs. When we arrive at move 22, most programs will start to notice what is going on, as the opening of the h- or g-files is within their horizon, and at this point they begin to show evaluations that favour White. However, it takes some time to reach this position, and the programs do not possess the planning abilities to do that. There are 25 plies from move 13, when the g-pawn is pushed, to move 25, when White starts to open files on the kingside. It is not that the programs dislike the h- and g-pawn push. The consequences, however, are beyond their horizon, and therefore they have no especial reason to play these moves. I do not believe that this defect is difficult to fix, as the programmer can assign pluses to moves like g4, h4, ...b5 and ...a5 when the two sides have castled on opposite sides. Some programs, like Gandalf, have included this in their evaluation function. However, when you analyse positions like this with another top program, you will find that it is surprisingly hard to get them to play these natural-looking moves.

Building Fortresses

The poor planning abilities of computer programs is evident in all kind of positions. As mentioned before, closed positions where long-term planning is required tend to be especially troublesome for them. Also in the endgame the programs have problems with planning. One example is that they have no way of recognizing when their opponent is trying to set up a fortress, and this often becomes important when playing against strong human players. In general, I believe this theme is underestimated by the programmers. When some of them display messages in newsgroups, they seem to have the impression that a fortress position is something that could occasionally crop up in a game against a strong master. However, it is much more than that. The famous chess coach Mark Dvoretsky

has called the fortress "one of the most important methods of defending in the endgame".

The main problem is that when discussing fortress positions it is difficult to set up rules that do not have numerous exceptions. For this reason, an understanding of fortress draws has not been implemented successfully in any program yet. Let us take a look at some examples.

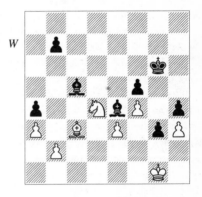

I. Smirin – Hiarcs 8
Internet 2002

Hiarcs 8 had been putting strong pressure on Smirin in this game, but now Smirin managed to set up an impregnable fortress, without Hiarcs understanding anything of what was going on. Hiarcs is not the only program to have trouble with this, however. All leading programs give a score of around –2 in the final position (after White's 60th move), when the game is a dead draw.

The game concluded:

48 ♗b4!

Most programs do not like this move, as it doubles White's pawns.

48...♗xb4 49 axb4 ♔f7 50 ♘b5

The knight is transferred to c3 and the entrance path for the black king is closed.

50...♔e6 51 ♘c3

White has reached the fortress position. The black king has no way to enter, and the game is drawn. Some more moves were played, but it does not change the picture.

51...♗c2 52 ♔g2 ♔d6 53 ♔g1 ♔c6 54 ♔g2 b5 55 ♔g1 ♗d3 56 ♔g2 ♗e4+ 57 ♔g1 ♗c2 58 ♔g2 ♗d3 59 ♔g1 ♗e4 60 ♔f1 ½-½

The computer evaluation of the position shows that it is beyond the scope of the best engines to understand that the black king will **never** enter the white fortress. They will just keep analysing new sequences of moves instead of taking a general look at the position, as humans do. In chess endgames there are many fortress positions where one side has more material but is unable to penetrate the opponent's position. When material up, the programs can often enter a 'fortress draw position' believing that it is won, while when playing the weaker side, they may miss that their position can be defended by arranging their pieces so that the opponent has no way to enter.

Another example of this inability to understand fortresses was found in the following game.

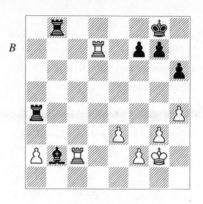

B

V. Anand – Fritz 6
Frankfurt rapidplay 1999

Fritz is leading in material, but it is probably quite difficult to win the position. The following move puts an end to all hope for Black, as the program walked into a permanent pin:

1...♖xa2? 2 ♖dd2 ½-½

The b2-bishop is pinned, and Black cannot make any real progress as his rooks cannot move. Today's programs will all take on a2, walking into the pin and evaluating the position as a two-pawn plus for Black, which is normally equivalent to a decisive advantage.

The aim of this example is not to discuss whether Black could have won in some other way. The point is that the programs keep on evaluating these positions wrongly, positions in which there is no reasonable plan. They do not realize that Black will **never** be able to move his bishop, as their analysis is not infinite. You could call this 'the concept of never', which is a concept that computers do not understand. Computer programs need to have a maximum value for the length of their variations and for most modern programs this limit is around 60-70 plies. Theoretically, however, the stronger side can prolong the winning attempts for a much longer period, and for this reason the program will not reach the evaluation of 0.00 before it sees no way to escape the 50-move rule, which can be much more than 100 plies away.

Closely related to the above-mentioned position are positional draws in endgames where the stronger side can make no progress.

that I have tested give a five-pawn or six-pawn advantage for Black, but none of them can come up with a winning 'plan' for Black, since computer programs do not plan.

Another example of an endgame draw is this:

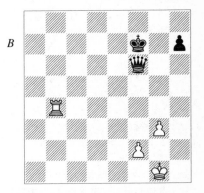

V. Kramnik – Deep Fritz (analysis)
Match (6), Bahrain 2002

In this position, White will keep shuffling his rook between f4 and h4, and he has created a fortress and ensured a draw. All the top programs give Black a big, and decisive, advantage in this position.

In this position a human will understand that the black queen alone cannot mate the white king, and that the black king is not capable of entering the battle since the white knights keep it imprisoned. Any attempt at sacrificing the queen ends in a draw, as one white knight will still be able to stop the black pawn. All computer programs

Another example of an endgame draw came in the same match of Deep Fritz versus Kramnik in game 1, when the program exchanged into a drawn pawn endgame in the following position (*see diagram overleaf*).

It is not so obvious that Black can draw this endgame if White, for instance, brings the king to e4 and forces

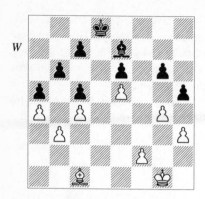

Deep Fritz – V. Kramnik
Match (1), Bahrain 2002

through f4-f5. The program, however, played a strange-looking move:

25 h4?

Now Black draws immediately:

25...hxg4 26 ♗g5 ♗xg5 27 hxg5 ♔e8 28 ♔g2 *(D)*

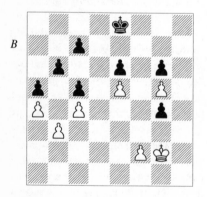

½-½

White will regain the pawn on g4, but the pawn endgame is completely drawn since neither king can penetrate the enemy territory. The white pawn

sacrifices f5 or b4 do not work unless Black decentralizes his king and puts it on a7, for example. None of today's programs are able to understand that the final position is just a dead draw. They give White scores ranging from 0.3 to 1.2, and the programs will enter completely blocked positions like this if their evaluation functions regard them as advantageous.

After 25 h4? Black also had the drawing option of 25...♗xh4 26 g5 ♗xf2+! 27 ♔xf2, when White has no way to penetrate the black position and nothing to use his extra piece for. Once again, any program will tell you that White is leading by between +1 and +2, when the evaluation actually ought to be 0.00.

Finally, I will conclude this small section on fortress draws and positional draws with a composition by former World Champion Vasily Smyslov.

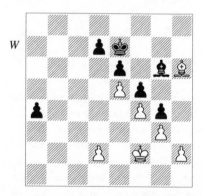

V. Smyslov, *New in Chess* 2002
White to play and draw

1 ♗g5+

1 d4? loses to 1...♔f7.

1...♔e8

After 1...♔f7 2 ♗d8 a3 3 ♗a5 a2 4 ♗c3 the bishop gets back in time to stop the pawn.

2 d4 a3 3 d5 a2

3...exd5 is met by 4 e6 with the idea of ♗f6, which is also a draw, as White covers all the important squares on the a1-h8 diagonal.

4 d6 a1♕ 5 ♔g2 *(D)*

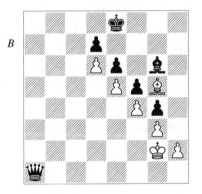

The position is drawn. Note that 5...♕a8+ 6 ♔g1 ♕d8 changes nothing. After 7 ♗xd8 ♔xd8 Black's king escapes the prison, but he will still not be able to win the h2-pawn with the king alone, and the black bishop cannot be activated. No program will suggest the queen sacrifice (6...♕d8), but they all still believe Black to be winning after this manoeuvre.

In the position after White's fifth move all programs consider Black to be winning (assessments range from −9 to −12).

I tested this position on Fritz 8 on a computer with an AMD 850 MHz processor and 432 Mb RAM set for hash tables. The output after 7½ hours was the following:

5...♔f7 6 ♗f6 ♕b2+ 7 ♔g1 ♔g8 8 ♗e7 ♗f7 9 ♗h4 ♕d4+ 10 ♔f1 ♕d3+ 11 ♔f2 ♕d2+ 12 ♔g1 −+ (−9.34) Depth: 24/68 07:31:09 19220186kN

This means that the program gives the move 5...♔f7 as the best with a score of −9.34, a decisive advantage to Black equal to a queen. Fritz 8 has analysed 24 plies in the main lines and up to 68 plies in selective searches. It has looked at around 19,220,186,000 positions at this point of the analysis, but apparently it still does not realize that Black has no way to penetrate the white fortress.

As this example shows, the problem is not that the computer is too slow or that it looks at too few positions. The problem is that it does not understand what it sees. It has no proper way to evaluate these positions, since material evaluation will tell it that it is nearly a queen up, and it does not understand that White could have any kind of compensation for this. Having already looked at nearly 20 billion positions, there is no reason to believe that the program would reach a significantly different conclusion, even if it were going through trillions of positions with a much faster processor. This leaves an interesting problem to solve for the programmers. If the programs cannot be taught to understand the whole area of fortress draws and positional draws, then strong human players will too often be able to escape with a draw in a lost position. This will happen even if the coming years show marked increases in computer power.

Basically, all of the examples above exploit the fact that computer programs are not able to plan and that they cannot recognize positions where there is no way to proceed, even if one side has a big lead in material. Since the birth of computer chess, the programs have lacked the ability to plan, and the programmers do not seem to have made significant advances in this field. In the case of fortress draws, some experiments have been made, but none of the top programs have implemented anything that looks like fortress recognition. As these issues are not new to programmers, you may ask why nothing has been done about it.

First of all, the concept of planning and the concept of recognizing fortresses are obviously very difficult to 'explain' to a computer. The second reason has to do with the competition between the computer programs. Many chess-players may believe that the programmers are mostly concerned with being able to beat human beings, but as the best programs can play at a level which is comparable to a human grandmaster, this is not really the main issue. The market value of being number one amongst computer programs is what really counts. For this reason new versions of a program are mainly

tested against other computer programs, and when the programmer analyses the lost games and draws, he will not see any examples of long-term positional planning or construction of fortresses, as none of the computer opponents are able to do this. Thus he will only consider this issue when once in a while the program plays a game against a strong human master who uses some of these methods. It is easier and far less expensive to play a lot of games against other programs than paying an international master or a grandmaster to test the strength of your program. The results you get from playing a large amount of games between computer programs will be statistically significant, but only in the area of computer vs computer. Playing against humans is an entirely different matter.

Materialism and King Safety

Some years ago you could be sure that if you were playing against a computer, it would accept every sacrifice you made and ignore almost anything else: positional factors, king safety, the opponent's attacking possibilities, etc.

In the latest generation of chess programs things have changed significantly. Even if there are still a lot of programs suffering from the old computer chess disease of materialism, we now have programs like Junior 7 sacrificing pawns and pieces on every occasion.

The problems with materialism can often be connected with underestimating the safety of the program's own king, as the following game between Shirov and Fritz shows. Shirov chooses a good strategy against the computer in this game. He plays the main-line Ruy Lopez and stays true to his own style. As a top player he does not have to fear Fritz's opening book, because he knows a lot about the typical aspects of the positions that arise in the Ruy Lopez. Garry Kasparov adopted a very different strategy in the 1997 match against Deep Blue, when he tried to get the program out of book as soon as possible by playing, e.g., 1 d3 in the third game. In this way he effectively gave away the possibility of getting an opening advantage with White, and as the match showed, this was not a good strategy.

In this game Fritz was using 8 processors running in parallel at 700 MHz and was capable of analysing 2.8 millions positions per second. The computer was dubbed 'The Fridge' by the players because of its volume.

A. Shirov – Fritz
Frankfurt rapidplay 2000

1 e4 e5 2 ♘f3 ♘c6 3 ♗b5 a6 4 ♗a4 ♘f6 5 0-0 ♗e7 6 ♖e1 b5 7 ♗b3 d6 8 c3 0-0 9 h3 ♘a5

One of the main lines in the Closed Ruy Lopez.

10 ♗c2 c5 11 d4 cxd4 12 cxd4 ♕c7 13 ♘bd2 ♘c6 14 ♘b3 a5 15 ♗e3 a4 16 ♘bd2 ♗d7 17 a3 ♖fe8 18 ♗d3 ♕b7 19 ♕e2

Up to this point we have been on more or less well-known territory, but now Fritz gets 'impatient' and wants to resolve the tension in the centre.

19...exd4?!

The more patient move 19...♖ab8 is a better choice, covering b5 and preparing counterplay on the b-file, or with ...exd4 and ...♘e5.

20 ♘xd4 d5?!

Part of a mistaken plan. The exchange ...exd4 should normally be connected with putting a knight on e5, but as this is not possible due to the loose pawn on b5, the whole idea backfires. The powerful light-squared bishop on d3 wakes up, pointing against the black kingside and introducing the possibility of a kingside attack. Fritz could 'argue' that it did not open only the b1-h7 diagonal, but also the f8-a3 diagonal. However, these two diagonals have a very different value. This game shows very clearly that computers do not have a sense of danger in the same way as humans. When attacked, they will often only realize that they are in trouble when it is too late.

21 ♘xc6

21 ♗xb5? loses to 21...♘xd4, and Black has active play for the pawn after 21 ♘xb5?! ♘e5.

21...♗xc6 22 e5 ♘e4 23 ♗d4

Burying the bishop on c6. It is possible that Fritz did not have any code for bad bishops at the time. In that case it might have avoided the previous moves. To humans it is now obvious that Black's attempts to resolve the central tension have not been very successful.

23...♘g5 24 ♘f3 ♘e4 25 ♘d2 ♘g5 26 ♖ec1!

Playing for a win.

26...♘e6 27 ♘f3 ♗d7 28 ♗e3 b4 29 ♘d4 ♘c5 (*D*)

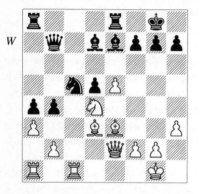

30 ♗f5!

An interesting exchange sacrifice by Shirov. Being well aware of how computers play, he probably knew that they almost always take 'gifts' like this if there is no clear refutation within their horizon. The strategy is of course risky as play becomes complicated, but on the other hand the computer's evaluation function will not work properly after the exchange sacrifice, and this contains a lot of advantages. Shirov looks at the attacking possibilities while the program counts material. This game underlines that

material is not everything. If your king is under attack, you should not worry about a pawn on the queenside. This is basic knowledge for most human chessplayers, but it is not so easy for Fritz, as the computer program wants very clear reasons for declining a material gain. In this concrete case, however, the program does not seem to have much choice, as White still has the initiative after 30...♘e6, for instance.

30...♗xf5 31 ♘xf5 ♘b3 32 ♕g4 g6

White provokes a weakness in the black king's shelter, but 32...♗f8 33 ♘xg7 ♔xg7 34 ♗h6 f5 35 exf6 ♖e4 36 ♕g5 ♘xa1 37 ♖xa1 ♖ae8 38 ♗xg7 ♖e1+ 39 ♖xe1 ♖xe1+ 40 ♔h2 also looks dangerous for Black, although there may be chances to survive.

33 ♘h6+ ♔g7 34 ♕f4 ♗d8 35 ♘g4 bxa3 36 bxa3 ♘xa1

Fritz takes the exchange and is probably quite happy with the position. However, the attack is growing more dangerous.

37 ♖xa1 ♖a6 38 ♖d1 ♕b3?

The computer shows an extreme greediness, which seems to cost the game. It wastes time by taking the a3-pawn while its king is under heavy fire. 'Just mate me if you can. I can't see anything', it seems to say. This is typical computer play. More chances of saving the game are offered by 38...h5, but in the millions of positions calculated by 'The Fridge', there was still no sign of danger and therefore it saw no reason not to grab material.

39 ♖c1 g5?

The game gets even more insane. Fritz advances the pawns in front of its king. The program is not worried about the safety of its king as long as it sees nothing within its horizon. Black could have tried something like 39...♕d3 to offer a queen exchange on e4 or f5 at some point. However, it is an open question if this would be enough to save the game.

40 ♕f5 ♕xa3 41 ♖c8 ♕a1+ 42 ♔h2 h5?! *(D)*

The program still displays no signs of fear and flings forward the pawns in front of its own king. Black could have tried to return some material with 42...h6 43 ♕d7 ♖ae6 44 ♖xd8 ♖xd8 45 ♕xd8 ♕c3, protecting against White's attacking possibilities with ♗c5, but after 46 f4! White's attack continues.

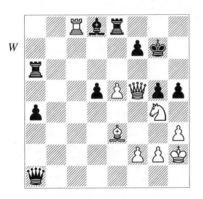

43 ♖xd8!

Another exchange sacrifice which removes one of the last defenders. In an attacking game like this a static material evaluation is of little relevance, but taking the dynamic attacking chances

of the position into consideration is of great importance.

43...♖xd8 44 ♘f6

It is too early to cash in with 44 ♕xg5+? since after 44...♖g6 45 ♕xd8 hxg4 Black has fended off the attack. White has to wait for the right moment.

44...♕c3 45 ♗xg5 ♔f8

Around this point, most of today's top programs will start to notice that Black is in trouble, because it is now within their horizon that Black will lose material some time in the near future. At this point, White is two exchanges down, but this is not the most important factor of the position. When conducting an attack, the value of the pieces depends very much on their activity and proximity to the king. A simple material count, assigning 300 (or 3) to a bishop or knight, and 500 (or 5) to a rook, would have Black leading with 400 (or 4) points here. In reality White has a winning position, and now he takes time to cover the e5-pawn before proceeding with his attack.

46 f4! h4 47 ♗xh4 ♕a5 48 ♕h7 ♔e7 49 ♘g4+ ♔e8 50 ♕g8+ ♔d7 51 ♕xf7+ ♔c6 52 e6!

Note that Shirov does not pay much attention to the fact that he can cash in with 52 ♗xd8 – a very non-materialistic way of thinking.

52...♖da8 53 e7 ♔c5 54 ♗f2+ ♔c4 55 e8♕

Shirov had only one minute left at this point, but the position is winning.

55...♖xe8 56 ♕xe8 ♔b3 57 ♕e2 ♖c6 58 ♕d1+ ♖c2 59 ♘e3 ♕d2 1-0

The operator resigned for Fritz in view of 60 ♕xc2+ ♕xc2 61 ♘xc2 ♔xc2 62 ♗c5, when the f-pawn wins.

"What was everybody worried about?", Shirov asked after the game. "It wasn't so difficult."

More on Sacrifices

The game above shows that computer programs still have a long way to go when playing against the top players, even if they calculate variations at a very high speed. They simply have to calculate much deeper in order to grasp the dangers of long-term positional attacking sacrifices like these, or the programmers will have to change their evaluation function so that they value attacking chances higher than small material gains. In the last two to three years a few of the top programmers have worked on the problems with materialism, and the latest generation of computer programs seem to have improved in this area. Especially the programmers of Junior have done some interesting work with material evaluation. The latest version of their program, Junior 7, starts to show positive evaluations for White as early as move 40 in the game above.

Let us take a look at another game in which some of the same problems with materialism and king safety appear. Moreover, we will witness that the programs can sometimes have

problems when calculating long lines containing sacrifices.

Fritz – V. Kramnik
Frankfurt rapidplay 2000

1 c4 e5 2 ♘c3 ♘c6 3 ♘f3 f5 4 d4 e4 5 ♘g5 ♗b4 6 ♘h3 ♘f6 7 e3 ♗xc3+ 8 bxc3 d6 9 ♘f4 0-0 10 h4 ♕e7?!

This is not a very good move, because White has a tactical point that takes advantage of the queen's position. In this position the idea for Black is to play ...c5 to keep the centre closed and exploit White's doubled c-pawns. 10...♘e7 with the idea of ...c5 is a better way to go.

11 c5! ♘d8

The point is that 11...dxc5 does not win a pawn, as White gets the material back with 12 ♕b3+ ♔h8 13 ♗a3 b6 14 dxc5 bxc5 15 ♕b5 ♗d7 16 ♕xc5, securing an advantage.

12 ♕b3+ ♘e6 13 ♗c4 ♖e8 14 ♗a3 *(D)*

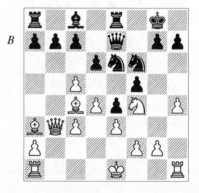

14...♔h8!?

Kramnik is under pressure and decides to release the tension by sacrificing the b7-pawn – a good strategy, especially against a computer program. As we saw in the Shirov game above, material sacrifices tend to 'disturb' the evaluation function of the program, and humans can benefit from this. The alternative to the text-move would be 14...♖b8, but passive defence is not a wise choice against a computer. Objectively speaking, Black does not have enough for his pawn in this position, but as the game develops he gradually gets more chances, as Fritz ignores Black's chances of counterplay.

15 ♗xe6 ♗xe6 16 ♕xb7 d5

Kramnik closes the position, usually a good idea against computers because it limits the tactical possibilities. Moreover, in this particular situation the closing of the centre means that it will be harder for the white pieces on the queenside to rescue the king if it is attacked.

17 ♖b1 ♗f7 18 ♖b3?

Black was preparing ...♘h5 and kingside play with his last move, and I believe White should try to counter these plans with 18 h5. However, the computer program probably sees that it will be able to win the black a-pawn some time in the future, so it starts mobilizing its forces on the queenside.

18...♖ec8 19 c6 ♕d8 20 ♕a6

White is busy with his plans of winning a pawn on the queenside, but at this point White should probably start to take Black's counterattack into

consideration and play 20 ♕b4, trying to exchange queens on e7. In some variations this could cost the pawn on c6, but it is definitely better to give back a pawn than risk getting mated.

20...♘h5 21 ♘xh5 ♗xh5 22 ♖b7 *(D)*

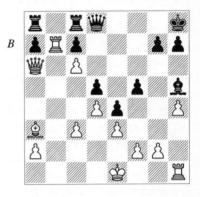

22...♕f6

Black now gets ready to attack, and he is aided by the fact that the bishops are of opposite colour. This favours the attacker in the middlegame.

23 0-0

Again, Fritz does not fear the upcoming attack. Black was already getting a lot of play for his pawn, but castling directly into the attack makes matters worse. White has no pieces that can defend his kingside, while Black's bishop and queen are ready to attack, and a rook can join the attack via e8-e6. This is a clear example of how programs can underestimate the safety of their own king and it also shows that chess programs can be very dogmatic. Nearly all programs award a bonus for castling, especially castling kingside as this is supposed to secure the position of the king. However, the king is not always safer after castling, and in this particular position the white king would actually have been better off in the centre.

However, at this point the position is not so easy for White anyway, as Black can launch an attack with ...f4. The best possibility is probably to try to stop the attack with the antipositional-looking 23 g3, conceding the light squares, but opening up the possibility of putting the king on d2, where it would be safer than on the kingside. Black definitely has a lot of play for his pawn at this point, but kingside castling by White hastens the end. Kramnik now slowly prepares the attack by ruling out possibilities of back-rank tactics.

23...h6 24 ♗c5 ♔h7 25 ♗xa7

An automatic move for a computer program, while for humans it seems somewhat foolhardy to hunt pawns like this.

25...♕xh4 26 ♖fb1 *(D)*

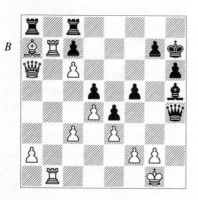

26...♗f3!

A key move in the black attack and probably an idea that Fritz 'underestimated'. As explained in Chapter 2, computers tend to skip lines that contain sacrifices, because of the null-move algorithm. In this way the computer can get rid of a lot of potential junk lines, e.g. where one side gives away a queen for nothing. Sometimes, however, these sacrificial lines may indeed be viable, and this is a good example of how tactical key lines can be missed when they contain sacrifices.

27 ♕f1

After 27 gxf3 exf3 28 ♕f1 ♖e8 the black rook joins the attack via e6-g6 with devastating effect.

27...♖e8 28 ♗b8 ♖axb8!

Another sacrifice, which makes it less likely that the computer program would consider this line in depth some moves earlier. Black has to play this move as White threatens ♗xc7, when the bishop would be able to join the defence on the kingside. Without the bishop there are no pieces left to defend.

29 ♖xb8 ♖e6 30 ♖f8 ♖g6 31 ♖xf5 ♖xg2+ 32 ♕xg2 ♗xg2 0-1

Black loses a rook after 33 ♔xg2 ♕g4+ 34 ♔f1 ♕xf5.

While the programs have a certain blindness in sacrificial lines based on long-term ideas, it is very important to note that they still see every short-term sacrifice and tactic. The problem arises when they do not see the material being regained within their horizon. In this case they have no reason to sacrifice, or no reason to believe that their opponent will do so, and this is what happened in the last part of the game above.

After the game, one of the Chess-Base programmers was quoted as saying that the Fritz king-safety evaluation was not optimized for rapid games, as the program usually is tuned to compete with other programs about being number one on the computer rating list (apparently he considered king safety to be less important in computer vs computer games). Whatever the reason may be, Fritz underestimated its king safety (like most other programs do) and even the latest version of the program feels comfortable until Black's 26th move lands on the board.

Aggression and Lack of Planning

Most chess programs play chess in an aggressive way and this earns them a lot of points when playing against amateurs. However, this aggression is not always justified as the opponents can exploit the weaknesses it creates.

V. Kramnik – Deep Fritz
Match (2), Bahrain 2002

1 d4 d5 2 c4 dxc4 3 ♘f3 ♘f6 4 e3 e6 5 ♗xc4 c5 6 0-0 a6 7 dxc5 ♕xd1 8 ♖xd1

In this match Vladimir Kramnik used the same strategy as he did in his match with Garry Kasparov two years earlier. He exchanges queens as soon as possible, as this limits the tactical possibilities in the position. We have already touched upon the subject that computers do not know how to plan, but quiet positions like this require good planning, and this is definitely to the advantage of Kramnik.

8...♗xc5 9 ♔f1 *(D)*

A move especially designed to take the computer out of its opening book. Until this point Kramnik had only played 9 ♘bd2 in this position.

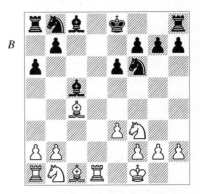

9...b5?!

This is an example of a move which is too aggressive, but it is a very typical move for a computer program. Fritz probably awarded a plus for gaining a tempo for development and preparing ...♗b7, but 9...b5?! weakens the queenside, as we shall see in the game. Black should put his pawn on b6 instead and get ready to finish development with

...♗b7, ...♘bd7 and ...0-0. The plan with ...b6 instead of ...b5 has been played by strong players such as Kasparov, Karpov and Lautier in similar positions.

10 ♗e2 ♗b7 11 ♘bd2 ♘bd7 12 ♘b3 *(D)*

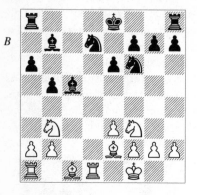

12...♗f8?

A very odd move and a difficult one to explain. One suggestion is that Fritz was over-estimating the value of fianchettoing the bishop with ...g6 and ...♗g7. Another explanation is that Fritz did not get the idea behind Kramnik's last move and was expecting White to retreat the knight with 13 ♘bd2, to prepare b3 and ♗b2 in which case the computer could have replied 13...♗c5, repeating the position. Whatever the reason, this is a clear error as Black cannot waste time in the development phase. He had to play 12...♗e7 with the idea of castling kingside.

13 a4!

A key move in White's strategy. If Black advances his pawn to b4, it will weaken his control of the queenside, and the important c4-square will fall into White's possession. This is all a player of Kramnik's strength needs. White gains a small but lasting advantage because of Black's weaknesses on the queenside. With the pawn on b6 this would not have happened as Black would still have the threat of ...b5 at his disposal if a white knight came to c4.

13...b4

After 13...bxa4 14 ♖xa4 the black a-pawn will come under serious pressure, but this is probably a better choice anyway.

14 ♘fd2!

Another strong move from Kramnik, who prepares to put the knight on c4 and make inroads on key queenside squares such as d6 and b6. It is now obvious that the advance of the black b-pawn has not really helped Black, but only weakened squares on the queenside, especially c4. It would have been better to have the pawn on b6 than on b4.

14...♗d5 15 f3 ♗d6 16 g3 e5 17 e4 ♗e6 18 ♘c4 ♗c7 19 ♗e3 a5

This further weakens Black's light squares on the queenside, but other moves are no better; e.g., 19...0-0 20 ♘c5 ♘xc5 21 ♗xc5 ♖fb8 22 a5 and White has a strong initiative on the queenside.

20 ♘c5!

Kramnik keeps the pressure and prevents Black from finishing his development with ...0-0.

20...♘xc5 21 ♗xc5 ♘d7 22 ♘d6+ ♔f8 23 ♗f2 ♖xd6 24 ♖xd6

White's advantage is materializing as he has now gained the bishop-pair. The two white bishops constitute a strong asset here as they control most of the squares on the queenside.

24...♔e7 25 ♖ad1 ♖hc8 26 ♗b5

White gains a strongpoint for his bishop on the queenside. His position is excellent, but Fritz now initiated some tactics that surprised Kramnik. However, the world champion found an excellent way of preserving his advantage.

26...♘c5! 27 ♗c6 ♗c4+! 28 ♔e1 ♘d3+ 29 ♖1xd3! ♗xd3 30 ♗c5! ♗c4 (D)

Not 30...♗c2 31 ♔d2 ♗xa4? 32 ♖d5+ ♔f6 33 ♗xa4.

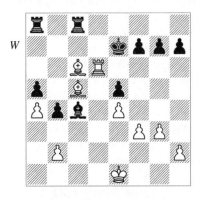

31 ♖d4+ ♔f6 32 ♖xc4 ♖xc6 33 ♗e7+ ♔xe7 34 ♖xc6

After a long forced sequence the game has turned into a simple-looking rook endgame. For most computer programs, and probably many humans as

well, it may have been difficult to see from afar that White has a usable advantage here. However, as Kramnik demonstrates, the active rook is of crucial importance and the fact that Black has difficulties in seeking counterplay gives Kramnik real winning chances. If the position is difficult in itself, Fritz is not helped by the fact that it is reluctant to give up material to get active counterplay.

34...♔d7

One attempt to get counterplay is 34...♖d8, trying to sacrifice the a-pawn to activate the rook via d3 and b3. However, White can simply cut out the counter-chances by 35 ♔e2!, when Black has not achieved anything.

35 ♖c5 (D)

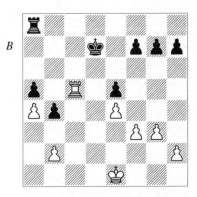

35...f6?

The computer misses the last chance to activate its rook and after this move it is forced into passivity for the rest of the game. 35...♖c8! is the best chance, giving up a pawn to get an active rook. White can achieve no more than a draw after 36 ♖xc8 ♔xc8 37 ♔d2 ♔d7 38 ♔d3 ♔d6 39 ♔c4 ♔c6 when Black has the opposition: 40 f4 exf4 41 gxf4 f6 achieves nothing as Black threatens to create an outside passed pawn with ...g5, while 40 h4 g6 41 g4 h5 42 g5 ♔d6 43 ♔b5 f6 44 gxf6 g5! results in a draw.

White is still better after 36 ♖xa5 ♖c2 37 ♖d5+ followed by ♖d2, but Black's rook is more active in these lines. It is interesting that Fritz apparently feared this line because of the material loss.

The game showed that passive defence leads to material loss as well, but in a variation that was not within the horizon of the computer. At that point there were no chances of getting compensation by activating the rook. A human master would normally recognize the necessity of sacrificing a pawn to achieve activity in a rook endgame, but it does not seem that the evaluation functions of the current programs are sophisticated enough to evaluate this correctly yet.

36 ♔d2 ♔d6 37 ♖d5+ ♔c6 38 ♔d3 g6?!

Black should just wait with 38...♖a7. Advancing the kingside pawns only creates further weaknesses.

39 ♔c4 g5 40 h3 h6 41 h4 gxh4 42 gxh4 ♖a7 43 h5 ♖a8 44 ♖c5+! ♔b6 45 ♖b5+ ♔c6 46 ♖d5

White loses a tempo to achieve zugzwang.

46...♔c7 47 ♔b5 b3 48 ♖d3 ♖a7 49 ♖xb3

Now White picks up the pawn that Black refused to sacrifice 14 moves earlier. In this position there are no chances of activating the rook as compensation.

49...♖b7+ 50 ♔c4 ♖a7 51 ♖b5 ♖a8 52 ♔d5 ♖a6 53 ♖c5+ ♔d7 54 b3 ♖d6+ 55 ♔c4 ♖d4+ 56 ♔c3 ♖d1 57 ♖d5+ 1-0

The pawn endgame is lost; e.g., 57...♖xd5 58 exd5 ♔d6 59 b4 axb4+ 60 ♔xb4 ♔xd5 61 ♔b5 ♔d6 62 a5 f5 63 a6 ♔c7 64 ♔c5 e4 65 fxe4 fxe4 66 ♔d4 ♔b6 67 ♔xe4 ♔xa6 68 ♔f5 ♔b6 69 ♔g6 ♔c6 70 ♔xh6 ♔d7 71 ♔g7.

Closed Positions

Positions of a closed nature are amongst the most troublesome for computer programs. The improvements in the evaluation of these positions have been scarce so far, mainly because no programmer has succeeded in giving his program the ability to plan. Many programmers seem to have given up on this issue and now give their programs a bonus to keep the position open.

Let us look at some examples of closed positions in games between humans and computers.

L. van Wely – Fritz
Dutch Ch, Rotterdam 2000

1 c4 e5 2 g3 ♘f6 3 ♗g2 ♘c6

3...d5 is a move that better suits a computer program, as it opens the position.

4 ♘c3 ♗b4 5 a3!?

Van Wely probably wanted to take the computer out of book with this move. The normal moves are 5 ♘d5 and 5 ♘f3 followed by 0-0.

5...♗xc3 6 bxc3 0-0 7 e4!

A strong move, initiating a good strategy against a computer program. It is now getting difficult for Black to open the position as White is controlling d5. Black should try to strike in the centre now with 7...♘e7 followed by ...c6 and ...d5, but White can counter this plan by simply playing 8 d4 with a better position. Now, the computer starts to make some strange moves, because of the closed nature of the position.

7...a6 8 a4

Stopping any ideas involving ...b5. White's strategy in this game seems to be to parry all attempts for counterplay before proceeding with his own plans.

8...d6 9 d3 ♗g4?!

The computer is trying to provoke a 'weakness' by luring the white f-pawn forward, but White wants to play f4 anyway, so this does not make any difference. 9...♘e8 followed by ...f5 seems to be the best way to counter White's kingside plans.

10 f3 ♗d7 11 ♘e2 ♕c8 12 h3

White will not allow ...♗h3, simplifying the position.

12...b6?

A very strange, passive move. Black should still try to achieve ...f5 by playing a preparatory move like 12...♘e8.

13 f4 *(D)*

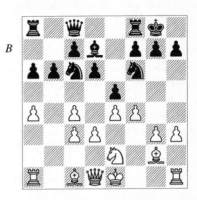

13...♗e6??

A horrible move, since Black hands over tempi for White's kingside attack. It should be said Fritz's programmer must have tried to work with this issue, since Fritz versions later than Fritz 6 do not play this move. Its big brother Fritz 7 suggests 13...♖b8 at a tournament time-limit, but it is not clear if this is a part of a plan as the main line it displays goes 14 f5 ♕d8?! 15 0-0?! (no reason to play this move as the king was safe in the centre, but all programs give bonuses to castling) 15...h6? 16 ♗e3 ♘a5 17 ♕c2?! (White should attack on the kingside) 17...♕e7 18 ♖f3 ♖b7? – very odd. It looks like Black could be preparing ...b5 with this last move, but in that case the knight's location on a5 is completely wrong as it hangs after axb5.

This whole line does not make sense, but it clearly shows that in closed positions there is no reason to rely on computer analysis, even if you have the best engines. They have no planning abilities and the possibility of a long-term attack on the kingside is far beyond their horizon. In the line above it seems like the program was choosing the moves randomly by throwing a die, as there is no connection between the moves whatsoever. Watching a main line like this, it is not surprising that the computer soon lost the game.

14 f5 ♗d7 15 g4 ♘e8 16 ♘g3 ♕d8 17 g5 ♗c8?

With what plan? Of course Black is close to being lost, but moves like this accelerate the end.

18 h4 f6 19 ♕h5 ♘a5 20 ♖a3! *(D)*

A very cool move from Van Wely, cutting out the few counter-chances connected to ...♘b3 before continuing with the attack. 20 ♖b1 would have left the a-pawn undefended.

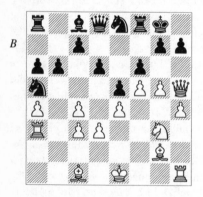

20...♕e7 21 ♘f1 ♘c6

Shuffling the pieces back and forth, but Black is losing anyway.

22 ♘e3 ♕d7 23 g6 h6 24 ♘g4 ♖a7 25 ♖g1! 1-0

With the deadly threat of ♗f3, followed by ♗xh6 and winning. A truly horrible game by Fritz.

I am sure that thousands of games like this have been played by computers, but the programmers still have problems to make them understand how to avoid getting squashed in this manner. We will return to these positions later, but here is one game showing that it is not as easy as Van Wely made it look.

E. van den Doel – Fritz
Dutch Ch, Rotterdam 2000

1 c4 ♘f6 2 ♘c3 e5 3 e4 ♗c5 4 g3 0-0 5 ♗g2 ♘c6 6 ♘ge2 d6 7 d3?

Not a good move, as it allows Black to get the initiative and the possibility of executing the plan of ...f5 with tempo – a very big difference compared to the Van Wely game.

7...♘g4 8 0-0 f5 9 ♘a4 *(D)*

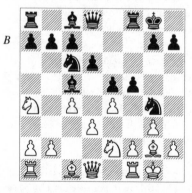

9...♘xf2!

White is close to being lost after only 9 moves of play. Now the computer gets the possibility of showing its strength in an open position with attacking possibilities.

10 ♖xf2 ♗xf2+ 11 ♔xf2 f4! 12 gxf4 exf4 13 ♘g1 ♕h4+ 14 ♔f1 f3!

The attack rages on with great precision.

15 ♘xf3 ♕xh2 0-1

The threat of ...♗h3, with the idea of ...♕h1+ and ...♘d4, is decisive. An impressive demonstration by Fritz.

White never got to close the centre in this game and the effect was astonishing. One wrong move and the game was close to being over. An important point to note here is the huge difference in playing strength when the same program plays an open and a closed position. To me it looks like the difference between an amateur and a super-grandmaster!

Fritz also had problems with closed positions in other games in the same tournament.

Fritz – H. Grooten
Dutch Ch, Rotterdam 2000

1 d4 c5

A good opening choice against a computer engine. Black provokes a position of a closed nature.

2 d5 e5 3 e4 d6 4 ♘c3 ♗e7 5 ♘f3 a6 6 a4 ♗g4 7 ♗e2 b6 8 ♘d2 ♗c8

Black avoids exchanging the light-squared bishops as this should favour White.

9 ♘c4 ♘f6 10 a5?

Initiating a mistaken plan. 10 f4! gives White a good position. White wants to win the bishop-pair, but it is not really important in this closed position.

10...b5 11 ♘b6 ♖a7 12 ♘xc8 ♕xc8 13 ♕d3 0-0 14 ♕f3?

Where is the queen going? White should play 14 0-0 and prepare f4 with g3 while keeping an eye on Black's queenside expansion plans with ...b4 and ...c4. Now White starts to move his queen aimlessly around, which results in Fritz slowly drifting into a passive position.

14...♘e8 15 0-0 ♕d8 16 ♕h5 *(D)*

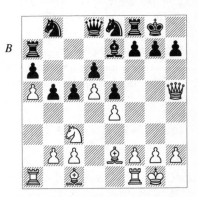

B

White wants to stop ...♗g5 with the plan of exchanging the bad bishop on e7 for its white counterpart.

16...h6 17 ♘d1 ♗g5 18 ♘e3 g6

Now Black slowly expands on the queenside.

19 ♕h3 ♘f6 20 ♕f3?

Once again moving the queen without a plan.

20...♘h7 21 c4 ♕d7 22 ♗d3?!

This move permits Black to lock the queenside. 22 cxb5, with the intention of opening some lines, should have been tried.

22...b4 23 ♗c2 h5 24 ♕d1 h4 25 h3 ♕d8 26 b3 *(D)*

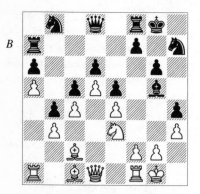

Pointless, like the following white moves. Fritz 7 believes White to be better here, but it cannot help its little brother when it comes to finding a plan.

26...♘d7 27 ♖e1 ♘df6 28 ♗b1 ♗f4 29 ♗b2 ♕e7 30 ♗c2

White has been moving his pieces aimlessly around for at least 5 moves, yet Fritz 7 still believes that White has an advantage. Black's plan is to prepare ...f5, and he can take his time as White seems to have given up any idea of playing actively. GM Thomas Luther suggests that Black should simply play 30...♖b8 in this position, send his king to the queenside, and then later play ...f5. This idea makes sense, especially against a computer program,

as it is often a good idea to prepare an attack very slowly. You have to be ready with all your forces when tactics begin. However, Black now puts his king on h8, which does not seem to be the right location. If the position opens up, there are the two bishops at b2 and c2 pointing towards the black king.

30...♔h8? 31 ♘g4 ♘g8 32 ♕e2 ♕g5 33 ♘h2 ♕h6 34 ♖ad1 f5 *(D)*

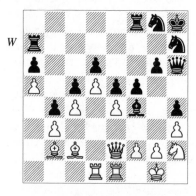

Black could have chosen not to play this move, and then the game could well have ended in a draw, as White was not displaying any activity. However, Black decides to take the chance and launch an attack. As mentioned before, the location of the king on h8 is not optimal and with the tactical power of the computer program, you can be sure that it is going to use any potential tactic exploiting the long a1-h8 diagonal.

35 ♔h1 ♖af7

35...♗xh2 36 ♔xh2 f4 is probably just a draw, but Black seems to be playing for more.

36 exf5 gxf5 37 ♖g1 ♖g7

37...♘e7 38 ♖de1 ♖g7 39 ♘f1 ♖fg8 is a better way to go. However, it is very difficult to conduct the attack with the two bishops at b2 and c2 that can 'wake up' at any moment.

38 ♘f3 ♛f6 39 ♘e1 ♘e7 40 ♘d3 ♘g6 41 g3 ♗h6 (D)

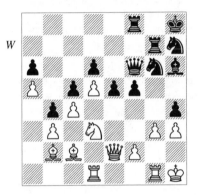

42 f4!

The 'sleeping' bishop on b2 is waking up again, and Fritz starts playing chess. Black is facing some problems on the long diagonal, and the position starts to get highly unpleasant for him.

42...hxg3 43 fxe5 ♛h4 44 ♛g2 f4 45 e6 ♘f6?

45...♘g5! is the best choice, when 46 ♘xf4 (defending against ...♘xh3) 46...♘xf4 47 ♛xg3 ♛xh3+ 48 ♛xh3 ♘gxh3 49 ♗xg7+ ♗xg7 50 ♖gf1 offers approximately equal chances. Black has a slight material edge, but White's passed e-pawn is strong.

46 ♖df1 ♛g5

46...♛h5 threatening ...♘h4 is better. Then 47 ♗d1 ♛g5 48 ♘e1 ♘h4 49

♘f3 ♘xg2 50 ♘xg5 ♘e3 51 ♘f7+ ♖gxf7 52 exf7 ♖xf7 53 ♖f3 leads to a rather unclear position.

47 ♘e1 ♘h4 48 ♛e2 ♖e7

If 48...f3 (with the point 49 ♘xf3 g2+), then 49 ♖xf3 ♘xf3 50 e7 ♖e8 51 ♛xf3 and White is winning more material.

49 ♘g2 f3 (D)

49...♘xg2 50 ♔xg2 ♔g8 is better, but White is of course still much better due to the powerful bishops and the passed e-pawn.

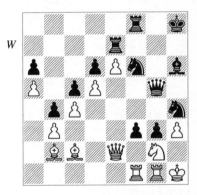

50 ♖xf3 ♘xf3 51 ♛xf3 ♗g7 52 ♗c1

The two bishops decide the game.

52...♛h5 53 ♛xg3 ♖g8 54 ♘f4 ♗h6 55 ♛xg8+ ♘xg8 56 ♘xh5 ♗xc1 57 ♖xc1 1-0

A very typical man vs machine game. At first the human outplays the computer positionally, and then outplays himself tactically. The program does not win the game – the opponent loses it. The computer plays the first part of the game like a total amateur, but wakes up to execute an elegant finish with very precise calculations. One lesson to learn from this game is to take a lot of time building up the attack and put all your pieces in optimal positions before launching the final breakthrough. When the final attack comes, the attacking force should be so overwhelming that nothing can stop it – not even the best calculation powers.

Activity of the Pieces

Some elements of positional thinking seem to have been too sophisticated to include in computer programs until now. Although some programs count the mobility of the pieces, it is still difficult for them to understand when a piece is out of play. If, for instance, a black knight ends up on h1 after a tactical sequence, it still counts in material evaluation, even if it is trapped and its loss is inevitable. However, its actual capture may be beyond the horizon of the program.

In the following game Rebel does not seem to understand the kind of trouble it gets into when its bishop is suddenly 'reduced to a pawn'.

R. Scherbakov – Rebel Century
Internet 2000

1 d4 d5 2 c4 c6 3 ♘f3 ♘f6 4 ♘c3 dxc4 5 a4 ♗f5 6 ♘e5 e6 7 f3 ♗b4 8 ♗g5

The main line goes 8 e4 ♗xe4 9 fxe4 ♘xe4 10 ♗d2 ♕xd4 11 ♘xe4

♕xe4+ 12 ♕e2 ♗xd2+ 13 ♔xd2 ♕d5+ 14 ♔c2 and White probably has a small edge. However, in his notes to this game Scherbakov remarked that this line would most likely be too complicated to play against a computer, as the position of the white king is somewhat unsafe.

8...h6 9 ♗h4 c5 10 dxc5 ♕a5 11 ♕d4 ♘c6

An alternative is 11...♗xc5 12 ♕xc4 0-0 13 e4 ♗h7 14 ♘d3 ♗e7 15 ♕b5 ♕c7 16 ♗g3 ♕c8 17 a5 ♘c6 with equal chances, as in Yusupov-Timman, Reykjavik 1988. Black has some active ideas based on, e.g., ...♘h5 and ...f5.

12 ♘xc6 bxc6 *(D)*

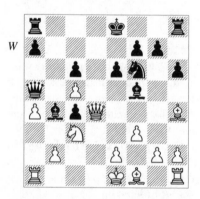

13 e4

The main idea in this line is to shut out the light-squared bishop. White's chances of an advantage will usually depend on whether he succeeds in this task.

13...♗xc5 14 ♕xc4 ♗g6 15 ♕a6 ♕xa6 16 ♗xa6 ♖b8 17 ♗xf6

A new move. Until this game only the passive 17 ♘d1 was played, with the continuation 17...♘d7 18 ♖c1 ♗b4+ 19 ♔f2 ♘c5 20 ♗e2 ♘xa4 21 ♖xc6 ♗c5+ 22 ♘e3 0-0 and Black had a strong position in Adianto-Kramnik, PCA rapidplay, London 1994.

17...gxf6 18 0-0-0 ♔e7 19 ♔c2 ♖hd8?

Black has fine play with 19...♖b4 20 b3 ♖hb8 21 ♗c4 f5, when the light-squared bishop enters the game again. However, Black's counter-chances will be smaller with only one set of rooks on the board.

20 ♖xd8 ♖xd8 21 ♗d3 *(D)*

Trying to keep the g6-bishop out of the game by stopping ...f5.

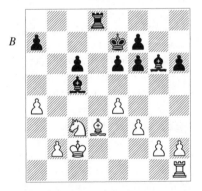

21...e5??

Unbelievable. Nearly any other move would do, but this one shuts out the bishop for the rest of the game. Even though today's top engines do not suggest that Black should play 21...e5, none of them change their evaluation significantly when this move is played,

and for this reason it is likely that they could play similar moves in other positions. Most of them consider the position about equal after 21...e5 and some even prefer Black. Maybe they like the bishop-pair!?

It is difficult to 'explain' to a computer what the problem is in this position, as the bishop is not bad in a traditional sense, i.e. limited by its own pawns. 21...e5 does not reduce the mobility of the bishop, but it completely cuts out any idea of an ...f5 break. It is quite clear, at least to humans, that the bishop now has no future as it cannot escape its prison. After his next move, White is effectively a piece up. The bishop still has a few squares at its disposal (h7 and g8), but this does not change anything.

22 g4! h5 23 h3 h4? *(D)*

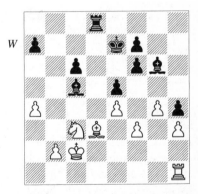

Another mistake. Any hope of king-side counterplay is connected to the threat of opening the h-file at some point. White wants to play on the queen-side, but if he is distracted by the possibilities of kingside counterplay, this may prove difficult, and Black has chances to save the game.

24 ♖d1 ♖d4?!

We have reached one of those positions where planning is required, and as you might expect the computer starts playing senseless moves. When the endgame has a closed character most programs are usually in trouble. 24...♖b8 is more resilient, trying to stop White's expansion on the queenside. Black has better chances to put up a fight with the rooks on the board.

25 b3 ♖d6? *(D)*

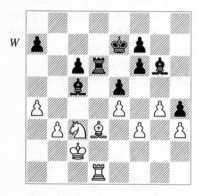

26 ♘e2

26 ♗a6!, as suggested by Scherbakov, is slightly more precise as it forces the rooks off at once.

26...♗e3 27 ♗a6 ♖xd1 28 ♔xd1

With fewer pieces on the board the bad position of the g6-bishop is emphasized. Most of the top engines consider White to be slightly better here. That is a big understatement. The game is effectively over.

28...♔d7 29 ♔c2 ♔c7 30 b4 ♗g5 31 ♗c4 ♔d6 32 ♔d3 ♔d7 33 ♘c3 ♗h6 34 ♘b1 ♗f8 35 ♔c3 ♔d6 36 ♘d2

Scherbakov takes his time because he wants to reach the time control at move 40, before advancing on the queenside.

36...♗h6 37 ♔d3 ♔c7 38 ♗b3 ♗f8 39 ♔c4 ♗g7 40 ♔d3 ♔d7 41 ♘c4 ♗f8 42 ♔c3 ♗h6 43 a5 ♔c7 44 ♗a4 ♗f4 45 a6 ♗g3 46 ♔d2 ♗f2 47 ♘a5!

Setting a small trap: 47...♔b6 48 ♗xc6 ♔xa6 49 ♘c4 and mates with b5. Pretty.

47...c5 48 b5 ♗g1 49 ♔d3 ♔b6 50 ♘c4+ ♔c7 51 ♗b3 ♔b8 52 b6 axb6 53 ♘d6!

Threatening to promote the pawn with ♘b5, ♗d5 and a7.

53...♔a7 54 ♗c4 b5 55 ♗xb5 c4+ 56 ♔xc4 1-0

White will slowly start to pick up the pawns on the kingside with ♘e8xf6, etc., and Black has no hope left.

Zugzwang Positions

We have already covered the technique of building a fortress in the endgame, and the engine's inability to understand this theme. Another important idea in the endgame is zugzwang, the situation where the player's obligation to make a move becomes a liability: whatever move you make will worsen your position. As most chess-players know, this has serious consequences in the endgame.

In general, computer programs are not familiar with the concept of zugzwang, and for this reason some endings may be unnecessarily difficult for them, because they are reduced to sheer calculation. The following position is an example of this.

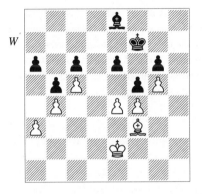

If you analyse this position only by calculating variations, you will probably have to go beyond 50 plies to demonstrate that White can promote a pawn. The computer programs may have some knowledge about what to do in the endgame, but this knowledge is not necessarily of much help here. One rule is to put your pawns on the opposite colour from your bishop. Many programs know about this rule. However, in this particular position it only confuses them, as some may want to play e5, even though this closes the position completely and makes the draw certain. Try to analyse the position for a while before reading on. You could even try to play out the position against your computer program to see

if you can win (in Chapters 8 and 9 I go more into detail about playing out positions against your computer).

When analysing an endgame position like this, a strong human player naturally does not try to calculate 50 plies. He analyses the position in terms of where to put the pieces and looks for the possibility to reach a zugzwang position. First of all, he would never even consider playing e5, closing the position. The e5-square is a perfect entry-point for the white king, as Black has to put his king on e7 to keep the king out of f6 and d6. At this point, with the black king tied down to e7, zugzwang is not so far away. After this White can manoeuvre his bishop to the a2-g8 diagonal and exchange on f5 at some point. Black cannot recapture with the g-pawn as this will give White a passed g-pawn. When he recaptures with the e-pawn, however, the white bishop will have some chances to enter Black's position via g8 and h7. An important feature of the position is that White has more space and therefore has the possibility of losing a tempo, which is a crucial factor when forcing a zugzwang. Let us take a look at how some of the top engines play from this position. All the following games were played with 10 minutes for the rest of the game and some of them show that the programs may be tricked by their 'knowledge' about good and bad bishops. We begin with a program that has won the world championship title several times.

Shredder 7.04 – C. Kongsted

1 e5?

Drawing the game, as the white king has no way to penetrate the black position.

1...♔e7 2 ♔d3 ♔d7 3 a4 ♔c7 4 ♔c3 ♔d7 5 ♔d3 ♔c7 6 ♔d4 ♔d7 7 a5 ½-½

Nimzo 8 – C. Kongsted

1 e5? ½-½

Chessmaster 9000 – C. Kongsted

1 ♔e3 ♗d7 2 ♗d1 ♔e7 3 a4 ♔f7 4 a5 ♔e7 5 ♗c2 ♗e8 6 ♔d4 ♗d7 7 ♔e5 ♗e8 8 ♗d1 ♗d7 9 ♗f3 ♗e8 10 ♗e2 ♗d7 11 ♗d3 ♗e8 12 ♗f1 ♗f7 13 ♔d4 ♗e8 14 e5? ½-½

Crafty 19.01 – C. Kongsted

1 ♔e3 ♔e7 2 ♗d1 ♗d7 3 ♗b3 ♗c8 4 ♔d4 ♗d7 5 exf5

Crafty does things slightly differently from the method described above. It exchanges on f5 before bringing the king to e5, but the result is the same. It is just a transposition.

5...exf5 6 ♔e5 ♗c8 7 ♗a2!

The program finds the main idea in the position. White loses a tempo to get Black into zugzwang. The alternative variation 7 ♗g8 ♗d7 8 ♗h7 ♔f7 9 ♔d6 ♗e8 10 ♔e5 ♔g7 11 ♔d6 ♔f7 (11...♔xh7? 12 ♔e7) 12 ♔c7 ♔g7 gets White nowhere (13 ♔d8? ♗f7!),

so Black's bishop must be on d7 before the white bishop enters the position.

7...♗d7 8 ♗g8 ♗e8

After 8...♗c8 9 ♗h7 ♔f7 10 ♔d6 ♔g7 11 ♗xg6 ♔xg6 12 ♔xc6 Black is unable to fight against White's passed pawns.

9 ♗e6!

Black is close to zugzwang. If the bishop moves, it will be exchanged and then White wins the pawn endgame easily. If 9...♔f8 then 10 ♔f6! and 9...♔d8 10 ♔d6!, in both cases with zugzwang.

1-0

Naturally, some of the programs may do better if tested with more time. I set Shredder 7.04 to analyse the position for a longer period, and after half an hour it decides not to play 1 e5? any more. Even though the program does not show signs of having found the right solution, it is generally possible that complicated zugzwang problems may be solved through sheer calculation, especially when computers get faster in the coming years. However, test positions like this give the impression that it is rather coincidental if the engine stumbles upon some of the zugzwang possibilities when calculating through the various lines. With a kind of 'zugzwang detection' these positions could be solved more easily, but so far I do not know of any program that has implemented this successfully although Fritz performs markedly better if its 'selectivity' is set to zero.

Note that the programs are actually handicapped by their endgame knowledge in this example, because of the fact that they like to put their pawns on dark squares when they have a light-squared bishop.

Lack of Endgame Knowledge

Concrete knowledge of theoretical positions is a part of the arsenal of a strong human player, and also of computer programs. However, the knowledge of the programs is normally quite limited compared to a strong human player. For simple programs it is more or less restricted to the perfect information in the endgame tablebases with five pieces or fewer – if the tablebases are installed (more about tablebases in Chapter 9). Usually, computers play quite well when they are close to these five-piece endings, as they can 'hit' the tablebases whenever they reach one of those positions in their analysis. However, this does not apply in cases where exchanges are unlikely.

Take a look at the following position.

Black's bishop does not have the same colour as the promotion square of the h-pawn and therefore he cannot win. This six-man ending is not yet included in the tablebases, and for this reason the programmers need to teach their program about these cases. Of the top programs only Junior and

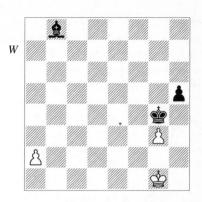

Crafty evaluate this as a draw, while the rest give position values that favour Black. Some believe Black has only a small advantage, while others return scores equal to a decisive advantage. The 'wrong bishop' is a familiar concept to strong human chess-players, and it is not that difficult to program a computer to understand this concept as well.

Another well-known position-type is this rook endgame:

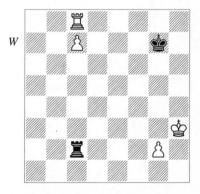

In this position there are six pieces including two pawns, and it is not

included in the currently available end-game tablebases. White cannot win, as it is impossible to force the black king away from the key squares g7 and h7. However, with the white pawn on f2 (instead of g2) the position is won since White advances the f-pawn to f6 and forces the black king to f7, and then he wins with the tactical trick ♖h8, meeting ...♖xc7 by ♖h7+. This is common knowledge for strong human players, and with the pawns on f- and c-files all programs can win the position quite easily. However, the evaluation of all the current top engines shows that they believe they can also win with the pawn on g2. Special cases like this have to be programmed specifically for the engine; otherwise they cannot understand them. Calculating every possible continuation from the diagram position is still beyond the reach of the current programs and will be for years to come.

Naturally, slightly more complex cases, such as the following one, are also hard for the computer engines.

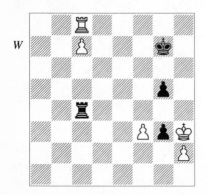

Here White has to play 1 ♔xg3! to preserve his f-pawn, followed by the pawn sacrifice 2 h4! and then advancing his pawn to f6. On 1 hxg3? Black replies 1...g4+!, eliminating the important white f-pawn after either 2 fxg4 or 2 ♔g2 gxf3+ 3 ♔xf3 – White cannot then win the game. A few engines may be able to find this idea if they are set to analyse for a very long period. The reason for this is that the winning variations in the line with 1 ♔xg3! could pop up within the horizon of the programs. Thus, by sheer calculation some positions may be solved. However, most programs will not have a chance if they do not have the necessary knowledge.

Endgame theory contains thousands of examples of these 'well-known' theoretical draws, but most of them will only be appreciated by a chess program if there are five pieces or fewer left on the board.

Positional Evaluation and Exceptions from Rules

Chess is a game of exceptions, and computer engines need to know not only about the rules, but also about the exceptions. As these are very frequent, it takes years to tune an evaluation function of a program to a reasonable level.

One typical problem that programmers face is how to evaluate passed pawns correctly, and misevaluating a passed pawn is common amongst the programs. Sometimes it needs to be assigned a very high value if it cannot be stopped, and in other cases when it is blocked or weak the advantage of a passed pawn can be neutralized.

In the following game the evaluation of a black passed pawn on its seventh rank caused problems for two engines.

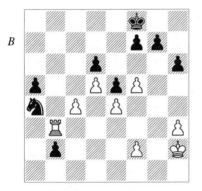

Chess Tiger 14.0 – Gandalf 5 beta
Test game

Chess Tiger 14 had just played 49 ♖g3-b3 and evaluated the position as favourable for Black: –0.86, comparable to an advantage of nearly one pawn, despite the fact that Black has only one pawn for the exchange. The Gandalf 5 beta replied:

49...♔e7

It showed an evaluation similar to that of Chess Tiger, –0.82. The game continued:

50 ♔g3 ♔f6 51 ♔h4 ♔e7

Gandalf now changed the evaluation to 0.00, but on the following

moves it returned to negative scores again. Chess Tiger was still showing negative scores.

52 ♔g3 *(D)*

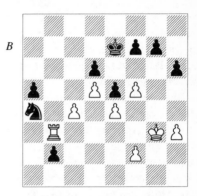

52...♔d7?

Gandalf did not want to repeat the position, but now it allows a breakthrough on the kingside. Staying put with 52...♔f6 is a better try. In that case White can try to reach a zugzwang position with 53 ♔g4 ♔e7 54 ♖b7+ ♔f6 55 f3! forcing Black to advance his kingside pawns. In that case White has the better chances as well.

53 f6 g6

Not, of course, 53...gxf6? as this will make the black pawns easy targets for the white king.

54 ♖b5

Now both programs returned scores about 0, i.e. nearly equal. Chess Tiger: 0.04, Gandalf 0.03.

54...♔c7 55 f4

At this point Chess Tiger jumped to 0.94, and Gandalf started to show more positive scores as well.

55...h5 56 fxe5 dxe5 57 h4 ♔d7 58 ♔f3 ♔c7 59 c5 ♘xc5 60 ♖xb2

...and Black resigned 13 moves later.

At move 60 both programs were evaluating the situation as much better for White: Chess Tiger: +1.5 and Gandalf: +1.6.

Let us look at the diagram position again. Why did both programs evaluate this position as good for Black?

Black has only one pawn for the exchange, but he has a passed pawn on its seventh rank and this is absolutely crucial for the programs. The pawn is covered by the knight on a4, and some programs award an extra bonus for this. Moreover, Black has two passed pawns (a5 and b2) that could, at least theoretically, be connected, and this may also give Black a plus.

Usually a pawn on its seventh rank is worth much more than a normal pawn, and this knowledge is included in all modern programs. There are of course exceptions, and this is one of them. The b2-pawn cannot advance since Black has no way to cover the promotion square. The black knight is tied down to the a4-square as it has to cover the passed pawn, but the white rook can still operate on several squares on the b-file, and additionally White has some chances to break through on the kingside, as we saw in the game. Moreover, and most important, the black king will never be able to go to the queenside and help the promotion of the pawn as long as White keeps his rook on the b-file. Connecting the black a- and b-pawn will never happen with the knight on a4.

However, these things are not so easy to explain to a program because it may interfere with other cases where a passed pawn can win the game. For this reason the evaluation of passed pawns remains troublesome for most engines. Of the top engines tested on the diagram position only two gave a positive score for White after one minute of analysis, while all others preferred to have the black pieces. The scores of different programs are not directly comparable, but at least they show that the majority believe Black to have a slight edge.

Hiarcs 8	0.55
Shredder 7.04	0.23
Junior 7	−0.27
Chessmaster 9000	−0.33
Nimzo 8	−0.42
Crafty 19.03	−0.39
Fritz 8	−0.47
Gambit Tiger 2.0	−0.58
Gandalf 5 beta	−0.82
Chess Tiger 14	−0.86

One thing to add is that the Gandalf version that played the game was from November 2002, and when I tested it the Gandalf 6 beta of March 2003, the evaluation had improved. It was now giving a +0.19 advantage to White after one minute of analysis. The evaluation of Chess Tiger 15.0 was not significantly different from that of the previous version (−0.68).

Some readers may ask if these evaluations are important at all. The answer is a clear 'yes', because evaluations decide for instance whether an engine chooses to go into an endgame which it believes to be advantageous. If this evaluation is wrong, it could exchange down to an endgame where the opponent that has the better chances – just as we saw in the example above.

The Good, the Bad and the Active Bishop

Some of the definitions in chess are not as clear as we may believe. When speaking about good and bad bishops there are many exceptions to be considered. A bad bishop usually means a bishop that has long-term problems with its mobility because it is blocked by its own pawns, especially centre pawns that are fixed on the same colour squares as the bishop. The programmer has to tell the program about this in 'simple' language. If we say, however, that the program should assign negative values to a bishop when, e.g., two of the pawns on the c-, d-, e- and f-files are on the same colour as the bishop, we will sometimes have nearly as many exceptions as we have examples of that rule actually working.

Let us begin with a classical example of a bad bishop (*see diagram*).

In this position the knight is far superior to the bishop and the advantage is big enough to win the game. After one minute's analysis, most programs

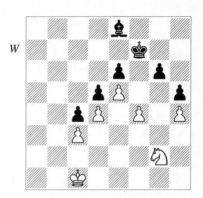

A. Burn – A. Alekhine
Karlsbad 1911

seem to believe White is slightly better here, and this indicates that the programmers have implemented code for a bad bishop. However, at this point none of them are aware of how decisive this advantage can be, as it is beyond their horizon that White's positional advantage should eventually lead to a material gain. The computer scores show that nearly all programs are aware that the knight is superior in these positions. Only the Tigers and Crafty have some problems here.

The scores are not directly comparable, but obviously a score too close to 0 is not a good result. If the scores are close to 0 it means that the engine might walk into an endgame like this as Black.

Shredder 7.04	0.89
Fritz 8	0.69
Nimzo 8	0.65
Gandalf 5 beta	0.54
Hiarcs 8	0.38

Chessmaster 9000	0.27
Junior 7	0.19
Crafty 19.03	0.01
Gambit Tiger	0.00
Chess Tiger 15	0.00

The game continuation emphasized the superiority of the knight in positions like this:

57 ♔b2 ♗a4 58 ♘e3 ♔e7 59 ♔a3 ♗c6

59...♗b3 with the idea of denying the white knight access to the other half of the board, is probably more resilient. However, after 60 ♔b4 White will advance his king and sooner or later the knight will reach the other half of the board. The combined forces of king and knight will drive the black king back, and eventually White will start picking up the black pawns. If the black bishop stays on b3 to stop the penetration by the white knight, then the knight can enter the other half of the board via g5-h7-f6. One sample line is: 60...♔d7 61 ♔c5 ♔e7 62 ♔c6 ♗a4+ 63 ♔c7 ♗b3 64 ♘f1 ♗c2 65 ♘d2 ♗e4 66 ♔c6 (gaining a move for the knight) 66...♗d3 67 ♘f3 ♗e4 68 ♘g5 ♗d3 69 ♘h7 ♗c2 70 ♘f6 ♗e4 71 ♘d7 ♗f3 72 ♔c7 ♗e4 73 ♘b6 ♗f3 74 ♘c8+ (Black is being pushed back) 74...♔e8 75 ♔d6 ♗g4 76 ♘e7 ♔f7 77 ♔d7 ♗d1 78 ♘c6 ♗a4 79 ♔d6 ♔e8 80 ♘a5 ♗d7 81 ♘b7 ♗c8 82 ♘c5 and White wins either the e-pawn or the black bishop. In lines like this is quite obvious how much more powerful the knight can be compared to the black bishop. However, these lines are far too long to calculate to the end from the diagram position. At least you do not need to calculate all this. You just have to know that the knight is much stronger.

The game went:

60 ♔b4 ♔d7 61 ♔a5 ♔c7 62 ♘c2 ♔b7 63 ♘b4 ♗d7 64 ♘a6 ♗e8 65 ♘c5+ ♔c6 66 ♘xe6 ♗d7 67 ♘g5 ♗f5 68 ♔b4 ♗g4 69 ♔a3 ♔d7 70 ♘f7 ♗e6 71 ♘d6 ♔c6 72 ♔b2 ♗g4 73 ♔c2 ♔d7 74 ♔d2 ♗e6 75 ♔e3 ♗h3 76 f5+ gxf5 77 ♔f4 ♗g4 78 ♔g5 ♗h3 79 ♘e8 ♔f7 80 ♘f6 f4 81 ♔xf4 ♗e6 82 ♔g5 1-0

There is a big difference between a game like this and the following position, which is an exception to the rule that a bishop is bad when the centre pawns are on squares of the same colour.

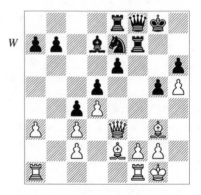

V. Anand – J. Timman
Dortmund 1999

Here the c3- and d4-pawns are on dark squares and according to the rule, the g3-bishop should be bad because it has limited mobility due to the three centre pawns on dark squares (the c- and f-files are regarded as centre files here). However, in this position the bishop is an important piece since it controls the key e5-square and other squares in the black camp. Moreover, its black counterpart has disappeared, and this makes the weaknesses of the dark squares even more evident.

The next diagram shows an even worse example when we try to apply our simple rule.

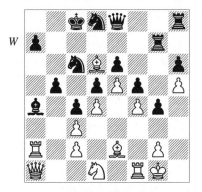

J. Fedorowicz – G. Rey
San Francisco 1998

In this case there are no fewer than four white pawns fixed on dark squares on the c- to f-files, so the bishop on d6 should be really bad. This is not the case however, as it plays an active role in this position. It is outside the pawn-chain and it is unchallenged on the dark squares because its opposite number has been exchanged. Moreover, it

is hitting many important squares in the black camp and it can become even more powerful if White succeeds in launching an attack against the black king. Actually that is what happened in the game:

28 ♘b2 ♕xh5 29 ♘xa4 bxa4 30 ♖b1 ♕h4 31 ♖ab2 g3 32 ♗f3 ♖hh7?

32...♔d7 is more resilient.

33 ♖b8+ ♔d7

If 33...♘xb8 then 34 ♖xb8+ ♔d7 35 ♕xa4+ ♘c6 36 ♕b5 and Black gets mated.

34 ♕xa4 1-0

If the exceptions from the rules are difficult to understand for humans, this is nothing compared to the problems that the engines are facing when evaluating bad bishops. Their excellent calculating abilities can sometimes compensate for this, but the quality of their positional evaluation is very variable. However, these examples show that defining a bishop as either good or bad is just too simple to evaluate positions correctly. For this reason some programmers have worked with what could be called the 'active bishop' which is a description that fits the bishop on d6 in the example above. Nevertheless, it is not so easy for a program to distinguish between a bishop that is active and a bishop that is just plainly bad.

The following chapter will display a few more computer weaknesses and describe how to exploit those when playing against the programs.

4 How to Beat the Computer

I'm sorry, Frank, I think you missed it. Queen to bishop three, bishop takes queen, knight takes bishop, mate.
HAL 9000, *2001: A Space Odyssey* by Stanley Kubrick

One thing is to know the weaknesses of the computer engines, another is to be able to use the knowledge when you play against them. The previous chapter could give the impression that computer programs do not know much about chess, but anyone with a copy of Fritz, Chessmaster or one of the other programs knows that this is not the case. The reality is that a large percentage of human chess-players have no realistic chances of beating the top modern chess programs. However, for those who still wish to pursue this goal, I will provide some advice in the following pages.

To play successfully against a computer program you need to know not only about its weaknesses, but also its strengths. The first, and most obvious, of their strengths is their tactical ability. The second is their consistency, their ability never to make big mistakes, but to play reasonable moves all the way through a game. In many human vs computer games the human builds up strong positional pressure or an attack, only to lose everything because of a missed tactical point. Moreover, the development of anti-computer chess seems to have resulted in many players playing very passively against computers, avoiding tactics at all costs. This is a very risky strategy, because the fear of missing a tactical point can be as important as actually doing it. It only leads to a passive position that will be lost anyway.

Most books about computer chess give the impression that with a quick fix and some good advice, you will be able to beat the computer rather easily. This is probably good for marketing purposes, but has nothing to do with reality. If you are rated below about 2100, I believe that your time will be spent much better by improving your general level instead of trying to beat the programs with some weird anti-computer strategies. Playing against computers may raise your tactical level slightly, but personally I prefer to play with humans whenever possible. I find it unnatural to play against something which never misses a tactical point (in the short term at least), but at the same time has great difficulties in understanding the dangers of a long-term attack. No humans play like this, at least none that I know of! Still, training games against the programs can be instructive, especially if you want to practice how to play a specific opening or play out a training position. I will explain how to do this in Chapter 7.

Anti-Computer Strategies

Analysing the recent man versus machine games, you can see a tendency amongst the top players not to play in the usual anti-computer style, but to play in their usual style. For strong players, I believe this is a good strategy, perhaps mixed with an awareness of the typical weaknesses that you may exploit. Adding a few anti-computer tricks may sometimes help you, as we will see in some of the following games. If you exaggerate, however, you may end up with some hideous losses.

On the Internet it is quite common for chess-players to post their wins against engines with the most bizarre strategies. An example of this is the following game, with Fritz playing on a P600 computer with 256 Mb RAM, and 128 Mb for hash tables, against a German player without an Elo rating:

Fritz 6 – Eduard Nemeth
Stuttgart 2000

1 d4 h5?!

The black player is not crazy; he is just using an obscure anti-computer strategy.

2 e4 e5 3 dxe5 ♘c6 4 ♘f3 ♗e7 5 ♘c3 a6 6 ♗c4 ♘h6 7 0-0 d6 8 exd6

♗xd6 **9 ♗d5 ♗g4 10 ♗xc6+ bxc6 11 h3 ♕e7**

Exploiting the fact that the program may underestimate the attack following the opening of the h-file. However, this attack is not really dangerous. The problem for the program is that it does not see any danger before it is too late.

12 hxg4 hxg4 13 ♗g5 f6 14 e5 ♕f7 15 exd6 0-0-0 16 ♘e5?! *(D)*

Getting a bit greedy. 16 ♗f4!, returning the knight, is superior, when Black's attack should quickly evaporate.

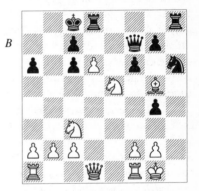

16...fxe5 17 ♗xd8 ♕h5 18 f3?

White can still win by 18 ♕d3! with the point 18...♘f5 19 ♗h4! ♘xh4 20 ♖fd1 ♘f3+ 21 ♔f1 ♘d4 22 d7+ ♔d8 23 ♘e2 ♕h1+ 24 ♘g1, when Black's attack is at an end.

18...g3 19 ♖e1 ♘g4 20 ♔f1 ♕h1+ 21 ♔e2 ♕xg2+ 22 ♔d3 ♘f2+ 23 ♔c4 ♘xd1 24 ♖axd1 ♖xd8

...and Black won.

The most important thing to say about these games is: don't try this at home! If you play like this you may win one out of twenty, if you are lucky. In addition, and more importantly, it will not improve your general level or understanding of the game, because it is an unrealistic way of playing.

During the few last years I have seen a lot of these anti-computer games, especially against Fritz 5 and 6, so when I got my copy of the latest Chess-Base creation Fritz 8, I was looking forward to checking its style, as I had heard that it should be more resistant to the usual anti-computer strategies. I usually only play training games in specific openings against the programs, but in the research phase of this book I decided to play some games in anti-computer style to analyse which ones work against a few of the current programs. I am sure that Fritz 8 is stronger than its predecessors, but it is far from immune to the usual strategies.

I apologize for using some slightly low quality blitz games here, but I have chosen to include them, as they illustrate some of the strategies humans have at their disposal without playing in the extreme style of the previous game.

I decided to play some games with a small increment as my earlier experience from playing with computers is that they like to play out long, drawn endgames. If you do not have an increment you will just lose on time, because the computer can move faster than you can.

C. Kongsted – Fritz 8 (version 8.0.0.8)
Copenhagen 2003
(4 min. for the game + 2 sec. increment per move)

1 d4 ♘f6 2 e3 e6 3 ♗d3 c5 4 c3 d5 5 f4

The Stonewall set-up is one of the standard anti-computer openings, both as White and Black. Normally, I do not play this way, but in a blitz game I do not want to use up too much time calculating tactics before it is actually necessary. The general idea is that White will prepare a long-term attack and save some time by playing automatic moves in the first phase of the game.

5...♘c6 6 ♘d2

Trying to trick Fritz out of the book with an unusual move-order, but unfortunately Fritz was still in book even after this move. 6 ♘f3 would be normal.

6...♗d6 7 ♘df3

Still aiming to get Fritz out of book, but with this move I am paying too high a price. It is usually a good idea to take the programs out of book, but only if you can do it with a natural move. Now Fritz was surely out of book! I was considering playing 7 ♘gf3 instead, but was disturbed by the fact that Black can exchange on d4, after which I have to recapture on d4 with the c-pawn, as f4 is not covered. When White chooses the Stonewall set-up, he normally wants to recapture on d4 with the e-pawn to avoid the opening of the c-file. Now, however, White loses control of the e4-square. 7 ♕f3 is an interesting alternative.

7...0-0 8 ♘e5

It would have been better just to develop the knight with 8 ♘e2.

8...♘e7 9 ♘e2 c4?!

This move puzzled me a bit. I know that most of the top engines are programmed to avoid closed positions, as they cannot find the long-term plans necessary to play these positions. Nevertheless, the latest incarnation of Fritz voluntarily walks into a closed position. Quite surprising.

10 ♗c2 b5 11 ♖g1

Getting ready to push the kingside pawns.

11...♗b7 12 g4 ♘e4 13 ♘g3 f6

White's opening has not been very successful, and now Black strikes back in the centre.

14 ♘f3 ♘g6 15 ♗d2 e5 *(D)*

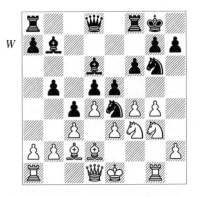

Usually you know that something has gone wrong when the computer

makes a counter-strike in the centre like this! At least I did not feel very confident at this point, and did not have any reason to do so either. Now White has to do everything to keep the centre closed.

16 f5 ♘h8 17 ♕e2 ♘xd2 18 ♔xd2

The king may as well stay in the centre, since it would probably not be safe after castling queenside. In that case Black could easily get an attack going with ...a5 and ...b4. When playing against a computer you should never give it the chance to execute clear-cut plans like this. If it has a clear idea of where it is going, it can strike swiftly and very accurately.

18...e4?!

Fritz likes to gain space, but at the same time it closes the centre, and now White's king is suddenly rather safe. I believe it would have been much better to play 18...b4 and get on with the attack, and preserve the option of opening the e-file later.

19 ♘h4 b4 20 ♘g2

White eyes the e6-square as a possible location for the knight.

20...bxc3+ 21 bxc3 ♘f7 22 ♘f4 ♘g5

Fritz gets materialistic and uses several tempi trying to put a knight on f3, which White can only avoid by sacrificing the exchange or playing the computer suggestion 23 ♘e6?, which loses a pawn. However, sacrificing an exchange is a small price to pay for the possibility of getting an easy-to-play attack on the kingside. If Black had played 22...♗xf4 23 exf4 White would have blocked e3 and had good attacking prospects on the kingside.

23 ♖gf1 ♘f3+ 24 ♖xf3

Well, I only need one rook to mate it, I thought! Now Black gets into a position where it is difficult for him to attack the white king, while all White's moves on the kingside are obvious.

24...exf3 25 ♕xf3 ♗xf4 26 ♕xf4 ♕e7 27 h4 ♖ae8 28 g5 ♔h8 29 ♖g1

White's kingside attack develops naturally.

29...♗c6 30 ♘h5 ♖f7? *(D)*

After this imprecise move, White's threats become really dangerous. The actual consequences of the attack were beyond the horizon of Fritz at blitz speed. Most humans would have realized long time ago that White's attack is not without sting and a very accurate defence is needed, but when I set Fritz 8 to analyse this position it is still displaying negative values of −0.9 (i.e. a positive score for Black) around this point due to its material advantage. After six minutes, however, the score changes to slightly positive values. The development of this game, and many other similar games, makes it very obvious that computers cannot 'sense' the dangers of a looming attack, because they see nothing of what is beyond their horizon. Black should play 30...♖g8!, when he has better chances of parrying the attack. In that case White can continue by 31 ♕f3, followed by ♘f4 with the threat of playing the knight to g6 at some point,

while it is difficult for Black to do something constructive.

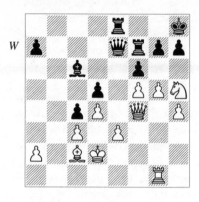

31 g6!

White crashes through.

31...hxg6?!

31...♖ff8 is probably slightly better, but the white attack continues with 32 gxh7 ♖f7 33 ♕g3 ♔xh7 34 ♘f4 and White should be close to winning, eyeing e6 and g6 for the knight. Alternatively he can put the queen on g6, the rook on g3 and start to push the h-pawn, while Black's counter-chances against the white king seem too slow.

32 fxg6 ♖ff8 33 ♘g3

Better is 33 ♕f3! with the point that 33...♔g8 34 ♘f4 f5 loses to 35 ♖g3! ♕xh4 36 ♖h3 ♕g5 37 ♕h1.

33...f5 34 h5 ♔g8 35 h6 ♗d7

Black lacks counterplay.

36 ♘h5 gxh6 37 ♕xh6 ♕xe3+

One of the nice things about playing against computers is that their tactical strength sometimes backfires. At this point Fritz simply gives up a rook for a pawn because it analyses that

Black is losing in all lines. The threat was g7 with deadly consequences. I had only 15 seconds left at this point (but still the two-seconds-per-move increment), so I was quite happy about this gift. Fritz could have tried to complicate matters with 37...f4 38 e4 dxe4 39 ♗xe4, but this is winning for White as well. The threat is ♗d5+ and, for instance, 39...♗e6 fails to 40 g7 ♖f5 41 ♕h8+ ♔f7 42 g8♕+ ♖xg8 43 ♕xg8#.

38 ♕xe3 ♖xe3 39 ♔xe3 ♗c8 40 ♔f3

Trying to gain a little time from the increment before proceeding.

40...♖d8 41 ♔f4 ♗d7 42 ♔g5 ♗e8 43 ♔h6 ♖d6 44 ♗xf5 1-0

I only had 10 seconds left, but the position is easily winning. Fritz recognized this and said: "I resign. Maybe humans are smarter after all." Probably true, but not so easy to prove in a blitz game. After this I decided to play some longer games so as not to get a heart attack while playing.

The next game I would like to show displays a slightly different development. In this game my opening was more successful, but later on Fritz showed its dreaded tactical strength.

C. Kongsted – Fritz 8
(version 8.0.0.8)
Copenhagen 2003
(10 min. + 2 sec. per move)

1 d4 d5 2 e3 ♘f6 3 ♗d3 ♘c6!

Fritz plays the opening differently this time. One of the improvements in modern programs is that they have a learning function in their opening library. If they score badly against you in one line, they will pick another variation in later games. This is what is happening here. Fritz lost in the opening 1 d4 ♘f6 2 e3 e6, so now it tries something different to make the task more difficult for its opponent. The move played by Fritz is a book move and it is the invention of the Russian master Chigorin. Black is preparing to play ...e5.

4 f4 ♘b4 *(D)*

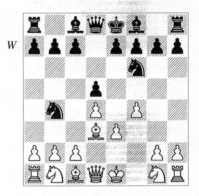

5 ♘f3

White has to part with his bishop as he would get a horrible position after 5 ♗e2 ♗f5 6 ♘a3 c5 7 c3 ♘c6. In the game White reaches a solid and closed position with control of the centre, and this is the most important thing when playing against a computer.

5...♘xd3+ 6 cxd3

White recaptures with the pawn to gain control of e4.

6...e6 7 0-0 ♗e7 8 ♕e2

This move is an attempt to take Fritz out of book and make it think on its own. In this particular case, I prefer the computer to be on its own in the opening phase rather than repeating the moves of a strong Russian master. If it plays too many moves from the book, it will often get its pieces out to natural squares, and therefore deviating a bit from normal lines can sometimes be profitable. I will get back to a discussion of this subject later. Now Fritz was indeed out of book.

8...0-0 9 e4

Possibly not the best plan, as it gives Black the opportunity to strike back in the centre. I believe that playing slowly with 9 ♘bd2, ♘e5, and after some preparation g4, would have been a slightly better choice.

9...a5?

Fritz does not seize the moment to open up the position with 9...dxe4 10 dxe4 c5!, when Black's position is fine. The explanation for Fritz's strategy could be that it did not want to help me to rectify the doubled pawns on the d-file. At this point however, the doubled d-pawns are not really a disadvantage, and Black would have been better off to open the position.

10 e5! ♘d7 11 ♗e3 a4

With this move and the following moves it looks like Fritz is playing according to a plan of getting counterplay on the queenside. Personally I believe that this counterplay is very slow, but it is interesting that all of the following moves are a part of the same plan. Earlier versions of the program would most likely have started to make senseless moves around this point.

12 ♘bd2 c6 13 ♗f2 ♕b6 14 ♖ab1 a3 15 b3 ♘b8

The knight is on the way to b4, which is a very slow plan when you consider White's possibilities of kingside expansion. I believe Black should play ...f5 this move or next move, to try to counter White's expansion on the kingside. White wants to play g4 and f5 at some point, but takes the time necessary to prepare it well.

16 ♔h1 ♘a6 (D)

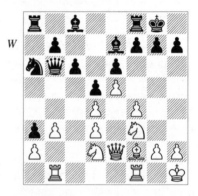

17 ♖g1

When building up an attack against a computer opponent, it is of crucial importance to get all the pieces on the right squares before the attack is initiated. When the tactics start you should have an overwhelming force, so that nothing can stop your attack – not even the computer's extraordinary calculating abilities. My last few moves have been aimed at playing g4, and this plan can easily backfire for White if it is not well prepared.

17...♘b4 18 ♘f1

Prophylaxis is very important, also against computers. Even though Black's counterplay does not look very dangerous, I should be aware of what my silicon opponent is trying to do. At this point I realized that it was preparing to put pressure on the d3-pawn with ...♕b5, ...b6 and ...♗a6. Thus, my pieces have to be ready to defend the d3-pawn.

18...♕b5 19 ♖d1 b6 20 g4 ♗a6 21 ♘e1 c5 22 f5 c4! *(D)*

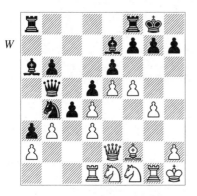

Just when I thought that Black had run out of counterplay, the program finds new resources. Exchanging on c4 is now taboo as it opens the long a8-h1 diagonal for the bishop, so I just have to get on with the attack on the kingside.

23 f6! gxf6 24 ♗h4 cxb3 25 axb3

Fritz's counterattack has now generated a dangerous passed pawn on the queenside. It is very difficult, however,

for a computer program to weigh the value of the passed pawn against a kingside attack. Not that it is easy for humans, but at least most humans respect when their king is under attack. At this point Fritz clearly prefers Black's chances, but soon the score starts dropping down.

25...♘c6 26 ♗xf6 ♗xf6 27 exf6 ♕xb3?!

Too greedy. Black has chances of surviving after 27...♔h8 with the idea of defending with ...♖g8-g6 at once. Also 27...♖fc8 with the idea of taking the king to the centre is very unclear; e.g., 28 ♕e3 ♔f8 29 ♕h6+ ♔e8 30 ♕xh7 ♕xb3 31 ♕g8+ ♔d7 32 ♕xf7+ ♔d6 when the black king is safer than on the kingside, and the strong a-pawn gives counterplay. On 27...♘xd4? White plays 28 ♕e3.

28 ♖g3 ♔h8

28...♘xd4? is again impossible due to 29 ♕e3 threatening ♕g5+.

29 g5

Now Fritz's evaluation starts dropping, but Black has already been in deep trouble for a while. It is characteristic for computer programs that Fritz does not realize how dangerous the attack against its own king is.

29...♖g8 30 ♕h5 ♖g6 31 ♘g2?!

Very precise play was needed at this point, but unfortunately I mixed up the move-order. 31 ♖h3! is correct, immediately setting up the mate threat, which forces 31...h6 (or 31...♔g8 32 ♕xh7+ ♔f8 33 ♖c1 and White wins due to the threats of ♖xc6 and ♕h8+ followed by g6!) 32 ♘g2, when the threat of ♘f4 forces Black to give up the queen with 32...♛xd1 33 ♕xd1. This position may look slightly unclear at first glance, but analysis demonstrates that White's attack hits Black before he can threaten to promote his passed a-pawn.

31...a2!

Without fear.

32 ♖h3 *(D)*

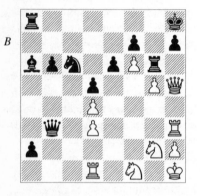

32...♔g8!

A very cold-blooded move. I was expecting 32...h6, when 33 ♘f4 wins. Black then has to sacrifice his queen in an attempt to save himself, but it does not work: 33...♛xd1 34 ♘xg6+ ♔g8 35 ♕xd1 fxg6 36 ♖xh6 ♔f7 37 ♖h7+ ♔g8 38 ♖g7+ ♔f8 39 ♕c1 ♗b7 40 ♕f4 and mating.

33 ♘f4?

Two inexact moves in this phase of the game are too much; now Black wins in short order. Better is the simple 33 ♕xh7+! ♔f8 34 ♕h8+ ♖g8 35 g6! (the idea that I missed during the game) 35...♛xd1 (on 35...fxg6? comes 36 ♕h6+ ♔e8 {36...♔f7 loses to 37 ♕f4!} 37 f7+! ♔xf7 38 ♕h7+ ♖g7 39 ♖f3+ ♔e7 40 ♕xg7+ ♔d6 41 ♖f7 with a winning attack) 36 g7+ ♔e8 37 ♕xg8+ ♔d7 38 ♕xf7+ ♔d6 39 ♕f8+ ♔d7 when White should probably be content with giving perpetual check on f7 and f8 with the queen.

33...♛xd1!

With three very precise moves in the critical phase of the game, Fritz manages to turn the tables.

34 ♕xh7+

I did not like 34 ♕xd1 ♗xd3 35 ♕xd3 ♘b4 followed by ...a1♛, when White's attack has disappeared. Now, however, the game ends even more quickly.

34...♔f8 35 ♘xg6+ ♔e8 36 ♕g8+ ♔d7 37 ♕xf7+ ♔d6 0-1

Excellent defence by Fritz.

I hope these games will make it clear that even with extensive knowledge about computer programs, everything can be spoilt with a little laziness in calculating variations when things become tactical.

After playing some games against any program, you find one main weakness that all of them have in common: they are highly repeatable. While the human can learn about the program's style and slowly find its weaknesses, the program learns nothing about you. It may be 'smart enough' to avoid the openings in which it has lost before, but it will not change its style. Computer programming has not reached the stage where programs are able to learn from their mistakes, and that means that they will repeat positional errors and other flawed conceptions.

After a few games with Fritz 8, I have already learned a few things. It does not avoid closed positions, and it has the usual problem of lacking a 'sense of danger' when an attack on its own king is under way. It is most likely stronger tactically than its predecessors, but as earlier versions of Fritz were already excellent tacticians it does not really change much. All things considered, some of the usual anti-computer strategies still work quite well.

The Computer's Opening Book

When playing a computer, the first question is what openings to use. Many players seem to fear the enormous amount of theory in the opening book of the programs, but it is important to note that quantity does not equal quality. Personally, I have got used to taking the computer program out of book as early as possible. This has been the recommendation of the best anti-computer players for several years.

However, there are also arguments for following the usual theory and playing 'normal' openings. If you know your openings well, it makes sense to stay with them, especially in longer games against the machine. Your experience and knowledge about certain middlegame positions that arise may prove valuable. The worst thing you can do is to play an opening you do not know; e.g., playing the French as Black without knowing the ideas behind the various lines. The second Kasparov vs Deep Blue match showed us what kind of trouble a player can get into if he tries too hard to play anti-computer openings. As Viswanathan Anand commented about this match, Garry Kasparov changed identity and became "Mr Anti-Deep Blue" instead of being Kasparov. This was partly due to the openings he chose, e.g. playing 1 d3 in one of the games in the second match, because he was overestimating the value of Deep Blue's book.

Opening books are often made as the last thing before release, and for the programmer it can be an annoying element when there is a lack of time. The opening books are made by the programmer himself or a chess-player who enters a lot of lines suggested by standard theory or databases, but often without giving the lines a critical check themselves. The opening book operators are not necessarily strong players, and thus they may have trouble identifying which variations are currently viable and which are not. Often there are lines in the opening book which are based on games from relatively weak players, and in that case it would be a better choice for the program to leave the opening book around move 10 and come up with its own ideas. On the other hand, it may also be following a game of Kasparov, Karpov or Anand or some other top player, in which case it is definitely a good idea for the computer's opponent to take it out of the book!

Generally, I do not believe that strong players have to fear the computer's opening book. One extreme example of a book error occurred in the decisive game of the playoffs of the computer blitz world championship between Nimzo and Fritz.

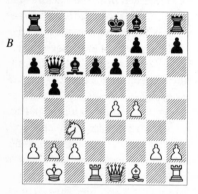

Nimzo – Fritz
Microcomputers blitz Wch 2000

In this position Fritz chose an odd move:

13...h6

The game continued:

14 &d3 h5 15 ♘d5 0-0-0?? 16 ♘b4??

Fritz put its queen directly *en prise*, but Nimzo did not accept the favour!

If the programs had been analysing the position by themselves this would of course never have happened, but both of them were following the same book with flawed data dumped in from a database. In the original game Black had played 13...♕c5 instead of the futile 13...h6.

As this example shows, the opening books are very far from being perfect.

Openings and Move-Orders for White

Nevertheless, there are opening set-ups which are generally regarded to be more successful than others when playing computers. The common stamp of those openings is that they achieve some kind of closed or blocked position in the centre by forming a wall of pawns.

1) The Stonewall Attack

This set-up is the one I tried to reach in two games against Fritz given earlier, and it is perfectly demonstrated in the games Van Wely-Rebel Century and Kramnik-Deep Junior below. It is possibly the most successful opening strategy against computer programs so far, and the engines must have lost thousands of games where opponents chose this set-up.

Basically, the set-up consists of putting pawns on d4, e3, f4 and c3, blocking the position and getting ready to expand on the kingside if Black castles kingside. If he is not disturbed, White will usually arrange his pieces like this: ♗d3, ♘f3, ♘bd2, 0-0 and then later moves like ♕e2, ♘e5 and possibly an expansion with g4, of course depending on the situation. Most programs like to castle kingside, so it is usually not so difficult to execute this plan. The normal move-order is 1 d4 ♘f6 2 e3 followed by developing the bishop to d3 on move 3. In Van Wely-Rebel Century 4, annotated later in this chapter (and also Van der Wiel-Rebel Century 3 in the notes to that game) we see White experimenting with a set-up where he develops the bishop outside the pawn-chain: 1 d4 ♘f6 2 c3 e6 3 ♗g5, only to complete the Stonewall later with e3 and f4.

After 1 d4 d5 2 e3 Black can obstruct White's plans by continuing 2...♗f5, developing the bishop outside the pawn-chain. White can of course just continue his plans by playing 3 ♗d3, exchanging bishops and continuing to set up the Stonewall with f4 and c3, but the exchange of the light-squared bishops favours Black since the light squares in White's camp are weak. An alternative is to develop the bishop on e2 after moves like f4, c3, and ♘f3 to reach a normal Stonewall position with reversed colours. In any case, the black bishop is better placed on f5 than on c8, and White should not expect to get any advantage out of the opening in this line. However, getting the right position against a program is often more important than getting an objective advantage.

I have seen suggestions that this set-up could best be reached via Bird's Opening, 1 f4. However, I will not recommend this, as you would have to deal with From's Gambit 1...e5!?, which usually leads to open positions and tactical play. This is not what you want when playing against a computer.

2) The 'English' Wall

This is a similar set-up, which involves putting pawns on c4, e4 and d3. For game examples see Van Wely-Fritz in Chapter 3, and Smirin-Deep Shredder in this chapter, while the game Van den Doel-Fritz shows some of the dangers if White is not aware of Black's counterplay against the weak point f2. The usual move-order for this set-up is 1 c4 e5 2 ♘c3 ♘f6 3 g3, finishing the wall with d3 and e4 later. In this line White will usually achieve his goal after 3...♗b4, because of 4 ♗g2 with good central control, while 3...d5 is the best move for a program as it changes the nature of the position to a more open one.

To counter this opening of the centre, White may choose to set up the 'English Wall' straight away with 1 c4 e5 2 e4, but it looks a bit ugly and in that case Black can develop his bishop to the natural square c5, eyeing the weakness on f2. If White chooses to play this variation he should be aware of possible counterplay against f2.

In the line 1 c4 e5 2 ♘c3 ♘f6 3 g3 the bishop is less likely to go to c5 as

3...♗c5 would be met by 4 ♗g2 and a set-up involving e3 and ♘ge2, when the bishop on c5 is in danger of proving misplaced.

3) King's Indian Attack

This is a universal opening system which is usually characterized by a set-up like 1 ♘f3 d5 2 g3 c5 3 ♗g2 ♘c6 4 0-0 e5 with King's Indian themes of preparing e4 with 5 d3. To play this system requires knowledge of the typical ideas in the King's Indian; otherwise you will probably just end up in a passive position.

White can also often play the King's Indian Attack when starting with 1 e4. Some examples:

The French: 1 e4 e6 2 d3 d5 3 ♘d2
Caro-Kann: 1 e4 c6 2 d3 d5 3 ♘d2
Sicilian: 1 e4 c5 2 ♘f3 and 3 d3

If White is not disturbed in the process, he will follow up with the standard King's Indian moves g3, ♗g2, ♘f3/♘bd2 and 0-0 with chances of achieving a blocked or fixed position in the centre, depending on whether Black plays ...d4 or ...dxe4 later.

Some readers may protest that some of these openings have a dull character, and that playing 'system chess' like this, always putting the pieces on the same squares in the opening, is not their style. Actually, this is the way I felt myself when I played the test games against Fritz 8. As I wrote earlier, I believe that playing in your own style and with your own openings can

sometimes be the best anti-computer strategy, provided that you know the openings well and you play with longer time-limits.

Game Examples for White

Now let us take a look at a few games, which are based on the opening ideas for White mentioned above.

L. van Wely – Rebel Century 4.0
Match (2), Maastricht 2002

1 d4 ♘f6 2 c3 e6 3 ♗g5

Getting ready to set up a Stonewall formation with the bishop outside the pawn-chain. The potential of this tricky move-order as an anti-computer system was first shown by the well-known 'computer killer' John van der Wiel.

3...h6 4 ♗h4 b6 5 ♘d2 ♗b7 6 e3 ♗e7 7 ♘gf3 c5 8 ♗d3 0-0 9 ♕e2 d5 10 ♘e5

It seems like Van Wely was well prepared for the battle against Rebel as he was copying the initial moves of an earlier game between Van der Wiel and Rebel Century 3.0. White is setting up the Stonewall-like pawn-structure after ♘e5 and f4 and gets ready to conduct an attack on the black king. Most computer engines are still defenceless against this strategy.

10...♘c6 11 f4 ♘e4 (D)
12 ♗g3!

Van Wely deviates from Van der Wiel-Rebel Century 3.0, Match (6), Maastricht 2000, which continued 12

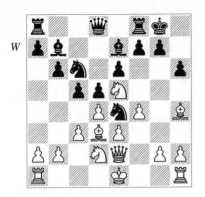

W

♗xe7 ♘xe7 13 0-0 f6 14 ♘g4 ♘xd2
15 ♕xd2 ♘f5 16 ♖f3 with good prospects for White on the kingside. Van
Wely's move is a very tricky one for
the computer. The bishop blocks the
g-pawn that is supposed to take part in
the kingside expansion, but Van Wely
must have known a lot about computer
weaknesses to play like this. Objectively speaking, it is not a good move.
Against a computer, however, it is an
interesting choice. For the program it
is very tempting to take the bishop, and
many other programs copy Rebel's
next move. They believe that they improve their position by winning the
bishop-pair and by giving White doubled pawns on the g-file. These factors, however, are of no importance
here. The only thing that counts is that
the h-file is now being opened for
White, who has easy play by attacking
on the kingside with g4-g5.

12...♘xg3?

12...♘xe5 13 dxe5 c4 14 ♗c2 f5 is
better. Then the bishop looks very
strange on g3.

13 hxg3 ♖c8?!

Too slow. Black should exchange
one of White's attacking pieces with
13...♘xe5.

14 ♘df3 ♗d6

14...♘xe5 is still better. Now White
launches a powerful attack.

15 g4! f6 16 ♘g6 ♖f7 17 g5 ♖cc7

Black has to sacrifice a pawn. If
17...fxg5 White plays 18 fxg5 ♗g3+
19 ♔d2 and the attack rages on.

18 gxh6

An alternative is 18 0-0-0, slowly
building up the pressure, as White can
cash in later. To me it is understand-
able, however, that Van Wely just plays
it simple and takes the pawn.

18...gxh6 19 ♖xh6

Now White has won a pawn, but his
attack is repelled, at least for a while.

**19...♖h7 20 ♖xh7 ♖xh7 21 0-0-0
c4 22 ♗c2 ♕e8 23 g4**

23 e4! is an alternative (23...♕xg6
is met by 24 e5 f5 25 exd6 with an excellent position for White), but Van
Wely continues playing simple chess
and keeps the position closed – a wise
strategy against a computer program.

**23...♖h6 24 ♘fh4 ♖h7 25 ♕g2 ♘d8
26 ♖h1 b5 27 ♘f3 ♖xh1+ 28 ♕xh1
♘f7 29 ♕h5 ♕d7 30 ♘gh4**

Faster is 30 ♘ge5! fxe5 31 ♕h7+
♔f8 32 g5 e4 33 g6, with an immediate win. However, Van Wely was still
choosing simplicity.

**30...♘h8 31 g5 f5 32 ♘e5 ♗xe5 33
dxe5**

Van Wely exchanges into a winning
endgame. He is a pawn up, and the

passed g-pawn, the d4-square for the knight and a good vs bad bishop are factors that ensure the win.

33...♗c8 34 ♘f3 ♕f7 35 ♕h6 ♕g6 36 ♕xg6+ ♘xg6 37 ♘d4 ♗d7 38 b3 ♔g7 39 ♗d1 ♘e7 40 ♔b2

The white king penetrates the black position.

40...♔g6 41 ♗e2 ♘c8 42 a4 a6 43 axb5 axb5 44 ♔a3 ♘e7 45 ♔b4 ♘c6+ 46 ♘xc6 ♗xc6 47 ♔c5 ♗e8 48 b4 1-0

White wins; e.g., 48...♔g7 49 ♔d6 ♗f7 50 ♔e7 ♔g8 51 ♔f6 ♔f8 52 g6 ♗g8 53 g7+ ♔e8 54 ♗h5+ ♔d7 55 ♗f7.

Another game that has become a model for players who like to play anti-computer chess was the encounter between Vladimir Kramnik and Deep Junior in the super GM tournament in Dortmund, 2000.

V. Kramnik – Deep Junior
Dortmund 2000

1 d4 d5 2 e3

White is getting ready to set up the Stonewall with ♗d3, f4, c3 and ♘f3. As mentioned before, this plan can be countered by 2...♗f5 to exchange the light-squared bishop. I believe this must be the best choice for a computer program, and this move has been included in many computer opening books after this game.

2...♘f6 3 ♗d3 e6

Now Black's light-squared bishop stays behind the pawns and White can set up the Stonewall without being disturbed.

4 f4 ♗e7 5 ♘f3 c5 6 c3 0-0 7 ♘bd2 ♘g4?

A very odd idea. Black invests a lot of tempi to close the centre, but this only helps White, since Black has no counterplay when White initiates his kingside expansion.

8 ♕e2 c4?!

A typical computer error: gaining space, but at the same time closing the position, and thus making White's task on the kingside much easier.

9 ♗c2 f5 10 ♖g1!

White goes directly for the attack instead of castling kingside. The idea is simply to play h3 and g4.

10...♘c6 11 h3 ♘f6 12 g4 ♘e4

12...b5, trying to get some counterplay on the queenside, is better, but the black position would still be difficult.

13 ♕g2 g6?!

Weakening the kingside cover. After 13...♗h4+ 14 ♔e2 the king is safe in the centre, so the best move seems to be 13...♖f7.

14 ♕h2 ♔h8 15 h4 ♘xd2?

This only helps White to develop. 15...fxg4!? 16 ♘xe4 gxf3 is more tenacious, but after 17 ♘f2 (17 ♘g5 e5! is less clear) White is still better, and he can continue the attack with h5.

16 ♗xd2 fxg4 17 ♘g5!

Junior may have been expecting 17 ♖xg4 e5 when playing its 15th move, but of course Kramnik will not allow the opening of the position.

17...♕e8 *(D)*

After 17...h6 18 h5 e5 (18...♗xg5 19 fxg5 ♕xg5 20 hxg6) 19 hxg6 ♗xg5 20 fxg5 ♕xg5 21 e4 White is winning.

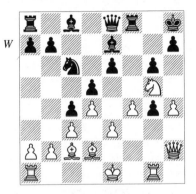

18 h5! gxh5 19 ♖xg4! ♖f6

If 19...e5, then 20 ♖h4 exf4 21 ♖xh5 ♗xg5 22 ♖xh7+ ♔g8 23 ♖h5! ♗f6 (or: 23...♕e7 24 ♖xg5+; 23...♔f7 24 ♖xg5 ♔e7 25 0-0-0 and the attack continues) 24 ♕g2+ ♗g7 (24...♔f7 25 ♗g6+) 25 ♗h7+ ♔h8 26 ♗g6+ winning the black queen.

20 ♖h4 ♖h6 21 0-0-0 a5 22 ♖h1 b5 23 ♗d1 ♖a7 24 ♗xh5 ♕f8 25 e4!

The attack develops logically.

25...♗d8

Or 25...dxe4 26 ♗g6! ♖xh4 (after 26...♖xg6 27 ♖xh7+ ♔g8 28 ♖h8+ ♔g7 29 ♕h7+ Black gets mated) 27 ♕xh4 ♗xg5 28 fxg5 ♕g8 29 ♗xe4, and again White has a winning attack.

26 f5! b4 27 ♗g6 ♖xh4 28 ♕xh4 bxc3 29 bxc3 ♗f6 30 ♕xh7+! ♖xh7 31 ♖xh7+ ♔g8 32 ♗f7+ ♕xf7 33 ♖xf7 1-0

White wins after 33...♗xg5 34 ♖c7.

I. Smirin – Deep Shredder
Internet 2002

1 c4 e5 2 ♘c3 ♘f6 3 g3 ♗b4

As mentioned earlier, 3...d5 is the right way for a computer program to play this position, as it opens up the game.

4 ♗g2 0-0 5 e4

Smirin chooses the same opening set-up as Van Wely in his game against Fritz given in Chapter 3. This set-up is very effective, as many programs do not prepare the necessary break in the centre, but give White a free hand on the kingside. We are now entering one of those lines that are still way beyond the understanding of even the best engines.

5...♗xc3 6 bxc3 d6 7 ♘e2 ♗g4?!

It is not exactly clear what Black intends to do with this move. The right plan is 7...c6 to try to get counterplay in the centre with ...d5.

8 f3 ♗e6 9 d3 c5?

This horrible move gives White a clear advantage because of the possibility of playing for a kingside attack without being disturbed in the centre. 9...c6, preparing to break in the centre with ...d5, is a much better choice, and would have made things more difficult for White.

10 0-0 h6?

Another move which has no point. Actually only White can benefit from a move like this, as the pawn on h6 becomes a weakness later when White starts his kingside offensive.

11 h3

Smirin builds up the attack slowly. He probably knows that the engine does not see the dangers of the white attack yet and by playing a quiet move like this he does not 'alert' it too early. The move is a preparation for a later g4, and thus it would probably have to be played anyway later.

11...a6 12 a4 *(D)*

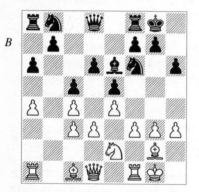

White stops all counterplay before proceeding with his own plans. Good prophylactic play usually has the effect that the computer program 'runs out of ideas' and starts playing senseless moves. We have already seen it in many games, and this one is no exception.

12...b6?

12...♘c6, preparing to answer 13 f4 with 13...exf4 keeping the position more open, is a better option, although White is still much better.

13 f4 ♘c6

13...exf4 is not possible now due to 14 e5!, so at this point there is no alternative to allowing f5 followed by g4, h4, etc., and the usual attack on the king.

14 f5 ♗d7 15 g4 ♕c7?

Black should try to hold back the attack a little longer with 15...♘h7. Now, after 15 moves, he is already close to being lost.

16 ♘g3 ♘a5 17 h4 ♘h7 18 g5

It is quite clear that the pawn on h6 only helps White to open files on the kingside.

18...hxg5 19 hxg5 ♕b7 20 ♗e3 b5

Black finally gets his queenside counterplay going. However, it is too late to create counterplay as White's kingside attack has grown too strong.

21 axb5 axb5 22 ♕h5 bxc4 *(D)*

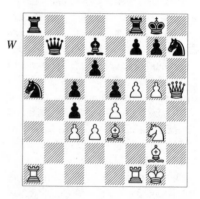

23 f6! ♖fc8

23...cxd3 is answered by 24 fxg7 ♔xg7 25 ♕h6+ ♔h8 26 ♘h5 ♖g8 27 ♖xf7, winning. 23...gxf6 loses to 24 ♕h6 with the idea of 25 ♘h5 or 25 gxf6 and the game will end quickly after 24...♔h8 25 ♘h5 ♖g8 26 ♖xf6! ♖af8 27 ♕xh7+! ♔xh7 28 ♖h6#.

24 fxg7 ♗g4

A desperate move, but Black was losing anyway; e.g., 24...♗e6 25 ♕h4! with the idea ♘h5-f6+ is decisive.

1-0

Openings and Move-Orders for Black

We have now studied a variety of set-ups for White that work well against the programs. What do you do as Black when playing against a computer?

We shall look at some possible systems against the two first moves that computers play the most, 1 e4 and 1 d4.

Against 1 d4

1) The King's Indian Defence

Naturally, the closed centre and the long-term attacking possibilities in many lines make the King's Indian a good choice against computer programs. In the Classical Main Line with 1 d4 ♘f6 2 c4 g6 3 ♘c3 ♗g7 4 e4 d6 5 ♘f3 0-0 6 ♗e2 e5 7 0-0 ♘c6 8 d5 ♘e7, the centre is blocked and Black gets ready to play ...♘d7/...♘e8 and ...f5, possibly followed by expansion on the kingside. If you play normal theory moves, the computer can follow its book lines for a long time and develop its pieces naturally. Thus in that case it is usually a good idea to play one single, slightly off-beat move to get the computer out of book. In

fact, when out of book, most programs will have serious problems understanding that they have to expand on the queenside with pawn moves like b4, c5 and so on.

In most man vs machine games the programmers try to avoid these positions by playing the exchange variation 7 dxe5 dxe5 8 ♕xd8 ♖xd8, which should only be dangerous for Black if he does not know the theory. When the queens come off early on, it is usually an advantage for the human player as it reduces the amount of surprising tactics, which is the area in which computers excel.

Nevertheless, there is a lot of theory in the King's Indian and it requires some study to play it, also against computers.

2) The Schmid and Czech Benonis

The completely closed centre in these openings is ideal for combating computer programs. After 1 d4 c5 2 d5 e5 3 e4 d6 (the Schmid Benoni), the pawns are already completely blocked against each other. Black has to check up on various attempts to keep the position open. The alternatives are 2 dxc5, 2 e3, 2 c3, and 2 ♘f3 but all of those are unambitious. If White plays 2 e4?! trying to transpose to an Open Sicilian, Black replies 2...cxd4 3 ♘f3 a6!, with a line of the O'Kelly Sicilian that is quite poor for White.

The Czech Benoni features the additional moves ...♘f6 and c4: 1 d4 ♘f6 2 c4 c5 3 d5 e5. However, in that case Black will have to check up what to do if White refuses to close the position and plays 3 ♘f3. One idea is the gambit line 3...cxd4 4 ♘xd4 e5 5 ♘b5 d5!? 6 cxd5 ♗c5, in which the centre is somewhat blocked, and Black has natural development and some space for his gambited pawn. Moreover, there are chances of playing for a kingside attack if White castles kingside.

3) The Stonewall

Obviously, the Stonewall can also be considered as an answer to 1 d4, but if you choose to play 1...f5, then be aware of the Staunton Gambit with 2 e4!?, and some other lines that often lead to an open position, notably 2 ♘c3. One way to avoid this is to play 1...e6 with a later ...f5, but in that case you have to be ready to play the French after 2 e4.

A third move-order is 1 d4 d5 2 c4 e6 3 ♘c3 c6, getting ready to play ...f5. However, this allows the gambit line 4 e4!? dxe4 5 ♘xe4 ♗b4+ 6 ♗d2 ♕xd4 7 ♗xb4 ♕xe4+, which is only a good choice against a program if you know the line very well. Black can try to side-step this complicated line by playing 4...♗b4.

Against 1 e4

1) Gurgenidze System

This line is a mixture between the Modern Defence and Caro-Kann. Black plays the moves ...g6, ...c6, and ...d5 almost regardless of White's set-up;

e.g., 1 e4 g6 2 d4 c6 3 ♘c3 d5. Black wants to encourage e5, after which the position gets a closed character. See the game Junior-Piket later in this chapter for an example of how to play this system.

I have also seen a few games by John van der Wiel where he plays the 'Gurgenidze counterattack' with success. This is 1 e4 c6 2 d4 d5 3 ♘c3 and then 3...a6, preparing ...b5 and attempting to finish setting up a light-squared wall with ...e6. It is very difficult for computers to understand how to play against something like this.

2) The French

In general, the closed nature of the French seems to cause computer programs some trouble. I have seen the line 1 e4 e6 2 d4 d5 3 ♘c3 ♗b4 4 e5 b6 (or 4...♕d7) being used many times by anti-computer players, but the drawback of this line is that Black may sometimes end up in a somewhat passive position. In my view, the Classical line, 3...♘f6, is a good and solid choice. Seirawan showed one way to play this opening in the game Dragon-Seirawan below.

3) The Berlin Defence

This line has been used with success against computers, because there are fewer tactical tricks when the queens come off. Long-term planning and understanding of the resulting endgames are the most important factors. The main line of the Berlin Defence goes

1 e4 e5 2 ♘f3 ♘c6 3 ♗b5 ♘f6 4 0-0 ♘xe4 5 d4 ♘d6 6 ♗xc6 dxc6 7 dxe5 ♘f5 8 ♕xd8+ ♔xd8. Once again, this is not an opening that you can just play without preparation. You have to study the strategy and the plans of the positions arising, and once you have done that, it will be a good pick for an opening in a game against a program.

Game Examples for Black

Let us look at some examples from recent games where grandmasters have played Black against a computer. In the AEGON tournament in 1997 the anti-computer expert Yasser Seirawan demonstrated one way of getting into a closed position with the French.

Dragon – Y. Seirawan
AEGON, The Hague 1997

1 e4 e6 2 d4 d5 3 ♘d2 ♘f6 4 e5 ♘fd7 5 f4 c5 6 c3 ♘c6 7 ♘df3 c4!?

When I saw this move the first time, I thought that this was something you would only play against a computer. My database reveals, however, that the move has been played by Petrosian, Botvinnik and Korchnoi in normal games. The position is now closed, and as we have seen earlier, this is clearly an advantage for the human player. A more standard approach is 7...♕b6, followed by ...cxd4 and ...f6, putting the white centre under pressure.

8 ♘e2 b5 9 g4 ♘b6 10 ♘g3

At this stage of the game both players follow logical plans. Black prepares ...b4 and White prepares f5.

10...h6!?

Part of a plan which becomes obvious on the next move. Black wants to prevent White's knight from coming to g5.

11 ♗e2 *(D)*

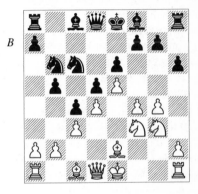

11...♔d7!?

An interesting idea. Most programs have a huge positive jump in the evaluation for White when this move is played. The reason is that they award White a big bonus because Black has lost his castling rights. Apparently, the programs have no code to make them understand that castling is less important in a completely closed position like this. Actually, playing 11...♗e7 followed by castling kingside would be quite risky (but typical for a computer) as White will easily get an attack going after f5. Castling queenside would also be inappropriate because Black needs his rook on the b-file, which will be opened up after the prepared plan ...a5, ...b4 and ...bxc3.

12 ♗e3 a5 13 ♕c2 ♔c7 14 f5 b4 15 ♖g1?

White has played reasonably until now, preparing and playing f5, but I find it odd that the program puts the rook on g1 instead of f1. It seems obvious that White should put one or two rooks on the f-file and then open it with fxe6. After 15 0-0 White has a good position. His king will be safe on h1 and he can get ready to break through on the kingside.

15...♕e8 16 ♖g2?

Obviously, White completely loses the plot at this point. White's position is fine after 16 b3!, opening files on the queenside where Black's king is located. The idea is 16...bxc3 17 a3!, and after this ♕xc3 with a good position.

16...a4 17 ♗f1? (D)

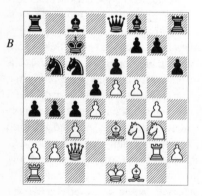

It is not clear what White is trying to do.

17...b3 18 ♕b1 bxa2 19 ♖xa2 ♘a5

Black eyes the hole at b3, and he now has a firm grip on the queenside. White's only chance is to break through on the kingside.

20 ♘h5 ♔b8 21 f6?

For unknown reasons White chooses to close the kingside – not a wise choice as Black has all the play on the queenside. The following phase of the game is the fight between a grandmaster and an amateur when it comes to positional chess. When playing against a computer, "what you want are messy strategic conditions", Seirawan was once quoted as saying. In this game he has succeeded pretty well in doing that.

21...g6 22 ♘g7?

I do not really understand this move, as it just seems to lose a pawn. Perhaps the program saw some compensation in the fact that Black exchanges his good bishop, but I do not see any way that White can exploit this. 22 ♘g3 at least does not lose a pawn. However, in that case, it is not clear how White's expansion on the kingside should proceed.

22...♗xg7 23 fxg7 ♖h7 24 ♖a3 ♕g8 25 g5 h5 26 ♔f2 ♕xg7

Black is now a pawn up, and he starts to form the winning plan. The black queen and rook on the kingside have to be transferred to the b-file to put pressure on b2, and after that the bishop goes to e8 to cover the only black weakness at f7. The program just starts making random moves, and 24 moves (or 48 plies) later, the pawn on b2 is lost. For humans, long-term planning like this is not that difficult. However, it is very hard for a computer program to counter strategic play of this kind, as long as there are no tactical shots. It is way beyond the horizon of any computer program what Black is trying to do here.

27 ♔g1 ♖h8 28 ♖f2 ♖e8 29 ♘d2 ♖e7 30 ♗e2 ♕g8 31 ♖f3 ♗d7 32 ♗f2 ♕c8 33 ♕c1 ♗e8 *(D)*

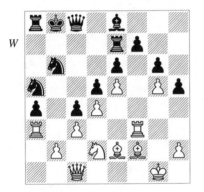

Excellent manoeuvring by Seirawan. He covers the f7 weakness and then proceeds to put pressure on the queenside.

34 ♕d1 ♖b7 35 ♗f1 ♕c6 36 ♗g2 ♘c8 37 ♕a1 ♖aa7 38 ♖f4 ♕b6

Getting ready for the final breakthrough.

39 ♖a2 ♘b3

At this point most programs start realizing that White has some problems, and that he may lose the b2-pawn. But it is too late now. Black gains control over the a-file, and this decides the game.

40 ♘xb3 axb3 41 ♖xa7 ♖xa7 42 ♕c1 ♖a2 43 ♗f1 ♕a5 44 ♗e1 ♖a1 45 ♕d2 ♖b1 46 ♗g3 ♕a1 47 ♖f2 ♘b6 48 ♕e2 ♔c8 49 ♕d2 ♘a4 50 ♕e3 ♘xb2

Black finally wins the b-pawn and, with it, the game.

51 ♖f3 ♘a4 52 ♕f4 b2 0-1

White is lost; e.g., 53 ♕f6 ♔d7 54 ♕g7 ♖xf1+ 55 ♖xf1 ♕xf1+ 56 ♔xf1 b1♕+. A well-played anti-computer game by Seirawan.

Against a computer playing 1 d4, the King's Indian Defence is an excellent system. In the following game the Australian player Nick Speck (nickname on ICC: Insight) shows a typical way of playing the opening. He has an Elo rating of 2389 and he has spent some years on the Internet Chess Club (ICC), developing various anti-computer strategies.

Crafty – N. Speck
Internet Chess Club 2000

1 d4 ♘f6 2 c4 g6 3 ♘c3 d6 4 e4 ♗g7 5 ♘f3 0-0 6 ♗e2 e5 7 0-0 ♘c6 8 d5 ♘e7 9 ♘d2

In another game between Crafty and Speck the program tried 9 ♘e1 ♘d7 10 ♗e3 f5 11 f3 f4 12 ♗f2 b6!? (it is normal to continue the kingside expansion with 12...g5, but against a computer this move makes sense as it takes the program out of book and makes it more difficult to achieve the c5 advance) 13 ♘d3 g5 14 ♕c2 ♖f7 15

♖ad1 ♗f8 16 ♖d2 (the program starts playing nonsense moves) 16...♖g7 17 ♘e1 h5 18 ♕d1 ♘f6 19 h3 ♘g6 20 ♘d3 ♗d7 21 b4 ♕c8 22 c5 ♗xh3 23 c6 g4 24 fxg4 ♗xg4 25 ♗f3 ♗e7 26 ♖b2 ♘h7 27 ♗e2 ♔h8 28 a3 ♘h4 29 ♗xh4 ♗xh4 30 ♖d2 ♕d8 31 ♘b2 ♗g3 32 ♗xg4 hxg4 33 ♘e2 ♕h4 34 ♘xg3 ♕xg3 35 ♕e1 ♕xe1 36 ♖xe1 g3 37 ♘c4 ♘g5 38 ♖d3 ♖h7 39 ♘d2 ♔g7 40 ♘f1 ♖ah8 41 ♘xg3 fxg3 42 ♖xg3 ♔g6 43 ♔f2 ♖h1 and Black won.

9...♘e8

9...a5 is the main line here. In the King's Indian, however, it is usually a good idea not to follow main lines in order to take the program out of its opening book more quickly. When on their own, most programs often have a hard time, and they do not find it easy to break on the queenside with moves like b4, c5 and so on.

10 b4

This transposes to a sideline of the Bayonet Attack. After Black's next move there is only one game left in my database, and the program was probably out of book by the 11th move.

10...a5 11 bxa5 ♖xa5 12 ♘b3 ♖a8 13 ♗e3 b6 14 a4 f5 15 ♕c2 f4

Against a human it is possible that Black would have waited before playing this move, but when the opponent is a computer it is best to close the position before it gets the idea of playing exf5.

16 ♗d2 g5 17 a5 ♖b8!?

This funny little move is designed to trick the computer into believing

that it gets a strong passed a-pawn. The strategy is of course a bit risky, because the pawn may turn out to be strong at some point. But in this game it just goes to a7 and is solidly blockaded.

18 a6?!

18 axb6, to open files on the queenside, is preferable, but of course Black still has the kind of closed position that he wants.

18...♖a8 *(D)*

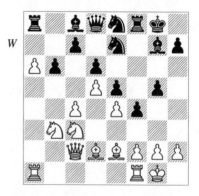

19 a7

Most programs just love to play a pawn to the seventh rank. They award a lot of pluses for that.

19...♘f6 20 ♖a2

If White could just break through on the queenside, then he would be able to exploit his passed pawn. However, it is not obvious how this could be done, and especially not for a computer. Now Black slowly improves his position without White being able to do anything about it.

20...♖f7 21 ♖fa1

The program has reached the usual nonsense stage, because it sees no obvious plan in the position.

21...g4 22 ♕d3 h5 23 ♔h1 ♗h6 24 ♔g1 ♖g7 25 ♕c2 ♔h7 26 ♕c1 ♕e8 27 ♗d3 ♕g6 *(D)*

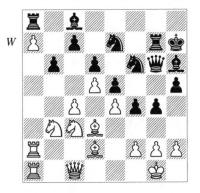

Seeing that White has no constructive ideas, Black takes his time and puts all pieces on optimal squares before the attack.

28 ♕f1 ♔h8

Now that all the black pieces are on good squares it seems obvious just to continue the attack with moves like ...h4 and ...g3 or ...f3. However, Speck has another strategy – he waits! I asked him about this idea, and he told me that quite often it is not so easy to conduct the attack even though Black's pieces look like they are excellently posted. This is due to the impressive calculating powers of the modern programs.

Instead he waits and waits, and because the computer believes it is better because of the passed a-pawn, it will

never accept a draw. Thus, when nearly 50 moves have been played without a pawn moving, the program will finally move one of the pawns in front of its king to escape the draw. But at the same time it will ruin its defensive stance. Personally, I am not sure that I agree that this is a good strategy, but at least it has worked many times. However, it demands a lot of patience.

29 ♔h1 ♘h7 30 ♘b5 ♘g8 31 ♕e1 h4 32 c5!

The program finally finds a way to get counterplay and thereby forces Black to launch his attack.

32...bxc5 33 ♗a5 *(D)*

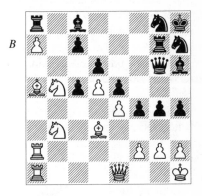

33...g3!

At last!

34 fxg3

34 ♗xc7, to break open the queenside, is better. 34...gxh2 can then be answered with 35 f3 h3 36 ♗f1, when White has chances of hanging on.

34...hxg3 35 h3 ♘g5

The knight gets ready to sacrifice itself on h3 to destroy the white king's pawn-cover – a typical idea in the King's Indian.

36 ♗xc7 ♘xh3! 37 gxh3 f3 38 ♗f1 ♕h5 39 ♗xd6 g2+(?)

39...♗xh3! forces mate.

40 ♗xg2 fxg2+ 41 ♔g1 ♕xh3 42 ♗xe5 ♗e3+ 43 ♕xe3 ♕xe3+ 44 ♖f2 ♕xb3

Black is not in a hurry to cash in. With 44...♗h3, holding on to the g-pawn, preparing ...♖f8 and planning to answer 45 ♘c7 with 45...♖xa7!, Black could end the game even more quickly. White cannot parry all Black's threats.

45 ♘c7 ♖xa7 46 ♗xg7+ ♔xg7 47 ♖xa7 ♕b1+

47...♗h3, holding on to the passed g-pawn, is slightly better.

48 ♔xg2 ♕xe4+ 49 ♔g1 ♕e1+ 50 ♔g2 ♔g6

Black won 30 moves later with the help of his passed c-pawn.

In the 2000 Dortmund Super-GM tournament, the Dutch grandmaster Jeroen Piket played the Gurgenidze System against Deep Junior.

Deep Junior – J. Piket
Dortmund 2000

1 e4 g6 2 d4 ♗g7 3 ♘c3 c6 4 ♘f3 d5

A good choice of opening. When playing White, it is easier to get into a closed position, but with Black it is a bit trickier. The strategy behind this opening is to tempt White to play e5, blocking the position, when strategic understanding will prevail.

5 h3 a6

This move seems designed to take the computer out of its book. Moreover, it also has the function of supporting ...b5 in a later queenside offensive.

6 ♗f4 ♘f6 7 e5 ♘fd7

Black has tempted the e-pawn forward, and he is now one step closer to setting up the position that he wants.

8 ♕d2

Better is 8 h4!, immediately playing on the kingside, where White has the initiative. If 8...h6 then 9 e6! and White will get excellent compensation for the pawn because of Black's pawn weaknesses.

8...e6 9 ♗g5?

Not the best. White should exchange the bishops at once with 9 ♗h6! to exploit the weak dark squares in the black position, and after that move he would have an excellent position. Now he allows Black to close the kingside with ...h6, and then it becomes much harder to break through.

9...♕b6 10 0-0-0 h6 11 ♗e3 ♕c7 12 h4! b5 *(D)*

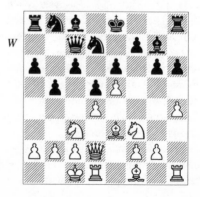

13 ♗f4?

The previous move was a part of the right plan, but now it becomes clear that the white player is a computer program. White loses a tempo with the bishop and it is not obvious that it should be better placed on f4. On the contrary, it seems to block the white f-pawn. Better is 13 h5, and when Black answers 13...g5, White would probably like to play 14 ♘h2 straight away, with the ideas of opening lines on the kingside with f4 and later bringing the knight to the f6-square (via g4). The only problem is that Black can counter in the centre with 14...c5, when the knight is slightly misplaced on h2, and White has some problems defending his centre. It is probably better to prepare this with 14 g3!, getting ready to strengthen the centre with f4, after ♘h2. The difference, compared to 14 ♘h2, is that when Black exchanges on f4, White can recapture with the g-pawn and keep his strong centre intact. If Black continues with the same plan as in the game, White will strike hard on the kingside. 14...♘b6 15 ♘h2 ♘c4 (other moves seem to be way too slow) 16 ♗xc4 bxc4 17 f4! gxf4 18 ♗xf4 with a fine position for White. Black is underdeveloped and it will take time before he can exploit the open b-file. White, however, strikes very fast with ♘g4, eyeing f6 and putting pressure on h6. Black may choose to strike in the centre with 14...c5 instead, but exchanging and opening files in the centre should favour White as he is better

developed. One sample line is 15 dxc5 ♘c6 16 ♘d4 ♗xe5 (16...♘dxe5 is also met by 17 f4, giving White a good position) 17 ♘xc6 ♕xc6 18 f4 gxf4 19 gxf4 ♗f6 and White may try to emphasize the position of Black's bad light-squared bishop on c8 by exchanging the dark-squared bishops. 20 ♗d4! ♗xd4 21 ♕xd4 ♖g8 22 b4! with a clear plus for White due to his space advantage, better development, and superior placement of several pieces. In particular, the c8-bishop is not worth much.

13...♘b6 (D)

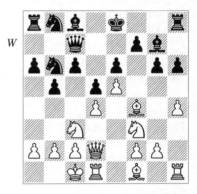

14 a3?

There is no reason to play this move, as it weakens both the queenside cover and the c4-square. Moreover, the move makes it easier for Black to open files when his attack gets going. For a computer engine, however, it is not so obvious that Black is going to attack on the queenside later on. His pieces do not really constitute a threat at this moment. It would still have been better to try 14 h5 g5 15 ♗g3 losing a tempo because the bishop was on f4, but the idea of breaking through on the king-side with ♘h2, f4 and ♘g4 is still strong.

14...♘8d7 15 ♔b1 a5 16 ♘a2 ♕a7 17 g4?!

This looks like a very nice and active move, but in fact it does not achieve anything as Black will just answer g5 with ...h5, keeping the position closed. I believe that White is already in trouble at this point as Black's attack is developing very harmoniously. 17 h5, with the same ideas as before, is still the best try, but White has already wasted too much time and he will have to face a dangerous attack.

17...♗f8 18 c3 ♗a6 19 ♕e1

White is getting ready to defend the position, while the sad description that fits his kingside pieces could be 'all dressed up, but nowhere to go'.

19...♘c4 20 ♗d2 ♗e7 21 ♘c1 ♘db6 22 h5

Finally advancing on the kingside, but at this point it only closes the position further.

22...g5 23 ♘a2 ♔d7

Like Seirawan, Piket chooses the d7-square for his king in this closed position, and as mentioned earlier, this can tease the evaluation function of some engines that do not know that losing castling rights is of very little importance in a completely closed position like this. Note how Piket is putting every single piece on the right square before breaking with ...b4. This

idea has often been described as 'inviting everyone to the party'.

24 ♗c1 ♖hb8 25 ♔a1 *(D)*

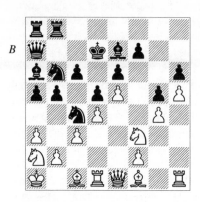

25...b4!

Now, with all his pieces optimally placed for the attack, Piket makes the final breakthrough. It is a good idea to take note of this strategy and use it when you play against a computer program yourself. Your attacking force should be so overwhelming that nothing will be able to stop it when files are opened up.

26 ♘d2 ♘xd2 27 ♗xd2 ♗xf1 28 ♖xf1 ♘c4 29 ♖b1 b3 30 ♘c1 ♗xa3! 31 ♕d1

White is also lost after 31 bxa3 b2+ 32 ♔a2 bxc1♕ 33 ♕xc1 ♖xb1 34 ♔xb1 ♖b8+ 35 ♔c2 ♕b6 36 f4 ♘b2! (threatening ...♕b3+) 37 ♗e3 ♕b5 38 ♔d2 ♕d3+ 39 ♔e1 ♘c4, and Black wins material.

31...♕b6 32 bxa3 b2+ 33 ♔a2 bxc1♕ 34 ♕xc1 ♕xb1+ 0-1

After 35 ♕xb1 ♖xb1 36 ♖xb1 ♘xd2, Black is simply a knight up.

After the game Piket told an interviewer that he would never have played like this against a human opponent, as the chances for White would have been excellent with an opponent who could pick the right plan. He was also quoted as saying that it is not the objective evaluation of the position that counts against a computer. The most important thing is that you get the kind of position you want, and in this game Piket certainly succeeded in doing that.

The strategy of playing a blocked but somewhat passive position can easily backfire, as we shall see in the following game.

Rebel Century – L. van Wely
Match (3), Maastricht 2002

1 e4 e6 2 d4 d5 3 ♘d2 ♘c6 4 ♘gf3 ♘f6 5 e5 ♘d7 6 ♘b3 ♗e7 7 ♗b5 ♘cb8

Van Wely chooses a closed line in the French, aiming to exploit his superior strategic understanding in the position that arises. However, the whole line is slightly passive and in this game Rebel Century succeeds in using its space advantage very well.

8 0-0 b6 9 ♕e2 a5

Black is aiming to reduce White's attacking potential by exchanging the light-squared bishops with ...♗a6. In this way, Black gets rid of the 'French' bishop on c8 which may sometimes be bad (although personally I like this bishop, as it can usually be activated). In exchange for this White has a lot of space and some attacking possibilities if Black castles kingside.

10 ♗e3 ♗a6 11 a4

We are now out of theory, and with this move White attempts to recapture with the a-pawn, if Black should choose to exchange on b5. This would seriously harm Black's development, so he forces White to make the exchange.

11...c6 12 ♗xa6 ♘xa6 13 ♖fc1 0-0 14 c4!

The opening phase is over, and White has emerged with a small advantage. The white pieces are slightly better placed as White has a space advantage, and this gives him better possibilities of manoeuvring his pieces onto the right squares for a kingside attack.

14...dxc4 15 ♖xc4 *(D)*

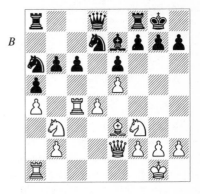

15...♘db8

Black's exchange on c4 has given him a weak pawn on c6, but more important, also the option of putting a knight on d5. A lot of manoeuvring is needed, however, before Black can put a knight on d5, and during this time White prepares a kingside attack.

16 ♘bd2 ♘b4 17 ♘e4 ♘8a6 18 ♘fd2!

An excellent move from Rebel. For a computer it is very unusual to play very well in the build-up phase of an attack, when the tactical consequences are often too far ahead to be calculated. White now shifts the action from the queenside to the kingside and opens a path for his queen to take part in the kingside attack.

18...♘c7 19 ♕g4 ♔h8 (D)

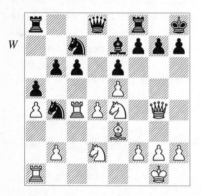

20 ♖a3!

An excellent move, based on a tactical point that becomes clear some moves later. The white pieces are getting ready to join the attack, and the rook enters the game via the third rank.

20...♘bd5 21 ♗g5!

White pins the e7-bishop in order to prevent it from taking the a3-rook and at the same time opening the third rank for the rook – a beautiful idea. The

d5-square is not important if Black is mated on the kingside.

21...f6 22 exf6 gxf6 23 ♖h3! ♕e8

23...fxg5 loses to 24 ♕h5 – this is the tactical justification for the rook manoeuvre.

24 ♕h4 ♖f7 25 ♗h6 b5!

Van Wely fights back and tries to get counterplay on the queenside. If he manages to repel the attack on the kingside, he has chances of creating a queenside passed pawn which is beautifully supported by the black pieces.

26 axb5 cxb5 27 ♖c1 a4 28 ♖g3 (D)

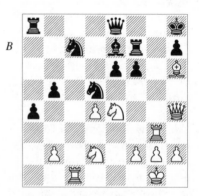

28...a3?!

Stronger is 28...b4! 29 ♘f3 a3 30 bxa3 bxa3 31 ♕h5 ♗f8 (not 31...a2? 32 ♘h4! a1♕ 33 ♘g6+ ♔g8 {33...hxg6 34 ♗g7+ ♔xg7 35 ♖xg6+ ♔f8 36 ♕h8#} 34 ♘e5+ ♔h8 35 ♘xf7+ ♕xf7 36 ♕xf7 mating) 32 ♘e5! ♖e7 (32...fxe5? 33 ♕xe5+ ♘f6 34 ♘xf6 is winning for White), and then:

a) 33 ♕xe8 ♖axe8 34 ♗xf8 ♖xf8 35 ♘c6 ♖g7 36 ♖xa3 ♘f4, and Black hangs on due to the double threat on e2 and g2.

b) 33 ♘xf6!? leads to some long forced lines. 33...♘xf6 (33...♛xh5 34 ♖g8#) 34 ♛h4! (threatening ♛xf6+ and also ♗xf8 followed by ♘g6+) 34...♗xh6 35 ♛xf6+ ♗g7 36 ♖xg7 ♘d5! (36...♖xg7 37 ♖xc7 ♛f8 38 ♘f7+ ♔g8 39 ♘h6+ ♔h8 40 ♖f7! ♛xf7 41 ♘xf7+ ♔g8 42 ♛f3 ♖b8 43 ♘h6+ ♔h8 44 h4! and Black cannot keep his a-pawn and at the same time parry the threats to his king; e.g., 44...a2 45 ♛a3! ♖b1+ 46 ♔h2 a1♛? 47 ♛f8+ mating) 37 ♖xe7+ ♘xf6 38 ♖xe8+ ♘xe8 and White is better due to the extra pawn, but he has to keep an eye on the a-pawn.

29 bxa3 ♖xa3 30 ♘f3 b4? *(D)*

30...♗f8 is the last chance to try to repel the white attack.

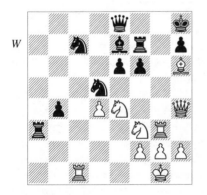

31 ♛h5! ♖xf3

Van Wely sacrifices the exchange since 31...♗f8 32 ♘e5! ♖e7 (32...fxe5 33 ♛xe5+) 33 ♘xf6! ♘xf6 34 ♛xe8 ♘cxe8 35 ♗xf8 ♖xg3 36 ♗xe7 ♖c3

37 ♖b1 is just a bad endgame, but still better than the game continuation.

32 gxf3! ♗f8 33 ♔h1 ♖e7 34 ♖cg1! 1-0

White wins because of 34...♛xh5 35 ♖g8# or 34...♗xh6 35 ♛xh6 ♖f7 36 ♖g7 mating.

Summary of Anti-Computer Strategy

Here is an overview of the strategies you can use to beat the best of today's programs:

1) Try experimenting with the opening set-ups for White and Black described in this chapter. Form walls of pawns and achieve blocked and closed positions and watch out for possible ways to prevent the computer from opening the position.

2) Do not fear the opening book of computer programs as they may contain errors and are sometimes based on games of relatively weak players. On the other hand, if you feel you are playing an opening where the computer would do worse without its book, do not hesitate to play one slightly off-beat move. However, this should only be done in a way that does not compromise your position.

3) From closed or blocked positions, slowly build up a massive attack against the computer's king. Remember to 'invite everyone to the party', i.e. to put all pieces on their optimal squares before the final breakthrough.

See Deep Junior-Piket in this chapter for an example of this idea.

4) Apply a maximum level of concentration when things get tactical and use more time at these critical moments. Even when all other parts of your anti-computer strategy are perfect, you will still lose games because of tactics. Without working hard on improving your tactical ability, you will never be able to beat the best of the modern programs.

5) Do not fear tactics when playing against the program. The fear of missing a tactic will lead you to inferior and passive positions and will eventually lead to a loss anyway. Most games **will** get tactical sooner or later, and sometimes you have to pick a tactical and complicated line to exploit your advantage.

6) Prophylactic play is extremely important, also against computers. You should always take into account what your silicon opponent is up to. If you are successful in repelling the most obvious attacking possibilities, you can sometimes reach a stage where the program starts playing senseless moves, as it does not have the ability to make long-term plans.

7) In general, try to work as much as possible with long-term planning as this area is still not within the reach of the computers.

8) If you do not succeed in closing the game it is often a good idea to swap some pieces to simplify it, if you can do so without compromising your position. Especially a queen exchange helps to reduce the amount of random tactics. Kramnik used this strategy to perfection in the first half of the match against Deep Fritz in Bahrain.

9) Read about the blind spots of the programs in Chapter 3, and be aware of all the ways in which you can exploit them. Personally I have experienced that it is much easier to play against the programs when you know these weaknesses by heart and have a thorough understanding of how they reach their conclusions. Performing computer-assisted analysis will help you to develop an understanding of the specific weaknesses of each program. One program may have problems with passed pawns, another does not know about opposite-coloured bishop endings, a third underestimates weak squares in the centre and so on.

10) If you have got into an inferior position, try to look for possible drawn fortress positions in the endgame, where the computer could still believe that it is winning.

11) Computers are still greedy, and offering them pawns for initiative and positional pluses is a good way to jam the evaluation function of the computer. They often underestimate sacrificial lines because of the null-move algorithm, and this means that you can sometimes surprise the programs with an intuitive piece sacrifice to open up the pawn cover in front of the king. Moreover, computers often underestimate the dangers to their own king.

This strategy is of course risky, as computers are excellent defenders, and they will usually find defensive resources quite quickly – if they exist. A good example of sacrificing for a kingside attack was seen in Shirov-Fritz in Chapter 3.

12) Once you identify the weaknesses of a program and succeed in executing a winning strategy, you can use this technique over and over again. Computers repeat their mistakes; they cannot learn. Humans are able to learn, and this ability should be used in the battle against the programs.

Naturally, all of this is just words, and you will have to practice a lot to be able to implement these strategies intuitively.

A suggestion for further studies is to analyse the computer games played by anti-computer experts such as Yasser Seirawan, John van der Wiel, Vladimir Kramnik and Viswanathan Anand for opening ideas and anti-computer strategies. In most databases computers usually have the prefix 'Comp', so you can find, e.g., Seirawan's games against various engines by searching through the database with the words 'Seirawan' and 'Comp'.

I have given some Internet addresses for further reading about anti-computer chess in the Bookmarks section of the book (see page 184).

5 Hardware, Software and Databases

I find ideas? No, Fritz finds the ideas.
Evgeny Bareev, grandmaster and world no. 8 with 2729 Elo on the January 2003 list

Despite the fact that the top modern programs play at a level comparable to a human grandmaster, it is surprisingly hard to learn anything from playing against them. The computer programs play reasonable and active moves most of the time and they hit you very hard the first time a promising tactical opportunity arises. Even if you feel that you were never outplayed, you may lose ten games in a row, and the lesson will still be the same: you should improve your tactics.

My feeling is that average chess-players' experiences with computers make them respect the programs too much. In chess clubs you can often hear people saying "Fritz showed -1 at this point", believing this to be some kind of indisputable evaluation of the position. However, we know from the previous chapters that computer evaluation is far from being perfect, and it is much more valuable to be able to use human language like 'a weak square', 'control of the centre', etc., to

describe a position than using the numerical evaluation of the program. '-1' tells us very little about the position. One of the players could have sacrificed two pawns and have some compensation, which the program does not always appreciate.

My impression is that players who overvalue computer assessments will have difficulties improving, simply because they do not learn to think about chess in the right way, and they tend to look at a game of chess as just a series of moves, not as planning and strategy, which is actually the area in which humans are strongest.

Moreover, I have the impression that some players spend too much of their chess study time with the computer. I believe it is important to perceive chess computers as a supplement to other chess studies. Generally speaking, you should not spend more than half of your chess study time with the computer. The reason is that if you are serious about chess, one of your main tasks is to develop your own analytical abilities. Sometimes you have to look at a real board and some real pieces instead of looking at a screen with Fritz or another analytical engine running in the background. Otherwise your brain will be accustomed to a program that points out all tactical problems for you, and this will surely not help you when you sit down to play in the tournament hall. You may realize that 'analysing with a computer' too often changes into 'watching the lines that the computer analyses'. You stop thinking yourself, and this is certainly a large pitfall and something to be aware of when using computers.

However, with the above-mentioned warnings, we should now be ready to discuss how to improve and analyse with the help of the computer. The following chapters will give some suggestions for how to make best use of the computer's impressive capabilities.

Databases

Using game databases for studying the opening and studying your opponent's play is probably the most widespread use of computers amongst stronger players. Nowadays games of your future opponents are available worldwide a few minutes after they have been played, and this is a fact that every serious tournament player has to take into account. A novelty played in a grandmaster tournament in France can be repeated the day after in Slovenia.

The information age has affected chess a lot, and the effect of this can only be positive, if we know how to handle the huge amount of data. In general, our experience with the Internet shows that a lot of information does not necessarily make us smarter, and nobody is going to be a stronger player just by owning a 2 million+ database. Danish grandmaster Bent Larsen has been quoted as saying that he does not believe that the information age has had many advantages for chess-players. In his time, he only had a few books with the best games to look at, and this was all he needed for improving in chess. Although this point of view has some merit, I disagree with it overall. If you want to, you can easily make some searches in a database to find games of 2700+ players, and then you will have only the games of the best players. Therefore the main point is to extract the right information out of the databases. However, if these games are not annotated it can be difficult to understand what it is going on in them. Thus, databases should only be used as a supplement to other sources and other tools.

There are several commercial databases available. Some of those include more than 5 million games, but it is important to remember that quantity does not necessarily equal quality. If these collections include duplicates, incomplete games, games without a result, etc., it is hardly worth wasting your time on them. Some databases can be downloaded from the Internet and may contain interesting games that are not included in the main databases. I have given some URLs for good places to search for games in the Bookmarks section (page 184).

Most of the databases have some weaknesses in common, because of the varied quality of the original source. Games may be entered with the wrong result, with wrong moves, or with an incomplete game score. Moreover, you may also find that inconsistent spelling of names is common in several databases.

As for the commercial offerings, they do get rid of most of this junk data. ChessBase has the Mega Database which is updated every year and currently contains more than 2.3 million games. I believe this to be one of the best choices, but also one of the most expensive. It contains around 50,000 games annotated by top players. The annotations in Mega Database are certainly useful for understanding what is going on in a certain opening line, but they are of variable quality – the best game annotations are still to be found in printed magazines such as *New In Chess*. It is also worth mentioning the far less expensive Big Database, which contains the same games as Mega Database, but without annotations.

When choosing a database, an economical solution is to purchase Chess Assistant 7, which includes a 2 million+ database that comes with the program. Another alternative is Knut Neven's Research Database, which currently includes nearly 3 million games, and is updated every week. Like the ChessBase and Chess Assistant databases, this database also deals with the problems with inconsistent spellings, etc. The main reason why the Research database contains more games than the alternatives is that more correspondence games have been included. Moreover, in the Research Database, Neven has experimented with assigning historical ratings to players that were active before the rating system was invented. This means that you can more easily use Elo as a parameter when searching for quality games, but of course you have to take these old ratings with a grain of salt.

Surprisingly often, chess-players do not manage to get the right information out of the databases, and one of the reasons for this is that they do not have up-to-date information. It has happened quite often to me that after a game my opponent has said something like "I thought you played the King's Indian", etc. The reality is that chess-players do not necessarily play the same opening as they did three years ago. To find out which openings your opponent currently prefers, it is important to look specifically at the latest games he played.

The ChessBase Mega Database is only updated once a year, so serious players will have to update and add games more often. There are several sites on the Internet where you can get new games on a weekly basis. One of the best-known is The Week In Chess, and the games from this site can be downloaded easily by going to the 'Help' menu of ChessBase 7 or 8 and clicking 'Get new games'. However, they can also be downloaded by going to the TWIC website. ChessBase also publishes ChessBase Magazine six times a year, featuring new annotated games and much else besides.

Database Programs

As I have mentioned before, Chess-Base is the database program against which all others are measured. At the time of writing ChessBase 8 was the latest version of the program, and the following discussion is based on this version, but will doubtless apply to later versions of the program as well. The basic structure and functions have been the same through the latest upgrades.

Personally, I have been using Chess-Base for many years and I believe the program has everything I need. It contains all the normal database functions such as making searches based on names, positions, manoeuvres, headers, etc., and it has several analysis engines included. There is a chess 'tree', which makes it possible to merge a lot of games into one to view the general structure of an opening variation with all the statistical information included. ChessBase 8 also includes the very useful feature of giving access to an online database that contains around 2.5 million games. The database is updated on a weekly basis and thus it is a handy tool for players who want the latest information without actually doing the work of downloading the games themselves. As I have chosen ChessBase 8 for many examples throughout this book, I will not delve deeper into the many functions of the program now.

The main competitor of ChessBase is the Russian-developed Chess Assistant. If you think ChessBase is the program that has it all, then you should try the Russian equivalent. Chess Assistant 7 has just about every function a chess computer freak could think of. One example worth mentioning is the sophisticated analysis functions with which you can perform deep, interactive analysis. The best engine included in the Chess Assistant package is Chess Tiger 15, which is more or less on the same level as the strongest engines from ChessBase. Also freeware engines like Ruffian, Crafty and the weaker Dragon are included, and there is also the possibility of importing engines from the Internet.

When using the interactive analysis you can add your own lines for the engine to analyse (like in Fritz, described in Chapter 6). The brilliant thing is that you have a lot of options to use while the engine is analysing the various lines. You can make the engine skip a certain line and go on to the next branch, if the evaluation of the current position is obvious for you. You can adjust the analysis depth while it analyses, and make the engine go deeper into certain lines. If you want the engine to look only at certain positions, it is possible to insert markers and make it analyse only marked positions. When analysing a whole game automatically, there is also great flexibility. It is possible to decide if, for instance, the engine should focus on the middlegame and only go through the endgame very quickly, because things were already decided by that point.

It is also worth mentioning that the learning abilities of the engines work very well inside Chess Assistant. It has a learning function, which is important when performing computer-assisted analysis, as it means that the engine recalls what it has analysed before.

Let us assume that you analyse a position where you try to make a sacrifice work. The engine suggests a defence, but through analysis it is proven that this line is not sufficient to parry the attack. If the learning abilities work well, you can go back to the initial position, and the computer will remember that its first suggestion was not good enough to defend the position. In that case, it will immediately start looking for other variations, instead of repeating the analysis it has already performed. The learning abilities also depend on the size of the hash tables, which is a subject I shall discuss later.

The tree functions of Chess Assistant are also worth mentioning. It is possible to build a tree even from databases with millions of games, and this ability makes it very easy to track down transpositions in the opening.

Other positive aspects of Chess Assistant are that database searches are very fast with this program, and that it works with the DGT Board, an electronic chess board described in detail later in this chapter. It also has support for ICC (the Internet Chess Club) as an integrated part of the interface, and the program comes with a 2 million+ database, including CAP (Computer Analysis Project) data. The CAP project is an attempt to computer analyse the whole *ECO* (Encyclopaedia of Chess Openings) and specific parts of chess opening theory to find flaws, novelties and blunders. I think that it is an interesting project, but I have not found any use for the data yet, as I normally use manual computer-assisted analysis, or fully automatic computer alternatives such as Deep Position Analysis or Blunder Check in Fritz (both described later in Chapter 6) to find errors in games and analysis. One problem is that if you get a position where the CAP data gives an evaluation of -0.30, you have no information about which engine this assessment refers to. However, the general impression of Chess Assistant is that it is a program with an enormous amount of functions and facilities.

So which one is best, ChessBase or Chess Assistant? I suppose it depends on what you want. In ChessBase you get simplicity and a very nice interface. It includes access to the weekly updated online database, and there are excellent features like the 'Opening report' mentioned in Chapter 7. I also believe that the publishing features, both on the Internet and printed, are great. Personally I like the ChessBase interface, but it may just be a matter of what you are most used to.

Chess Assistant, on the other hand, is certainly a more economical solution. In addition to the database program, it includes possibilities of playing against the built-in engines (not possible in ChessBase), and a 2 million+ database. A ChessBase user will have to buy a playing program (Fritz) and the Big Base database to match this. So Chess Assistant is a 3-in-1 solution. On a short-term basis the enormous amount of functions in the program may seem slightly confusing. I believe, however, that when you get to know the program better, the time invested in learning how to use the program should pay off.

All in all, I am not going to recommend one program over the other. The discussion above shows that there are pros and cons of both. For new chess computer users, I should mention that both companies have 'light' versions of their programs which are downloadable from their respective websites. By checking out these demo-versions of the programs you can test which one you prefer.

Those who do not have funds for investing in one of the commercial programs should try the freeware database

program Scid, which comes with the freeware engine Crafty. It is also quite easy to import strong freeware engines like Ruffian, Yace or others available on the Internet. Moreover, a free reference database of 600,000 games should soon be available on the Scid website. All in all, you can have a decent database system with some strong engines included just by downloading a few program files from the Internet. All Internet addresses that refer to these programs and engines are given in the Bookmarks section of this book.

A program which can work as a supplement to both database and playing programs is BookUp by the American programmer Mike Leahy. BookUp is like the database programs, but its main use is to drill you in your opening repertoire. You can download BookUp Lite from the BookUp website to try this feature. The main idea is that you input the opening moves that you want to learn by heart, with all lines and ramifications. The 'Training' function in BookUp, found in the 'Command' menu of the program, will help you to get to know these lines by randomly picking one of the moves you have entered. Thus you will easily learn the different variations by playing over the lines with the program playing the opponent's move. When you encounter a line that is especially troublesome or difficult to remember, you can change the weight of the move so that the computer always plays this move. This is done by clicking the move, pressing Alt-U, to bump the desired line up in the variation display, and then pressing Alt-T to get the Training dialogue box. Then you select 'Computer Must Play Top Candidate', and the program selects the move in the top. Some people may argue that it is not a good idea to learn moves by heart, and that your time is better spent studying the ideas of the opening. Of course, you should know the ideas before actually learning move-orders. However, I have found that going through concrete move-orders with BookUp has given me a better feeling of the various positional ideas in an opening, and when to go for which plan. Moreover, if you know only the general positional ideas and are up against someone who knows the general ideas **and** the concrete move-orders, he will surely have an edge over you. If you are rated below 2100, however, I believe that specific move-orders are probably not that important, because most of your opponents will deviate from the known theory at an early point.

Playing Programs

Most modern computer programs play at more or less the same high level of strength, so for a new user the amount of functions available in the various interfaces is probably more important.

The Fritz interface from ChessBase may be the best-known playing program. As I have used the program for

the examples in this book, I will not discuss any specific functions at this point. Instead I will just give a short description of the many different strong engines that can be used within the interface. In this short survey I have analysed the latest versions of each engine, but the reader should be aware of that the programs are subject to change, and that the 'personalities' described here can change over time.

At the time of writing, **Fritz 8** is the main engine in the latest version of the interface. I believe that the Fritz engine has made a lot of progress since versions 5 and 6, which were mainly fast-searchers without much knowledge of endgames and positional play. Fritz 8 is a good all-round engine. It is has a very sensible and objective evaluation and rarely gets carried away in sacrificial lines like its 'cousin' Junior. Nevertheless, Fritz 8 it is much less materialistic than it was earlier and will still often give up a pawn for active play. The engine still has some of the general weaknesses that are common for all computer engines, such as not seeing that a long-term attack is dangerous before it is too late.

Junior 7 is one of the wildest and most tactical engines available. It gladly sacrifices one or two pawns, or even a piece, for an unclear attack, and this makes it a very dangerous opponent for humans. Sometimes the sacrifices are not sound, but it takes a lot of strength to show that this is actually the case. Junior seems to explore the limits of compensation, and thus, it is a very interesting analysis partner. On the other hand, it may be a good idea to combine its analysis with a more 'objective' engine such as, for example, Fritz. When analysing endgames or positional play, it is advisable to switch to one of the other engines for the best results. However, it is very good at quickly sorting out complicated middlegame tactics.

Hiarcs 8 is quite different from Junior as it searches much more slowly. Junior analyses up to ten times as many positions per seconds in some positions, but Hiarcs has enough knowledge to compensate for that. Hiarcs's main strengths are in positional play and endgames, and incidentally I have found that it is perhaps the best program for analysing rook endgames.

Shredder 7 is another slow-searcher with a lot of knowledge of endgames and positional play incorporated. Generally, this engine is known as the best endgame program, and I believe that this is a fair judgement. When playing against other programs, you will often see Shredder turn the tables and win from a more or less equal endgame. The tests I have made with the program so far show good results, and I have not been able to locate any weaknesses other than the common ones, described in detail in Chapter 3.

Nimzo 8 is one of the fast-searchers from ChessBase. While it is good in tactics, it suffers very much in positional evaluation and endgame knowledge.

Besides the commercial engines mentioned here, there are also a number of free engines that can be downloaded from the ChessBase website and used within the Fritz interface. Several of those are not so far from the commercial engines in strength. Among the strongest ones are List and probably also Crafty, but I can also recommend downloading a few of the weaker engines for training games; for example, EXchess, which I have used myself. These engines should be saved in the Engines folder under your ChessBase folder.

Alternatives to ChessBase Programs

The ChessPartner interface produced by the Dutch company Lokasoft is a quite simple interface, but it includes all the main functions of a chess-playing program. It has analysis functions, tools for book editing, database handling, automatic game analysis, importing engines downloaded from the Internet, playing chess over the Internet, move announcement, and support for the DGT electronic chessboard (described in detail later in this chapter). A small drawback is that the annotation facilities in the current interface (5.2) are not so advanced. You can write verbal annotations to a game, but the current version does not include Informator-style annotations ('+−' = decisive advantage for White, etc.). A demo-version of the Chess Partner interface is available from the Lokasoft website.

Gandalf and **Chess Tiger 15** are the two main engines in Chess Partner, and they are both of a similar level to the ChessBase engines. ChessPartner also has a weaker Lokasoft Standard chess engine, which can be used, e.g., for training games. **Gandalf** is an extremely aggressive and entertaining engine. It likes to give up material for initiative or attack, and I believe it is probably one of the strongest attacking engines available. It is a slow-searcher, which means that it has a lot of knowledge of positional play and endgames, but it also does very well in tactical tests. The Gandalf engine supports the UCI (Universal Chess Interface) protocol, and thus it can be exported to other interfaces, for instance the Fritz interface. At the time of writing (March 2003), Gandalf's status in Lokasoft is unresolved. My personal experiences with the first beta versions of Gandalf 6 have convinced me that the program will be amongst the very best when it is released. A Gandalf 6 beta version won the computer tournament CSS Online Masters in the winter of 2002/3 ahead of Deep Fritz, Shredder, Junior and many of the other leading engines.

Unfortunately, I do not have so much experience with **Chess Tiger 15**, but from the test games I have seen so far, it seems on a par with the other top engines. The engine is also the strongest of those included in the Chess Assistant package. The only slight drawback is that in some endgames its evaluation is not very precise, as its knowledge seems to be limited. Thus for endgames, you might do better to pick another engine.

Chessmaster 9000 is a very popular program produced by the American company Ubisoft. It is based on the engine The King programmed by Johan de Koning, which is also of a similar standard to the other engines mentioned in this survey. The Chessmaster program sells well, especially in the USA, and it is known for its many personalities, for instance a Morphy personality which plays the same openings and in the style of the legendary attacking genius. I find personalities an entertaining idea, but it is not terribly important when training with the computer. The program also has weaker personalities, and I shall discuss these in the section 'Handicapping the program' later in this chapter.

There are a lot of tutorials included in the program, ranking from beginner-level to advanced. The program also includes an audio chess course by International Master Josh Waitzkin, which is instructive and well done and relevant for most players, even up to master level. In general, this is probably the program you should buy if you have just started in chess, or if you want to teach your son or daughter to play chess. For more advanced players, I would recommend one of the alternatives, as there are only a few analysis functions in Chessmaster.

For those who do not want to invest in the commercial programs, there is an excellent freeware alternative, which can be downloaded from the Internet. The **Arena** interface is, I believe, not inferior to most of the commercial products, both regarding functions and layout. It is easy to install the interface and some engines to run in it, and, unlike other freeware interfaces, you do not have to be a chess computer freak to do this!

The Arena interface supports UCI (Universal Chess Interface) and Winboard, which are protocols for chess programs. In comparison with this, the Fritz interface only supports UCI.

Thus, Arena makes it very easy to choose from the hundreds of freeware engines available on the Internet and use them within the program. Currently engines like Yace, SOS, Ruffian and probably also the veteran Crafty are among the best, but new engines keep on coming up every month, so the picture is changing all the time.

Optimizing the Program

Once you have selected a program, you may want to know more about how to get the highest performance from it; e.g., when analysing your own games, or for getting the strongest opposition in training games. The latter should be relevant only for players at master level and up. The average player may instead want to know some more about 'handicapping' the program, and this topic is discussed later in this chapter.

Below you will find some advice on how to optimize the strength of the computer and the programs. For the examples I have used the Fritz interface, but similar options are available in other interfaces.

1) Close all other applications running on the computer while analysing with the program. This includes virus programs, instant messenger programs and others that you may have running in the background.

2) Let the program think on the opponent's time. This function is called 'Permanent brain' or 'Pondering', and is a feature that exists in all programs. It guesses the opponent's next move and starts calculating a reply. If the opponent plays the expected move, the program will often reply instantly. This saves time for later use. The program shows the move it is expecting in the engine window. In Fritz this function can be checked on or off in the engine dialogue box (F3).

3) Use the default engine parameters. Unless you are a very advanced user, it is difficult to tweak the parameters to obtain better results. The default values are the ones chosen by the programmer for best performance in most positions.

4) Use the right opening book for the program. When you buy a program,

it comes with an opening book which suits the program's style. You can often configure the book options, and in Fritz this is done by hitting 'F4'. In this dialogue box select 'Use book' and 'Tournament book' to get the optimal settings. Moreover, you can change the variety of play, influence of learn value and learning strength. The simplest thing to do is just to press 'Optimize', and you will see that the variety of play becomes much lower. In that case the program will play only the moves that it has been 'told' are the best.

5) Giving your program access to endgame tablebases (EGTB) will markedly improve its endgame play when there are only a few pieces left on the board. Most programs include some EGTBs on the program CD, and installing these will enable it to play positions with three-, four- and some five-piece endings perfectly. Some EGTBs, however, may be installed automatically with the program. Obviously, endings like ♔♖♙ vs ♔♖ and ♔♕♙ vs ♔♕, are of great importance for optimal performance by the program. Tablebases can be accessed from the CD, but installing them to your hard disk will speed up the process. Create a directory, e.g. C:\Tablebases, and copy the files from the CD, or a download site on the Internet, to this folder.

In Fritz you set the tablebase path by going to the 'Tools' menu, selecting 'Options' and clicking the 'Tablebases'

tab in the dialogue box. Click 'Browse' to find your tablebases directory, and note that the program gives you the possibility of locating the tablebases in three different directories. You can also set the cache memory to speed up the tablebase access during a game. According to ChessBase a value between 1 and 8 Mb is advisable.

6) Set the hash tables for optimal performance. Hash tables are memory areas in which the program can store positions and evaluations. If the program has analysed a position once before, it can check the hash tables to find the evaluation, instead of analysing the position all over again. This will seriously speed up the analysis process. Generally, fast-searching programs will fill up the hash tables much more quickly than slow-searching positional engines. For deep analysis and long time controls, large hash tables are needed. As a rule-of-thumb Chess-Base recommends 64 Mb RAM for games at blitz controls, and 256 Mb RAM or more for games at tournament time control, provided of course that you have this kind of memory available on your computer. Chess-Base gives a formula for the more technically oriented, which is:

$2.0 \times \text{Freq[MHz]} \times t[s] = \text{HT[KB]}$

In this formula 'Freq' is your processor speed in Megahertz, 't' is time in seconds, and 'HT' is hash tables in kilobytes. An example: a computer with a 2 GHz processor is playing a game at tournament time control, i.e.

around 3 minutes per move. What should the hash table size be? 2 GHz is 2000 MHz, and 3 minutes is 180 seconds. This gives us:

2.0×2000×180 = 720,000 Kb hash tables, or optimally 720 Mb for hash tables.

At the time of writing many computers have less memory than that, so you may have to go for a lower value. Usually you should keep nearly 100 Mb RAM free for other purposes if you are running Windows XP, while earlier operating systems are able to do with less. If you have a computer with 512 Mb RAM, do not use more than 420 Mb for hash tables with Windows XP as the operating system.

It is considered preferable, when possible, to use RAM in doubling increments, i.e. 1 Mb, 2 Mb, 4 Mb, 8 Mb, 16 Mb, etc. If you set your hash tables too high, you will know it when the engine starts analysing. If there is constant hard-disk activity, it means that the program has copied some files to your hard disk, and this slows down the analysis markedly. If, on the other hand, there is absolutely no hard-disk activity during analysis, you may want to increase the hash table size for faster analysis. You can try to verify the differences in analysis speed by experimenting with different sizes of the hash tables.

In Fritz or ChessBase, the size of the hash tables can be changed in the engine dialogue box (in Fritz you get this by pressing F3).

'Handicapping' the Program

As most of the modern programs play at an level somewhere between 2400 and 2700 Elo, they will prove to be a hard match for nearly anyone. For this reason, many chess-players have to consider the option of 'handicapping' the programs. Unfortunately, it seems to be very hard to program an engine to play weaker in a realistic way.

I tested some of the weaker 'personalities' in Chessmaster, and found out that, for instance, personalities rated around 1800 played in a very strange, random way, occasionally making piece sacrifices that make absolutely no sense at all. A human player rated at 1800 would not make nonsense moves like that, and thus after a few games, I felt that I had wasted my time. However, Chessmaster has hundreds of personalities, and you can also create your own personalities. You may be able to find or create some better ones than I did so far.

In the Fritz interface you have the opposite problem. If you use the Handicap function (Ctrl-H) and set the playing strength to 1600, the engine plays much better than 1600. Thus, if you want an opponent rated at 1600 it is a better idea to join your local chess club and play there, or use one of the Internet chess clubs. However, if you want to play training games in a particular opening and do not have a human training partner for doing that, then you have to use the handicapping functions.

In Fritz there are three possibilities. The first is Friend mode, which I would not recommend to use. The idea of Friend mode is that you give yourself a handicap of, for instance, 300, and then the engine will drop a piece, the first time it gets the chance (300 corresponds to three pawns or approximately a piece). After that it does everything it can to defend the position. Personally, I do not see the point of playing games like that, as it is a quite unrealistic style.

The second option is 'Handicap and fun', mentioned above, where you can choose some personalities like 'drunk', 'moron' and so on. After some experiments, my impression is that all the personalities play complete nonsense chess. Even drunkards and morons do not play like that! If, on the other hand, you set the rating yourself, the engine plays much stronger than the Elo indicated. Thus tuning the strength level of the program can be a difficult matter.

The third, and best, option is the Sparring mode, which you find in the 'Game' menu. Choose 'Levels' and then 'Sparring', and select the difficulty level in the dialogue that comes up. The idea of Sparring mode is that the program will play reasonable moves, depending on the level, but during the game it will give you a few chances to decide the game tactically. This is the closest you get to 'human play'. If you choose the level 'Very hard' the computer will generally play a better game, but it still gives you some possibilities of winning the game with a strong move once or twice during the course of the game. The only slight drawback is that a human and a computer do not always find the same things easy, i.e. a mate-in-seven can be easy for the program, while it may not be that obvious for the human. On the other hand, moves considered 'Very hard' by the computer can sometimes be simple to find for a human because of intuition.

For players rated around 2100 and above, it is possibly more instructive to play some training games against an engine operating at close to full strength. There are several ways of reducing the strength without actually using handicap mode. First of all, you can download a weaker engine on the Internet than the one that came with the program. Secondly, you can look at some of the features described in the section about optimizing the program and then turn the advice around. For instance, you can let the engine play without hash tables and without access to endgame tablebases. You change the engine parameters slightly or deselect the 'Permanent brain' option in the engine dialogue box (F3 in Fritz). You can also change the book options by pressing F4 in Fritz and choose 'Handicap'. This means that the program will pick a greater variety of opening lines, and it will not follow the book lines as far as normal. In the 'Book options' dialogue, you can change the value of 'minimum games' to tell the program how many games should be available in the book for it to play a specific line. If, after this tweaking, the engine is still playing too strongly, you should return to the normal handicapping options.

Tutorial Programs and Opening CDs

For the average chess-player, tutorial programs are a fun new way to learn about chess concepts. For both Chess-Base and Chess Assistant you can buy several tutorial programs, and Chessmaster has tutorials included in the program. Also other specific tutorial programs exist, such as Chess Mentor, of which there is a free demo-version available on the Internet. Moreover, ChessBase produces a lot of opening CDs. In general I believe these CDs should be measured by the quality of the material, not the medium, and the quality is not yet on the same level as 'normal' opening books. However, this may change. Currently, the authors of opening CDs rarely use the multimedia possibilities available on a computer, and thus having an opening CD is often like owning a written book on a CD, in which case I prefer reading a book rather than reading text on a computer screen. One of the advantages of having an opening CD is that

they sometimes include some additional games that are not included in the main databases, and besides that, they have an opening tree. The tree can be used as an opening book in Fritz to play training games in a specific opening. You can also construct a tree yourself to use as an opening book, and this is a feature I will discuss later in this chapter.

To give a complete overview of the tutorial software available here would be too space-consuming, so my general advice is to check out the reviews at the chess review websites. I have given some addresses of chess review websites in the Bookmarks section (see page 184).

Computer Hardware

The most important factors to consider regarding chess power in a computer are the processor speed and the amount of RAM (Random Access Memory). The speed of the processor determines the pace at which the processor can perform mathematical operations. If we compare two computers – one with a 1 GHz processor and one with a 2 GHz processor and all other factors equal – the latter will get close to double the speed of the former and analyse close to twice as many positions per second.

The size of the computer's RAM is important for the hash tables, as described in detail earlier in this chapter. Generally, you can run most chess programs with as little as 64 Mb RAM, but the performance of the programs will increase a lot with more RAM.

However, two computers with the same processor speed may still analyse at different speeds, because of other technical factors that I shall not mention here. In the Fritz interface you have the possibility of checking your configuration by making a benchmark test to measure the performance of your computer. This is called Fritz-Mark, and you find the function in the 'Tools' menu of the Fritz Interface. Select FritzMark from the dialogue and press start. The computer will now run a test and after some time you will see the result in the dialogue box. According to ChessBase, a typical Fritz-Mark for a 1 GHz Athlon processor with 128 MB hash tables is 620. When making this test, remember to close other applications that may be running on your computer, as this can have an influence on the performance of the system.

Electronic Chessboards

When playing computer chess, you may sometimes feel that you are missing something when sitting in front of a computer screen. I have already recommended that you set up positions and play through and analyse games on a real board, and an electronic chess board can make this an integrated part of your studies with the computer. I believe that whether you

have an electronic chess board or not, you should use a good part of your study time using real pieces and a real board, simply to adjust yourself to the situation in the tournament hall. Maybe it is a matter of taste, but I personally like the feeling of a real board much more, and I play and analyse a lot more seriously this way.

Several electronic chessboards are available. The best-known are those from Novag, Shahcom and DGT Projects, the latter being the most popular and the one used in most international tournaments. I have only had the possibility of testing the DGT board for this book.

The DGT board is a full-size traditional wooden chessboard and in comparison to the alternatives it has the most updates and new drivers for the various chess programs. I have tested the board and found it works well with Fritz, Chessmaster, Chess Partner and Arena, all programs with the move announcement option.

This feature makes it possible simply to turn off the computer screen and play against your computer, just by listening to the announcement of the moves. Chess Assistant also supports the DGT board, and thus it becomes easier to enter, for instance, some opening lines for later analysis. ChessBase 8 does not support the DGT Board, so ChessBase users will have to use the Fritz interface or wait for this feature to be included in a later version of the database program.

The DGT board has a general chess driver that supports other chess programs, and it also includes a specific driver for use in BlitzIn/ICC (the Internet Chess Club). Generally, it is more comfortable to be able to play opponents over the Internet with a real board, but for some reason most people in the Internet chess clubs only play games at fairly fast time-limits. I have found it close to impossible to play the usual 3-minute blitz games when you have to wait for the move announcements. Even in 5-minute games you lose too much time on this, so you will have to search for games with some increment, say 5 minutes for the game and 5 seconds added per move. Otherwise you will lose on time too often.

For training games against a computer opponent, an electronic board is very useful, and you can also use the board to record games you play against human opponents for later analysis. Moreover, you can use the electronic DGT clock in conjunction with the board, and the clock can also be used with a normal chess board.

6 Computer-Assisted Analysis

Not very long ago it wasn't easy for an average chess-player to get a solid analysis of a complicated position.
STEFAN MEYER-KAHLEN, author of the computer program Shredder

Being able to analyse a position with a computer is of great importance. To perform good computer-assisted analysis has a great many purposes. It is useful when analysing your own games, when checking new ideas in an opening, and when finding the best move in a correspondence game, etc. When done in the right way, the quality of computer-assisted analysis is usually far beyond what can be achieved by a human only, or a computer program working on its own. The reason for this is that humans and computers have a very different set of capabilities and the two complement each other excellently. I have already mentioned this before. While computers are excellent tacticians, strong human players often have more knowledge of the game and sometimes make better evaluations of the resulting positions. In situations where positional planning is required, strong human players are usually superior, as computers do not bother with positional planning. Of course, much of this depends on your level of skill.

If you have just started out in chess, you do not have the experience or intuition to add anything valuable to the computer analysis and probably you should not spend much time on it. Obviously, stronger players will be able to trust their own ideas more and can form an excellent team with a computer program.

My own experiences from playing correspondence chess in the ICCF Master Class gave me the impression that too many correspondence players switch off their brain when they switch on the computer. Most of them seem to let a computer program do an 'infinite analysis' overnight and then send the move recommended by the computer the next day. By letting a computer pick your next move, you do not learn much about chess, and your results will not be impressive either, especially if you are playing against someone who knows how to combine the force of human creativity and computer calculation. If it is done right, humans and computers working together can take chess analysis to a new level.

When analysing with a computer, your role as a human varies very much depending on which kind of position you are analysing. You need to have a well-developed feeling for what kind of computer weaknesses may be relevant in various types of position. This is important when deciding if you should follow the computer's suggestion or come up with your own. In general the human should perceive himself as the creative part of the team while the program performs the dirty work of analysis.

In positions where positional planning is needed, the human should come up with various plans and test them by 'playing them out' against the computer. Let us say that you have a plan of transferring a knight to a central square. Simply make the moves, and let the computer think for 10-20 seconds about each of the opponent's moves to see if it can find any valuable counterplay. In this way you can test if a plan makes sense. Often there will be a phase just after the opening when it is important to test the various plans. In this regard, the computer can be an excellent partner to try out different paths.

In positions of a more tactical nature the human also has to take an active role and direct the analysis by testing ideas and, especially, unclear sacrifices. Because of the null-move algorithm (described in detail in Chapter 2) computers will often discard material sacrifices unless they regain the material within their horizon or see sufficient positional compensation. Lines that involve giving up material are often not searched as deeply as other main lines because most of them simply make no sense. However,

humans often have an intuitive feeling about sacrifices that look like they could work, and computers are excellent partners for testing these lines. The main point here is that the user has to help the computer a bit by actually making the sacrifice on the board and thereby pushing the horizon of the program a bit further. If the program is analysing the position just before the sacrifice, it may spend only a small part of the allocated time analysing these lines, but when the position is on the board it simply has to analyse the lines. I will give a simple example of this from a blitz game I played against a beta version of Gandalf.

Expanding the Horizon

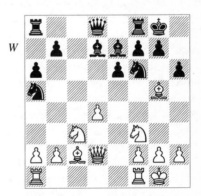

C. Kongsted – Gandalf 5 beta

The Gandalf 5 beta has just played 13...h6?, giving me the (for a human) obvious possibility of sacrificing a bishop for two pawns.

14 ♗xh6! gxh6 15 ♕xh6 ♘c6 16 ♘g5 ♕c7 17 ♗h7+ ♔h8 18 ♗g6+ ♔g8 19 ♘ce4 ♕xh2+

Desperation, because Black would otherwise get mated after ♘xf6+ and ♕h7#.

20 ♕xh2 ♔g7 21 ♘xf6 ♖h8 22 ♕g3 1-0

Gandalf resigned as it is too far behind in material.

Looking at the diagram position, I believe it is clear to most players at club level and above that 14 ♗xh6 is an interesting move to consider. As this was a blitz game, I did not calculate a lot of lines before taking on h6. For me, it was enough to know that I had two pawns for the bishop after the sacrifice as well as attacking ideas based on ♘g5 and possibly also a rook entering the attack via e1-e3. For a human it is often sufficient that it 'looks good', especially in a blitz game, while a computer has a different way of approaching the position. For a computer to play 14 ♗xh6 it simply has to be good, otherwise it will not play the move. I tried to set up this position on Fritz 8 and it took it 9 minutes and 40 seconds before deciding on 14 ♗xh6 as the best move in the position, showing a slight advantage to White with the evaluation +0.38. Until that point it preferred 14 ♗xf6. Many computer programs will discard the bishop sacrifice at an early stage due to the null-move algorithm, which is described in Chapter 2.

Let us assume that I want to analyse this position a little bit deeper and reach some conclusions about it. I execute the move 14 ♗xh6 on the board, and now my idea is to take the computer as far as possible in some of the critical lines. First of all, I note that accepting the sacrifice is not forced. I may get this idea by looking at the board myself, or I can ask the program to help.

For the following analysis I used Fritz 8 inside ChessBase 8, and I will discuss some of the analysis options that these programs contain. After 14 ♗xh6 I set Fritz 8 to analyse and for some time the program gives 14...gxh6 as the best move, with a value of 0.00. It sees that White can at least give perpetual check with the queen on the h- and g-files after taking on h6. Soon after, the evaluation starts climbing for White, and the program begins to consider other moves. In Fritz and ChessBase, you can press the '+' and '−' keys to change the number of lines shown. You can also press the 'y' key to stop it from considering the line that it currently believes is the best, and instead make it focus on the second best move. Pressing the 'y' key again makes the engine focus on the third-best move, etc.

I press the '+' key twice to make Fritz help me finding possible alternatives to accepting the sacrifice. After a few minutes I get the following analysis, showing that the program prefers White in all lines.

1) ± (0.66): 14...gxh6 15 ♕xh6 ♘c4 16 ♖fe1 ♘d6 17 g4 ♗c6

2) ± (0.75): 14...♘c4 15 ♕g5 ♘e8 16 ♕g3 ♗c6 17 ♗c1 ♘f6 18 ♖d1 ♕b6 19 ♘e5 ♘xb2

3) ± (0.97): 14...♗c6 15 ♘e5 gxh6 16 ♕xh6 ♕xd4 17 ♖fe1 ♘c4 18 ♕g5+ ♔h8 19 ♖ad1 ♕c5 20 ♕h4+ ♔g7 21 ♘xc4 ♕h5 22 ♕xh5 ♘xh5 23 ♗e4

Note that the lines cannot necessarily be trusted to the very end (e.g., 20 ♕h6+! ♔g8 21 ♘g4 +− is a big improvement in line '3'). I am mainly looking at the first moves in the variations and at the final evaluations.

Fritz has found two alternatives to the sacrifice, and even though the evaluation looks good for White, I should go back and check the lines later. My main interest at this point is what happens if the sacrifice is accepted. I move 14...gxh6 on the board and recapture with 15 ♕xh6 right away. Note that we have now taken the engine three plies deeper down this line. This may not seem a lot, but actually it is a big help for the engine, and the scores quickly start climbing for White.

How would you analyse this position if you did not have a computer program to help you? By finding the candidate moves, and analysing them in turn! This is exactly what you must do with the program as well. Take a look at the position to see what defensive options you see, and let us have a look at what Fritz says now:

1) ± (0.91): 15...♘c4 16 ♘e5 ♘d6 17 g4 ♘de8 18 g5 ♗c6 19 gxf6

2) +− (1.62): 15...♗c6 16 ♖fe1 ♘c4 17 ♖e5 ♘xe5 18 dxe5 ♘e4 19 ♘xe4

3) +− (1.94): 15...♖c8 16 ♖fe1 ♗a4 17 ♗xa4 ♘c4 18 ♗c2 ♖e8 19 ♗d3 ♕a5 20 ♗xc4 ♖xc4 21 ♖ac1

If you have other alternatives at this point, you should enter them and test them with Fritz. In this kind of position I generally trust the computer's defending abilities, so I will mainly help it to get deeper into the various lines. If some moves are forced – which means that all alternatives are clearly inferior – then it is even more important to enter the moves on the board and make the engine skip some plies.

The last of these lines (line 3) shows Black going into desperation mode to save the position, and the general picture is certainly that Black is having severe difficulties defending the position. Instead of just letting Fritz analyse the position at move 14, I have helped it to go some moves deeper, and now everything is becoming clear. 15...♘c4 looks like the best try, but I may get back to look at some alternatives later. Fritz suggests 16 ♘e5, but as my original idea was 16 ♘g5, and as I like this possibility better, I input the moves 15...♘c4 16 ♘g5 instead, and the scores keep on climbing:

1) +− (2.37): 16...♘d6 17 ♖fe1

2) +− (2.37): 16...♘d2 17 ♖fd1 ♘f3+ 18 ♘xf3 ♗c6 19 ♘e5 ♖c8 20 ♖d3 ♘h7 21 ♖e3

3) +− (2.66): 16...♗c6 17 ♖fe1 ♘d6 18 ♖e3

The program has now found my original idea of bringing the rook into the attack via the e-file and the third rank, and the advantage looks decisive. I take the engine a little further in the main line 16...♘d6 17 ♖fe1, and it is all over:

1) +– (8.06): 17...♕a5 18 ♖e5 b6 19 ♘ce4 ♘dxe4 20 ♖xe4 ♕e1+ 21 ♖exe1 ♖a7 22 ♗h7+ ♔h8 23 ♗e4+ ♔g8

2) +– (8.44): 17...♗c6 18 ♖e3 ♗f3 19 ♘xe6 fxe6 20 ♕g6+ ♔h8 21 ♖xf3 ♘fe4 22 ♖g3 ♖f7 23 ♘xe4 ♕g8 24 ♕h6+ ♖h7 25 ♖xg8+ ♖xg8 26 ♕xe6 ♘b5 27 ♖d1

3) +– (14.81): 17...♘f5 18 ♗xf5 ♕a5 19 ♗h7+ ♔h8

At this point I have gone through the most promising line for Black, but some of the alternatives may be interesting, and I could choose to go back and look at the candidate moves at move 14 and 15. After going through the various candidates, I have constructed a variation tree of the main lines from this position and I have a clearer picture of the possibilities after sacrificing the bishop on h6. The reason why computers are of such great help in this kind of position is their ability to go systematically through all the moves in a non-forcing position like the one at Black's move 15. Black does not seem to have enough resources to defend the position, and while humans may instinctively feel this, the program will help us establish this with a very high degree of

certainty. Ultimately, the result is some very trustworthy analysis, and if this was meant as opening analysis for a future tournament game, I would feel confident of sacrificing the bishop on h6. Note how effective it was to take the engine a little bit down the critical lines. This technique is of great importance, and it is worth taking note of when performing computer-aided analysis.

So 13...h6? was a mistake, and I set Gandalf to analyse the position at move 14. Being a strong tactical program, it took it only 9 seconds (!) to suggest 14 ♗xh6, which tells us that there can be great differences in the way programs evaluate the attacking possibilities after White's 15th move. As mentioned before, Fritz 8 was a bit more conservative and needed nearly 10 minutes before it decided on 14 ♗xh6.

Playing Out Positional Plans

If 13...h6? is not the move, then what should Black play? Fritz 8 suggests **13...♘c4** *(D)* threatening the queen and the b2-pawn.

Fritz suggests that White should go 14 ♕e2, indirectly covering the b2-pawn because the knight will be in trouble after 14...♘xb2 15 ♗b3 (15 ♗xh7+ is less promising). As a part of some opening studies, I had been looking at various grandmaster games

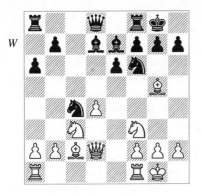

in this kind of position, and I believe that there is an interesting alternative to 14 ♕e2. The position can arise from the Caro-Kann, Panov Attack or the Queen's Gambit Accepted. The only slightly unusual thing about the position is the bishop on d7, which is usually developed via the moves ...b5 and ...♗b7, putting the bishop on the long diagonal and introducing the idea of ...♗xf3 in some lines. The bishop's location on d7 should favour White in comparison with the normal positions.

The standard idea is ♕f4-h4 with the simple threat of exchanging on f6 followed by mate on h7. An important point is that ...h6 is again often met by ♗xh6, while ...g6 may run into ♘e4 in some lines. Then Black has problems because of the undefended bishop on e7 when White's queen is on h4.

I let Fritz think for a while, but it did not hit upon this idea. It continued to propose 14 ♕e2, which does not lose material, but on the other hand does nothing to achieve an advantage either. So once again I will help the

engine by inputting the general idea and let the machine do the dirty work. I want to find out if the standard idea of ♕f4-h4 is viable in this position.

I enter 14 ♕f4 on the board, and obviously we have to look at 14...♘xb2, accepting the pawn sacrifice. Fritz suggests this move for some seconds, but then changes its mind to 14...♖c8, apparently because of the line 14...♘xb2 15 ♗xf6 ♗xf6 16 ♕e4 threatening h7 and b7.

15 ♗xf6 is of course not a part of my plan so I just enter the moves 14...♘xb2 15 ♕h4 and Fritz suggests 15...h6 as the best move with 15...h5 as the only, slightly inferior, alternative. 15...h5 simply looks too odd, so I decide to return later to refute it. I concentrate on the line 15...h6 16 ♗xh6 gxh6 17 ♕xh6 and now the story repeats itself. Fritz initially shows a 0.00 score because of the possibility of perpetual check, but soon the scores start climbing again and White's attacking possibilities seem promising. Now I go back to check 14...♖c8 and other candidate moves I looked at during the analysis to find out if there are other defensive tries that are more promising. In most of these positions there are several alternatives. Having gone through those lines, I find that the prospects for White are preferable, and Fritz's evaluations are getting still more positive the further down the road I go.

The interesting point is that Fritz had no idea of the plan ♕f4-h4 and could not hit upon the idea because of the computer's blindness in lines including sacrifices. It did not like to give up the b2-pawn and it did not, initially, like the prospects of the ♗xh6 sacrifice. However, with a little human help, inputting the main idea and thereby pushing the horizon further, it all became much clearer and the engine suddenly started to prefer White.

This example shows some of the main points when guiding a computer engine through the analysis. The human inputs positional ideas, pushes the program's horizon further, and tries out the sacrificial lines. When analysing with a program, you have the possibility of inputting the most speculative sacrifices to see if they work. After all, it is only analysis, and you can always try another line afterwards.

Automatic Computer Analysis

Two useful features in the Fritz interface are the Blunder Check and the Deep Position Analysis (Chess Assistant has similar functions as described in Chapter 5). When you have created a large tree of variations, you can leave the computer for some hours, automatically going through your work to see if it can find any improvements. All these analysis options are available from the 'Tools' menu in the Fritz 7 and Fritz 8 interfaces. Two of those, the Blunder Check and Deep Position

Analysis are quite similar. In this example I will focus on the latter, which is the most elaborate way of making automatic computer analysis.

Some computer users may have the impression that you get the best analysis from letting the computer study a position for a very long time – some hours, overnight or even for several days. In the Fritz interface this is known as 'Infinite Analysis'.

However, this does not solve the horizon problems computers have, and they may still not analyse sufficiently deeply to give the right evaluation of a position. When speaking about computer engines, it is a general rule that they need 3 times more time to go 1 ply deeper. Thus, if your program has used three hours to reach ply 14, it will display the next line when it reaches ply 15 after approximately nine hours. Analysing to ply 16 would take around 27 hours, and to ply 17 around 81 hours, etc. The programs gain relatively little going from ply 16 to 17, and thus it is hardly worth waiting the 54 hours it needs to do this. It is much more useful trying to play through some of these plies manually by finding possible candidate moves as in the example above.

However, the computer can do some of this work by itself, and this is what 'Deep Position Analysis' is for. One of the interesting things about this function is that the computer will look through all the moves and variations entered in the notation pane, even though it would normally not consider these lines itself. This means that in the example above the computer would analyse the lines with the ♕f4-h4 idea and the bishop sacrifice if I had entered them. Moreover, it will come up with additional solutions and other suggestions.

To understand how the Deep Position Analysis works I will set up a new position from a sharp line in the Sicilian:

1 e4 c5 2 ♘f3 d6 3 d4 cxd4 4 ♘xd4 ♘f6 5 ♘c3 a6 6 f3 e6 7 ♗e3 b5 8 g4 h6 9 ♕d2 ♗b7 10 0-0-0 ♘bd7 11 ♗d3 b4 12 ♘ce2 d5 13 exd5 ♘xd5 *(D)*

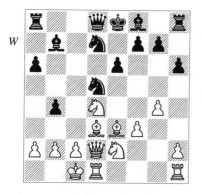

This is a line of the Najdorf Sicilian where White has tried 14 ♘f4 and the more aggressive sacrifice 14 ♘xe6!? to exploit the fact that the black king is still in the centre, while White is better developed and his king is safe.

I decide to make a Deep Position Analysis of this line, but first I take a look at the games in the database in this line. I find that accepting the sacrifice is obviously the main line, but 14...♕a5 threatening to take on a2 has also been played a few times, so I will have to consider this move as well. The first moves in the main line are forced:

14 ♘xe6!? fxe6 15 ♗g6+ ♔e7

I play out the moves on the board to expand the horizon of the program. The computer is already four plies down the main line. I only have seven games with this position in my database, and 16 ♘f4 was played in six of them – a move that looks logical to me. White wants to continue the attack by putting pressure on e6 and at the same time he starts clearing the e-file for a rook. I decide to play 16 ♘f4, but I will return to this position later if this move does not achieve anything.

16 ♘f4 *(D)*

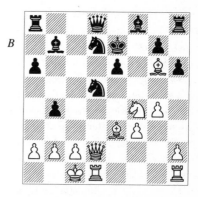

Now I believe I have reached a critical position.

Black has several ways of defending, and for this reason it seems right to initiate the Deep Position Analysis at this point. I go to the Tools menu in the Fritz interface, select 'Analysis' and then 'Deep Position Analysis'. After that I have some choices to make. As the position is complicated, I decide to let the computer analyse overnight. I give Fritz 8 300 seconds (= 5 minutes) to consider each move in the analysis. In the 'plus (root)' field I give it 3,600 seconds (= 1 hour) to consider the initial position, which I have decided is a critical position for the evaluation of the sacrifice. Next I can choose the branching factor at the first, second, third and fourth move. In this example I chose the values 3, 2, 2 and 2, which should give me a fairly large variation tree. If these values are changed, the output will be different, so it is worth experimenting with it on shorter time spans before making the actual analysis. Just below, 'Branching' lets me determine whether I want to get move alternatives for White, Black or both. I choose 'both' for this example, but sometimes it makes sense to opt for only one of the colours. In my game above against the Gandalf 5 beta the question was whether Black had any defence after 14 ♗xh6 gxh6 15 ♕xh6. In that case it would be relevant only to get alternatives for Black to see if the computer could find any defence for Black against White's best moves.

In the bottom of the dialogue box it is possible to choose the length of variations, which I set to 15 plies. The Evaluation Window is a value given in 100th pawn increments. I have picked the value '80', which means that if an alternative move is 0.8 pawn worse than the best move it will not be considered any further. I can also choose to have several engines analysing the position, but in this example I choose to stay with Fritz 8.

Next morning Fritz had not finished the Deep Position Analysis, but it had come up with the lines given below, with A11 given as the strongest line for both sides and a white advantage of 0.75. This evaluation shows that there is a clear difference between normal analysis and Deep Position analysis, which is much more elaborate. When analysing the diagram position initially, Fritz believes Black to have the advantage, but after a Deep Position Analysis it seems to prefer White.

The program suggests only two moves for Black at move 16, which means that it considers all other moves at least 0.8 pawns worse than the move considered best, 16...♕a5. Try to play through the variations and see if you can find any flaws. Fritz's main line is given in bold.

A) **16...♕a5**

A1) **17 ♕d4**

A11) **17...b3 18 axb3 ♕b6 19 ♗e4 ♕xd4 20 ♘g6+ ♔e8 21 ♗xd4 ♖g8 22 c4 ♖c8 23 ♔b1 ♗d6 24 cxd5 ± 0.75/14**

A12) 17...♕b6 18 ♕d2 (18 ♘xd5+ ♗xd5 19 ♕xb6 ♘xb6 20 ♗xb6 ♗xf3

21 ♗d4 ♗xh1 22 ♖xh1 ♖d8 23 ♖d1
♖d5 24 ♗e4 -0.47/15) 18...♕c6 19
♖he1 ♔d8 20 ♘xe6+ ♔c8 21 ♘f4
♘xe3 22 ♖xe3 ♗c5 23 ♖e8+ ♖xe8 24
♗xe8 ± 0.94/14

A2) 17 ♗f2

A21) 17...♔d8 18 ♘xe6+ (18 ♔b1
♘5f6 19 ♗f7 ♔c7 20 ♘xe6+ ♔c8 21
♕d3 ♕b5 22 ♖he1 ♕xd3 23 ♖xd3
♗c6 24 h4 = -0.03/13) 18...♔c8 19
♕d4 ♗c6 20 ♗e4 ♘7f6 21 ♕e5 b3 22
a3 ♗xa3 23 ♗e1 ♕a4 24 ♗xd5 =
0.00/11

A22) 17...♕xa2 18 ♕d4 (18 ♕e1
♕a1+ 19 ♔d2 ♘xf4 20 ♗h4+ ♘f6 21
♖xa1 ♘xg6 22 ♔c1 ♔f7 23 ♗xf6
gxf6 24 ♖f1 -+ -1.66/14) 18...♔d8
19 ♘xe6+ ♔c8 20 ♗e4 ♘5f6 21 ♘xf8
♖xf8 22 ♗xb7+ ♔xb7 23 ♕xb4+ ♔c8
24 ♗b6 ± 0.50/13

B) 16...♘e5 17 ♗f2 (17 ♕f2)
17...♔d7 18 ♗f5 (18 ♗e4) 18...exf5
19 ♘xd5

The computer was analysing the
lines with B, 16...♘e5, when I stopped
it, and it seemed to like White's position at that point, so I decided to come
back to that line later after looking at
variation A. When it gives 17 ♕f2 and
no further moves in line B, it means
that it suggests this as a possible alternative. However, I did not give it the
time to finish the analysis.

Why is this analysis better than
just letting the computer think overnight at move 16 for Black? The answer is that all of the moves in the
analysis above are checked and selected after an average of 5 minutes

for each move/position. The program
has analysed the position at the end of
the main line A11 for 5 minutes, and
that makes the assessment much more
credible than if the computer had just
analysed the position at Black's move
16 all the time. In the Deep Position
Analysis the computer is working on
expanding its own horizon, and thus
the quality of the analysis is generally
higher. However, there are still a lot of
things to check after the computer has
finished the Deep Position Analysis.
In fact the analysis has just begun. At
this point I normally print out the analysis and check the lines on a real chess
board. I do it this way because I want
to make sure that I am analysing the
position myself instead of watching
the computer lines on the screen. Afterwards I can obviously come back to
the computer and check the analysis.

The position is very messy and tactical and this is the reason why I chose
the program to sort this one out for me.
It usually does quite well in this kind
of position. However, when playing
through the analysis, a lot of questions
pop up. First of all, there are a lot of
lines and evaluations I have to understand. The program only displays the
moves which it finds to be the best, so
there may be a lot of hidden refuta-
tions of obvious but inferior moves
that I should work my way through. A
lot of the evaluations are not so clear
to me; e.g., the A21 line which is assessed with = or 0.00. Asking Fritz, it
gives me the line 24...♘xd5 25 ♖xd5

♗xb2+ 26 ♕xb2 ♗xd5 27 ♕xg7 b2+ 28 ♔xb2 ♖b8+ 29 ♔c1 ♕a3+ 30 ♔d2 ♕b4+ 31 ♔c1 ♕b1+ 32 ♔d2 ♕b4+ with perpetual check. Not that obvious!

Anyway, although lines like this seem convincing I should still keep a critical distance and go through this line as well as others. The 18 ♕e1 line of A22 is evaluated as giving a decisive advantage for Black, but the material distribution is uneven so in this case I will have to analyse a bit more to find out if the computer evaluation is valid.

The A11 line with 17...b3 is given as the main line, i.e. the best moves for both White and Black. Yet it is not apparent to me why Black should give up a pawn. I try to look at the alternative 17...♕b6, when the line 18 ♕d2 ♕c6 is given with a positive evaluation for White at the end of the line. But what about 18...♕a5 simply repeating the position? Even though this move appears obvious, it is not mentioned in the computer analysis!

You may ask how this could happen with the computer analysing every move thoroughly. I believe the answer is quite simple. When Fritz chose 18...♕c6 it was still under the impression that Black had a better position, and thus it was not trying to repeat the position. Later it turned out that the line was advantageous for White, but Deep Position Analysis does not include that the computer going back to look at positions it has already looked at. By contrast, a Blundercheck starts

from the end of each line, avoiding this problem.

After 18...♕a5 White is at his move 19 in the same situation as he was in move 17, and he has to decide if he wants to play 19 ♕d4 again given as the best by the program (but only repeating the position). If not, I should find an improvement on the 17 ♗f2 line or hit upon a third possibility at this juncture. Lots of work to do, even after the computer analysis!

When going through the analysis, it is also important to look for the kind of moves that computers overlook. After 16...♕a5 White has another speculative knight sacrifice with 17 ♘xe6!?. It is not mentioned in the computer analysis, but it is worth taking a look at. If the variations look promising I might consider doing a new Deep Position Analysis on the position after 17...♔xe6 18 ♖he1 and see if anything turns up. In fact, I have only been able to find a drawing line after this sacrifice, but nevertheless it is very important to keep an eye open for these possibilities, even though they may seem speculative at first.

The last kind of position I will mention here is the positional draw and the fortress. The final position of this example was mentioned in Chapter 3 as well (*see following diagram*).

White can make a fortress by sacrificing a rook for a knight and the b-pawn. The line from the diagram goes: **41 ♖c6 b5 42 ♖ee6 b4 43 ♖b6 ♔f7 44 ♖xf6+ ♕xf6 45 ♖xb4**

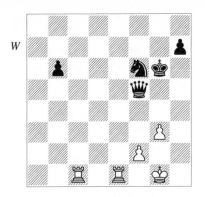

V. Kramnik – Deep Fritz (analysis)
Match (6), Bahrain 2002

Black has no way to make progress. Even the best of today's programs believe Black to be winning. Thus it is important to underline that only humans can find these possibilities and that we have to be alert, even though the programs tell us that Black is completely winning.

Summing up, the main points when analysing with a computer are:
- Be aware of all the general weaknesses of computer programs when you analyse.
- Analyse with a program you know well, so that you have a feeling about in which positions the program may have shortcomings.
- If you are analysing a position deeply, set up the position on a real board first, make your own analysis, and develop your own ideas about the position before going through the variations with a program.

- Play out forced moves and various candidate moves to expand the horizon of the program.
- Play out positional plans with the program to check if they are viable.
- Look out for, and try, speculative sacrifices when attacking.
- Be critical about the computer's positional evaluations, especially when material is unevenly distributed, or when very different positional factors have to be weighed against each other (e.g., attacking chances vs a passed pawn).
- When performing automatic computer analysis, choose Deep Position Analysis (or similar features in other programs) to push the horizon of the program.
- In endgames, be especially aware of positional draws and fortress positions. The programs will not find these possibilities.

Analysing Your Games with the Computer

After playing a game, I am always quite eager to see what Fritz or some other engine thinks about the moves played in the game, to discover if there were some hidden tactical shots which the players missed. Fritz – and most other playing programs as well – has the built-in function 'Full analysis', with which the program can automatically annotate a whole game, or even several games in a row. Fritz gives small verbal comments like "♖e8 was a viable option", and also some variations, evaluations and suggestions for improvements. While this can initially seem entertaining, it is of no use for serious chess-players. It is a far better idea to direct the analysis manually to make the computer think deeper at the critical point(s), while other less interesting phases of the game can be skipped altogether.

When entering the moves of the game it is important not only to check the positions that arose in the game, but also the variations that you were calculating at the board. A simple manual analysis may reveal a lot of missed opportunities and will make it easier for you to understand what was going on in the game and find the turning points.

According to Grandmaster Artur Yusupov there are four points to pay attention to when analysing your own games. You should:

1) Find the critical turning points in the game. These are the moments when mistakes were made, when opportunities were not exploited, or when the assessment of the position changed.

2) Find the reasons for your mistakes and try to find some patterns that you can work on correcting.

3) Look for new ideas, positionally and tactically – moves that you did not pay attention to during the game.

4) Pay special attention to the opening phase of the game and find possible improvements of your play.

How can the computer help you in this work?

I suggest your analysis should have three phases. In the first phase you enter the game into the computer, while you have an analytical engine running in the background to see if there were any blunders or obvious moves that you missed during play. At this point you should also check the variations that you were calculating at the board. Whenever the program finds something interesting, enter the analysis as a variation in the game. In ChessBase or Fritz a computer line is entered simply by pressing Ctrl-Space, while a single move is copied by pressing Space. After doing this, print the game and analysis and set up the chessboard to start your own analysis of the game. This is what I would call the second part of the analysis. It is important that the first computer-assisted part of the analysis is fairly brief, so that you do not get the impression that the computer has seen everything that was important about that game. Anyway, it never will – not at this point of the computer evolution at least.

The reason why I suggest that the second phase of the analysis should be with a real board and real pieces is that it is much easier to find new ideas, especially positional ideas, when you do not get distracted by computer lines. I have already mentioned the danger of your thoughts becoming too 'machine-like', when analysing with the program. You tend to look at moves instead of plans, and numbers instead of real positional evaluation.

The second phase of the analysis should be the most sustained part. You can start working on '1' and '3', and maybe you already know some things from the brief computer analysis. While analysing at the board, take note of interesting positional plans and tactical possibilities. Try to analyse everything yourself and then go to the third phase, which is the computer checking of the lines you have found, playing out positional plans and testing tactical lines. In the third phase you can also perform some detailed computer-assisted analysis on some of the critical positions, or you may choose to make a Deep Position Analysis. Eventually, your picture of what happened in the game should be much clearer and you will now be ready to make some annotations for your own benefit. These annotations should contain notes of '1' and '3', which you have worked out at this point. No computer program can help you to work

out '2'. Your reason for making mistakes can be manifold. You may have to improve your tactics, pay more attention to your opponent's plans, or there may be psychological explanations for hitting upon the wrong idea in a certain game. Anyway, this subject is somewhat beyond the scope of this book, so I will not go more deeply into it – it is covered in many other books. The important thing to note is that your annotations should address these subjects. You should make some short initial comments about what kind of mistakes you made in the game, why you made them, what you have learned from the game, and what you should do to eradicate these kinds of mistakes. Optimally, you should go through all of your games like this, but if you do not have so much time, then start with your losses and the draws.

I have now described how to use the computer for going through 1-3. Number 4, how to improve your openings, is the subject of the following chapter.

7 Improve Your Opening Play

When a player decides to change his openings, it's a sign that he's growing up!
VIKTOR KORCHNOI, grandmaster and former world championship challenger

The possibility of preparing for an opponent with a game database is one of the most useful features of a chess program. As mentioned before, handling the huge amount of data is of crucial importance, and in both ChessBase and Chess Assistant there are excellent opportunities for doing this.

Let us take an example of how to prepare an opening for a coming game. I am playing White and I have decided that I want to play 1 d4. Database searches in most database programs are quite similar, and I have used Chess-Base in the following example. If you have the program, I recommend that you go through the following steps while reading.

I search for a player's games by double-clicking my main database, and press Ctrl-F to get the search mask. If I suspect that there may be several different spellings of his name, I may try to find his games by clicking the 'Players' tab. This manual search is alphabetical, so I will only catch spellings that are quite similar in alphabetical

order, i.e. 'Jusupow' and 'Jussupow', but not 'Yusupow' or 'Yusupov'. I find that my future opponent 'Mr XY' mostly plays the Benko Gambit as Black, but sometimes picks the King's Indian Defence as well.

Let's suppose that I have one week to get ready for a game, and that I want to prepare well. First of all, I play through a lot of his games, especially the latest ones, to find out about his style and his potential weaknesses. Then I merge the games into a tree by pressing Ctrl-A (select all) and Shift-Enter. ChessBase will now show his games as a tree, and I will be able to see statistics of which lines he plays more often, and in which lines he scores well. While this information is quite useful, especially if he has a lot of games in the database, I should not become obsessed with the figures. It may be coincidental which games actually enter the main databases and thus one should be reluctant to draw any clear conclusions, in particular if there are only a few games, or if the games in the database are old. I should not choose my line against the Benko from seeing in which lines he scores badly, but rather choose which lines I would prefer to play myself. It is also important to make a statistical query only for his latest games, e.g. the last two years, to find out if he has altered his opening repertoire over time. If you discover, by merging all of his games in the database, that your opponent mostly plays 1 e4 as White, you may find out that he only played 1 d4 the last two years by merging his latest games. This merging process is done by selecting the relevant games with Shift and the arrow keys and merging the games with Shift-Enter.

When playing an opening like the Benko Gambit, with Black or with White, it is obviously of great importance to be familiar with the general positional ideas from both sides. Generally, I recommend to use computer and databases as a supplement to book studies, as you will find general ideas explained much better in most opening books than in the annotated games in any of the databases currently available. When deciding on which line to play against the Benko, I read some chapters of Steffen Pedersen's book about the opening, and this saved me some time. I quickly got an idea about what kind of positions the various lines lead to, and it would have taken me much more time to discover this through a database. It can of course be done, but when an author has already done a lot of work for you, there is no reason to reinvent everything.

First of all, I have to assign my main database as the 'Reference database'. This means that this is the database in which searches are conducted

by default. In the database window, select your largest database, right-click and select 'Properties' to get a dialogue box. In that dialogue you see a check box where you can select the current database as your reference database. Note that you can assign a smaller database as your reference database. If you are working with a specific opening and want to get search results only from that opening then it makes sense to construct a smaller database and search in this database only.

Constructing Your Own Databases

One problem with the commercially available databases is that they mainly include games taken from international events. Thus if you are a club player preparing a game against another club player who never took part in these tournaments, you will not find any of his games in the database. In that case you will have to take a look at the various club sites in your country to see if they have published any games from lower-rated tournaments that are not published in the big databases. In Denmark, where I live, I know that many clubs have sites with games from local clubs' tournaments, and I believe that this applies to other countries as well. It will take no more than one afternoon to download and construct a database with a few thousand games, and by doing this, you get much more information about your future opponents and better possibilities for preparing against them. In ChessBase it is very easy to merge several databases into one. You just open a database and drag and drop it into another database and so on. I recommend making a separate local club database to avoid confusion. In most database programs it is possible to search through several databases at once.

The next thing to remember is to be critical about the statistical information you can get from the database. Both ChessBase and Chess Assistant have functions to show you in what lines your future opponent scores well and in what lines he scores badly. It is very easy to be tempted to play a line in which your opponent has not done well. However, it is also quite dangerous. If you know nothing about the line, you will be in dire straits if your opponent deviates at a point where you did not expect it. In this way you can easily out-prepare yourself! Moreover, you should remember that the games in the database do not give the whole picture. Your opponent may have a lousy score in the French, when you look at the few games in the database, but in reality he could have played a lot of good games in this opening that were never published. This point is especially valid for non-titled players, for whom it is rather coincidental which games are included in the main databases.

When preparing for a tournament or an opponent, it is also worth noting which of your own games have entered the main databases. This is the information that your opponents will look through before a game. By looking at the games your opponent has at his disposal, you may have better chances of guessing what opening he might pick.

Studying Opening and Middlegame Ideas

Going back to the Benko example, I begin by making a search after the moves 1 d4 ♘f6 2 c4 c5 3 d5 b5. I search in my main database, the reference database, by pressing Shift-F7, and this returns 15,459 games. This is not even all the games with a Benko-like structure, as Black can play the ...b5 sacrifice at a later point from some of the variations in the King's Indian.

Clearly I am not going to play through all 15,459 games, so I should try to limit the number of games somehow. As I have the Mega Database, I try to search only for games with annotations. Again this is done by pressing Ctrl-F in the list of games, and choosing games with variations. Now I have 336 games, and I can cut down this number even more by selecting only games in which one of the players was rated above 2600. Now I have just 111 games, a more manageable number. If my goal is to get a better feel for the Benko positions, I should play through these games and take note of the various positional ideas in the games. I can also try to search for those of the 15,459 games that feature the highest rated players, and merge them into a tree to get a general idea of the structure in the various lines.

However, I have already decided that I want to play a particular line of the Benko which has its own characteristics, so I skip this phase and go on to the next step. The line I have chosen is **1 d4 ♘f6 2 c4 c5 3 d5 b5 4 cxb5 a6 5 b6!?** *(D)*, in which White gives back the pawn to stop some of Black's usual counterplay on the queenside.

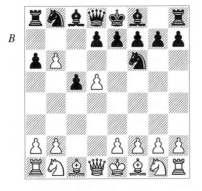

I make a search for this position and find 2,372 games. Once again, I can merge the games to be able to recognize the general structure of the variation. Afterwards, I search for annotated games and find that my database contains 55 of those. Playing through the annotated games is important in order

to understand some of the ideas in the position.

I find that in this line Black often plays ...♕xb6 and ...d6, and then fianchettoes his bishop with ...g6, ...♗g7 and then ...0-0. White tends to play ♘c3, e4 and often a4-a5 at some point, and he also frequently transfers the knight to the excellent c4-square with ♘f3-d2-c4. The c4-square is the key to controlling the queenside for White. Black may choose to counter White's plans with ...a5, but in that case he concedes the b5-square to White. The position arising is one where strategic manoeuvring is of importance and for this reason understanding the ideas is essential.

ChessBase has an interesting function that will quickly show the typical location of the pieces in a given opening. Try to select all 2,372 games from the search we have just made, right-click and select 'Piece probability'. I select the white knight for example, and the diagram shows that the knight is often located on the squares g1, f3, d2 and c4, indicating the knight manoeuvre that we discussed before. Although mainly a curiosity, this function may still be of help when trying to get a quick overview. You should, however, be able to reach the same conclusions pretty fast by playing through some of the most important games in this variation.

In the search after 5 b6!?, I also find around 500 games in which the sharper 5...e6 variation was played, when a completely different structure arises. The main line is 6 ♘c3 ♘xd5 7 ♘xd5 exd5 8 ♕xd5 ♘c6. Here rapid development is much more important than strategic manoeuvring, since the position has been opened up.

I believe that an opening book may help me to reach these conclusions faster, but playing through annotated master games will eventually lead me to the same conclusions. Of course, you should not only go through the annotated games, but also other high-rated games. If I have a lot of game material like in this case, I usually start out by looking at games in which one or both players were rated above 2600. However, there may of course be lots of interesting ideas introduced in games between lower-rated players, so when I study specific lines I will consider these games as well, still starting with the games featuring the highest-rated players.

The 'Opening Report'

ChessBase has a useful function which helps you to find game material and statistics quickly. First of all, you should assign your biggest, annotated game database as the reference database. After that, go to the 'Tools' menu in ChessBase and select Opening report in the position you want more information about. I choose to make an opening report on the position after 5 b6!?. This gives me a lot of information about this line. Most of the opening

report is self-explanatory, so I will just mention the main points here.

The first section of the report contains 'historical information' with links to the first games in the variation, the latest grandmaster game, and the latest game in the variation. Next there are some bar graphs telling me about the development of the variation statistically. According to the statistics the 5 b6!? line became very popular around 1990. Looking at the 'Fashion Index', it tops in 1991 with a score around 175%. The 'fashion index' gives the percentage of games relative to the entire database. In the middle of the 1990s the scores drop to around 100% again, but then the line seems to have regained popularity in the years 1999-2002. Most club players probably do not care if a line is 'fashionable' or not, but I believe that it should help players rated 2100 and above to know that a line is still considered playable by stronger players, which means that the line may give chances of achieving an advantage. Moreover, if the line is still 'fashionable' it means that I should look out for new games in this variation when importing the latest games into my main database. How to do this in the easiest way will be explained later, when discussing the repertoire database.

When looking at these figures it is important to know that there are far fewer games before 1985 and thus looking at statistics before this year is generally less useful.

In the next section there are links to games played by strong grandmasters in the line:

Alexei Dreev. Result=10/12 1990-2001 Elo-Ø: 2644. Games: 12

Anatoly Karpov. Result=3.5/5 1993-1999 Elo-Ø: 2733. Games: 5

Most of this is easy to understand. Dreev played the line in the period 1990-2001 with good results, and his average Elo in the games was 2644 (this is Elo-Ø).

Under this I find games of 'Other notable players':

Alexei Shirov Result=11/12 1989-2001 Elo-Ø: 2552. Games: 12

Giorgi Giorgadze Result=9.5/11 1989-1999 Elo-Ø: 2581. Games: 11

Some may ask why Alexei Shirov is only labelled a 'notable player' and not a 'strong grandmaster'. The reason is that, according to the database, Shirov mainly played this line in the period 1989-1991, when he was younger and had a lower rating. His average Elo in this period was 2552.

The opening report has helped me to single out some important games to play through. The next step is to look at the statistics, which tell me that White scores averagely and the percentage of quick draws (< 20 Moves) is low. Nothing unusual here. Normally you should only use this information to check if White has a very good or very bad score. In the case of an unusual percentage it is of course important to investigate the reasons behind this.

The fourth section is 'Moves and Plans', which gives me six different black answers to 5 b6!? with statistics on each move and games played by strong grandmasters. After this, a main line is given. In the case of 5...d6 6 ♘c3 the main line is 6...♕xb6 7 e4 g6 8 ♘f3 ♗g7 9 ♘d2, with a score of 64% in 181 games. The opening report also gives a critical line in each variation. In this case 6...♘bd7 7 ♘f3 ♘xb6 8 e4 g6 9 ♗e2 is considered critical with a 54% score to White.

Once more, we have to be aware of the nature of statistics. The score of 54% is calculated from only 12 games, and clicking the game link shows me that some of the games featured low-rated or unrated players. Of course, I should look at the best of these games, but the fact that this line is considered to be critical in the opening report does not necessarily make it so. The conclusion is based on slender statistical material.

The next part of the opening report is quite useful. It reveals the plans for White and for Black, with the number of games given in parenthesis. After 5...d6 6 ♘c3 the following plans are given for White with links to corresponding games:

e2-e4/♘g1-f3/♘f3-d2/a2-a4 (44)
a2-a4/a4-a5/♖a1-a4/e2-e4 (48)
e2-e4/♗f1-e2/0-0 (191)
a2-a4/a4-a5/f2-f4 (67)
♘g1-f3/♘f3-d2/♘d2-c4 (160)
a2-a4/a4-a5/e2-e4/♗f1-c4/♘g1-e2/0-0 (11)

And for Black:

♘b8-d7/g7-g6/♕d8xb6/♕b6-b7/♗f8-g7/0-0/♘f6-e8 (29)

♘b8-d7/g7-g6/♘d7xb6/♘b6-d7/♗f8-g7 (21)

g7-g6/♕d8xb6/♕b6-b4/♕b4-b7 (26)

♘b8-d7/a6-a5/g7-g6 (99)

♕d8xb6/♘b8-d7/♕b6-c7 (89)

♘b8-d7/♘f6-e8/♘e8-c7/♘d7-f6 (22)

These plans would of course become obvious if one played through a lot of games, but the opening report gives a quick overview. It only shows the first moves in the plan, so I would need another opening report at a later point to reveal where the knight goes after, for instance, ...♘e8-c7.

Some of the plans displayed above may seem somewhat strange, if you do not see the opponent's moves – for example the queen manoeuvre ...♕b6-b4-b7. The queen goes to b4 to lure the white rook to a4, but of course it has to retreat when the rook goes to a4.

After having looked at the six options, with statistics, critical lines and plans, we reach the last section, which is the opening key for this variation. The opening key is an index to games based on opening variations. This section will only be available if the reference database has an opening key attached to it. By clicking the key, you get an overview of the structure in the line, and if you keep on clicking through the various lines, you will encounter games at some point.

The opening report feature has also created a game tree in a separate window. In this you can follow all variations from the 2,372 games merged into one with various statistics available.

The Repertoire Database

Depending on your playing strength, you may want to keep yourself updated with what is happening in an opening line you play. Fortunately, ChessBase can do some of this work in an effective way and single out the games that may interest you by scanning through new material. First of all, you have to construct a 'Repertoire database', which includes all opening lines that are relevant for you. You go to the database window, press Ctrl-X to create a new database, name it 'Repertoire' and select 'CBH' as format. After that you right-click the icon of the database, select 'Properties' and a new dialogue box appears. In this you select the box next to repertoire database. Now you can start entering the opening lines that you play in this database with one game for each line.

I will enter two lines in the Benko. First I open the Repertoire database and then I press Ctrl-N to get a new board window. The first one to enter is the 5 b6!? main line: 1 d4 ♘f6 2 c4 c5 3 d5 b5 4 cxb5 a6 5 b6. I right-click the last move and go to 'Special annotation' and then 'Critical position – opening'. By doing this I tell the program that I am interested in getting new games where this position was reached when I scan through other databases. I save the game by pressing Ctrl-S, and I type "5 b6!? in the Benko" for the name of the white player, and 'as White' for the black player. This is the information that appears in the game list when I open my repertoire database.

The next line to enter is a move-order with ♘f3 that I will discuss below. I open a new board window and move 1 d4 ♘f6 2 c4 c5 3 d5 b5 4 ♘f3 and mark this position a Critical opening position and repeat the steps described above. In this way I can enter my whole repertoire, not only the Benko lines, in the database and make it easier to search through and extract information from new databases I download.

Let us suppose that I have downloaded the four latest databases from The Week In Chess and want to check if there are any games that are relevant to my repertoire. I select the databases by pressing Ctrl and clicking each database. Then, when all four databases are selected, I press Ctrl-F for searching, and in the search mask I click 'In repertoire'. In the search mask you can of course combine this search with other parameters, such as Elo rating of the players, for example.

Another way to search for relevant games is to make a 'Repertoire scan'. This is done by selecting a database, going to the 'File' menu, choosing 'New' and 'Repertoire scan'. In this case you will get the result as a database text with separate sections for each of the repertoire lines. This is especially useful if you have entered your whole repertoire in the repertoire database. The games are given as links and can be replayed by clicking at them, and they are sorted by player Elo and degree of annotation. One thing to note when working with the repertoire database is that if I do not assign a position as a 'Critical position' in the opening, the program will use the first branching point when searching for new games. If I have entered the two move-orders 1 d4 ♘f6 2 c4 c5 3 d5 b5 4 ♘f3 (4 cxb5) in one game, then the first position of my repertoire is the one after 3...b5. That means that I am not going to get games from a regular Benoni (i.e. 1 d4 ♘f6 2 c4 c5 3 d5 e6) for instance.

If you want to do a lot of work on improving your openings, one idea is to enter your whole opening repertoire into digital format, like a sort of 'living book', which can be updated all the time. Even if this work is very time-consuming, it certainly has a lot of advantages. First of all, reviewing is much faster in the digital format, and it is much handier having some files on a laptop than carrying around a suitcase of books when you go to a tournament.

You can start by working through one of your pet variations to see if this idea suits you. Start by going to your repertoire database, open a new game, and then enter the main lines of a variation, looking them up in an opening book or an encyclopaedia. You can add some annotations and evaluations and translate the relevant parts of a book into digital format. When you have the main structure of the line, you enter lines from other printed sources like *Informator*, *New In Chess*, etc. After this, you can start making database searches to make updates with the latest developments in the line. Press Shift-F7 to make searches in your repertoire database or use the Opening report at points where you want to go more into detail. When you play through a game, you can easily add it to your repertoire database by right-clicking the board and selecting 'Add to repertoire' (or the short-cut Ctrl-Shift-Alt-A). ChessBase will often suggest that you merge the game with another in your repertoire database, but remember to check if the game is merged at the right point. You cannot always be sure of this because of transpositional possibilities.

Eventually, you should have all important games in one line merged into one with annotations. You can now print the whole line in table-style ('ECO-style') by going to the 'File' menu and choosing 'Print' and 'Repertoire' and play through the lines on a real chessboard and try to come up with some new ideas. These can be analysed with a computer program and the viable ones could enter your

'book'. You can also get a computer engine to analyse through all lines by using the Blunder Check function described in Chapter 6. When entering moves in the 4 ♘f3 and 5 b6 lines, I had Fritz 8 running in the background, and it came up with a lot of suggestions in many variations. Some of them seem to be improvements, especially over the old lines given in *ECO* (Encyclopaedia of Chess Openings), or in positions that have not been reached many times at master level.

The advantages of this idea are obvious. You have your own, updated theory, which you can improve all the time, and you can make use of other advantages of having the material in digital format. For example, you can make an automatic Blunder Check of all the lines, and you can easily translate the whole of your 'living book' into a tree to play some training games with Fritz or another engine. In the Fritz interface, you create a new openings book by going to the 'File' menu and select 'New' and 'Openings book'. Give the book a name and then go to the Edit 'menu', select 'Openings book' and 'Add Priority Analysis', and then select the file from which you want to import your analysis. If you load this book, Fritz will play the lines that you have analysed from its new opening book, and thus you have the possibility of testing how well you know the opening or playing a few training games with the computer using the book. Another possibility of drilling you in your repertoire is to click the 'Training' tab above the notation pane in ChessBase. This feature hides the moves, and then you can try to remember which move to play.

The 'Training' feature can also be used for 'move guessing' later in the game. In this way you can test your own intuition and make sure that you are actively following the games you are playing through.

Transpositions

One important thing to look for when studying an opening are the transpositional possibilities. In Chess Assistant it is easy to find transpositions, as you can build a complete tree for a 2 million+ game database without problems. In ChessBase different methods have to be used. One idea is to take one of the main positions and check how many different move-orders lead to the following position, which can occur after 1 d4 ♘f6 2 c4 c5 3 d5 b5 4 cxb5 a6 5 b6 ♕xb6 6 ♘c3 g6 7 ♘f3 d6 8 ♘d2 ♗g7 9 e4 0-0 10 ♗e2 ♘bd7 11 ♘c4 ♕c7 (D).

A search in this position gives me 158 games in the database. I merge all of those games into a tree, go to the initial position and start playing through the first moves. As early as move 4 I see the first interesting transposition with 4 ♘f3. With this move I am able to dodge the critical lines with 5...e6 which seems to be the strongest line

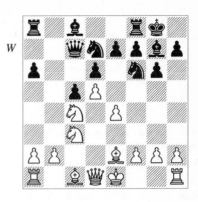

for Black against 5 b6!?. If 4...g6 5 cxb5 a6 6 b6, then ...e6 is no longer an option, because it does not fit in with ...g6.

However, I have to find out whether this gives Black other options, so I go to the position after 4 ♘f3 and make a new search. I find 2,243 games and by merging the games I see that 4...g6, transposing into the positional line given above, is by far the most popular move. However, the search shows that White will also have to examine moves such as 4...♗b7, 4...bxc4, 4...b4 and 4...e6!?. The last move in fact transposes to the Blumenfeld Gambit (1 d4 ♘f6 2 c4 e6 3 ♘f3 c5 4 d5 b5). Once again, a good opening book can help point out the most important transpositions and will save some time. When searching for transpositions in a database, the best solution is often to check every move or position against the database to find out if new transpositional possibilities come up. In ChessBase, however, this can be a slow process if you have less than 256 Mb RAM in your computer. With more memory than that, most of your reference database will be cached automatically and that increases the search speed by a factor of ten.

Some transpositions may also be tracked down by making pawn-structure searches. As mentioned before, there are a lot of Benko-inspired ...b5 sacrifices in the King's Indian that may or may not transpose into the usual Benko lines. These can be found by making a pawn-structure search.

Open the database you want to search in and press Ctrl-F. Click the 'Position' tab and set up the position in this diagram:

You can now click the game data tab and add other factors to search for; e.g., a certain rating span or selecting the ECO codes from E60-E99 to get positions from the King's Indian only. This will give you some more games with Benko Gambit themes, but of course you will also get some games in which ...b5 was not a sacrifice. The

position search is useful when there are a lot of possible transpositions. For instance, an opening like the Stonewall is characterized with the pawn-structure c3-d4-e3-f4 more than exact moves, as the Stonewall can be played as Black or White and against a variety of set-ups. In this case a pawn-structure search is a valuable tool. If you want search results for both White and Black with the Stonewall set-up, then remember to check the 'Horizontal' box. Position searches like this are of course possible in Chess Assistant as well.

Checking Variations and Creating Novelties

When playing a sharp line, I may want to check if the annotations in a certain game are viable. I have done this fairly often with Fritz, and the results are often surprising. A computer program can, without any help, find lots of mistakes in analysis, even GM analysis.

When going through annotations, you can use the Deep Position Analysis in Fritz (described in Chapter 6). This function will analyse all variations entered in the notation pane. Check if there are some variations that the computer does not need to waste time on. If there are, then delete them, or put a question mark in front of the first move in the line and the program will skip the line altogether.

The computer can also help you to come up with new ideas and suggestions when using the Blunder Check function. Through a database search you can find some of the main lines that you would like to play in a certain variation. Let's say that you have 5-10 games, some of them possibly with lines that you have entered yourself or with annotations from GMs. In Fritz, you select the games you want to analyse from the games list. After that you go to the 'Tools' menu, choose 'Analysis' and 'Blunder Check', and then the Blunder Check dialogue appears. Here you can choose either 'Time' or 'Depth'. I choose to analyse 5 games and use 60 seconds on average per move. Note that when you set the time to '60 seconds', the computer will often take a fair amount longer than that, because it is programmed to finish the ply that it started analysing. Thus you have to experiment a bit with this value.

'Threshold' is a number given in hundredths of a pawn, and it works like the 'Evaluation window' function mentioned when discussing the Deep Analysis function. If you want to use Fritz only for checking blunders, you should set this value at around 80. In that case, the program will alert you when a move makes the evaluation drop 0.80 or more. With this setting Fritz will only show you alternatives if it finds moves that are more than a '0.8 pawn' better than the move played in the game or given in the analysis.

I believe that in some positions it makes sense not only to look for blunders, but also for smaller improvements. If you set the value to '30', Fritz will display improvements that are 0.30 pawns better than the ones in the game/analysis, and in this way the program will help you by looking for minor opening improvements/novelties. The whole process may be accelerated by entering all relevant analysis in one game, cutting off the lines at move 20 or so, and performing a Deep Position Analysis, setting the 'Evaluation Window' to '30'. In that case no time is wasted on analysing endgames that are of no value when discussing novelties and opening improvements.

I know that some players may protest against letting the computer come up with new ideas, arguing that you should look for novelties yourself. I agree that this would be ideal, but I believe that the time factor and the huge amount of modern opening theory often makes it tempting to let the computer do some of the work for you. As the Bareev quotation at the beginning of Chapter 5 shows, this is even the case for very strong players. The last few years have seen great improvements in computer chess, and the programs are strong enough to find good improvements in many lines. One of the reasons for this is that the latest generation of programs (Fritz 8, Junior 7 and Shredder 7, etc.) are much better at evaluating compensation, for instance giving up a pawn in return for positional gains and thus 'understanding' more of the opening theory developed by humans. With the hardware speed increases expected in the next 10-15 years, there is no doubt that computer generation of opening novelties will be an even more important factor in the future.

In the sharp lines of the Sicilian Defence a computer program is an important partner when checking and discovering ideas. On the other hand, I do not think that the programs are quite so helpful in the positional lines of the Benko discussed above. Hence the usefulness of a computer program is very position-specific. The most important thing to remember is that the work has not finished when the computer suggests an improvement. This is when it all starts. Any automatic computer analysis should be followed by a manual check to expand on the idea. Moreover, even if the computer suggestions seem sound, it is still important to consider whether the suggested line suits you well. Some computer programs like to snatch a pawn and then set up a long, tough defence, but not all humans like to play positions like that.

Since the middle of the 1990s there have been many examples of GMs using suggestions from computer programs. Of course, the novelties are not all found by automatic computer analysis, but rather a manual computer-assisted analysis, which makes it easier for you to let the program focus on the critical points. However, an initial automatic analysis, possibly overnight, may help you to find critical points to explore further.

Learning a New Opening

When you have analysed an opening, played through grandmaster games and made some analysis, you should be able to single out 20-40 of the most important games in a given variation. These are the games by strong players that show you the current state of theory in this line. A good way to get an overview of the games is to merge them into one and print them in table-style (in style of *ECO* or *NCO*).

Having played over several grandmaster games, looked at positional ideas and learned a few of the main lines, you should have a better feeling about this variation. But you still need practice. The next step is to play some training games against a computer program, to get an idea of the middlegame ideas arising in this opening. Of course you can force the program to play this opening by making the moves for it, but if you want to play several games against it in the same opening, it is much easier for you if it plays the moves automatically.

This can be done by creating a small opening book for the program. Going back to the example from the Benko Gambit, I make a position search by entering the moves 1 d4 ♘f6 2 c4 c5 3 d5 b5 4 cxb5 a6 5 b6!?. Once again, I get 2,372 games. Then I search for games in which both players were rated 2450+, to limit the number of games, and I get 150 games.

In ChessBase I go to the database window and press Ctrl-X, a shortcut for creating a new database. I select the folder in which I want to store the book and change 'Save as Type' to 'Books (*.ctg)' in the pulldown window. Then I change the file name to 'Benko.ctg' and save it. Now I see a little icon with a tree in the database window, and if I want to, I can input lines manually by opening it, right-clicking and then select 'Allow editing' from the pop-up menu. However, I have already found the games that I want to include in my opening book and I can move the games from one place to another by using copy/paste: I go to the games list, press Ctrl-A (select all), Ctrl-C (copy) and then I go to the database window in ChessBase and select Benko.ctg and press Ctrl-V (paste). Then I have a Benko tree with 150 top games for a little opening book in Fritz.

I should add that an opening book can also by constructed within Fritz by using some of the same procedures. In most of the other playing programs it is possible to do this as well.

The next step is to open Fritz and load the book. This is done by going to the 'File' menu, selecting 'New' and 'Openings book'. Then I load the Benko book and start playing against Fritz. After just a few games, I have a

better feeling for the middlegames arising. The question as to whether you should 'handicap' the program depends mainly on your playing strength, but I believe players of 2100 strength and above should play against the program at full strength or pick a weaker engine, as suggested earlier. It has some value to see the program play the strongest moves it can find, and if you have problems winning (or drawing) you may choose to play the black side of the opening in some games to make the program give you some ideas for how to play the white side. Alternating the colours makes you more aware of your opponent's ideas, so make sure that you do this in some of the games. Generally, you should have a much better chance against the program than usual when you know the ideas of the opening and middlegame, and you will also find that your training games may help you to find out which kind of endgames arise from a specific opening.

When you have created a new opening book, you can make changes to it, if you want to. Open the book, click the 'Openings book' tab above the notation pane, and then right-click in the opening book and select 'Allow move adding'. This is helpful if, e.g., you want to add some transpositions. In the Benko example I had imported no games with the move-order 4 ♘f3, and that meant that the program was out of book at move four. With 'allow move adding' I can quickly add the transpositions I need just by entering the moves on the board. I can also add new games from other databases any time. If I have some games I want to add to a database, this is done by going to the 'Edit' menu, selecting 'Openings book' and 'Import games'. In that way I can add a whole database of games into my opening book. By clicking the 'Openings book' tab above the notation pane I can see which moves are in the book, and I can change the weights if I want Fritz to prefer one line over another. This is done by right-clicking on a specific move and changing the value of that move to 'Main move' or choosing 'Change weight' and assigning a weight between –125 and 125,

with positive values for the moves you want the program to play more often.

Note that you can also experiment with more book options by pressing F4, changing, among other things, the variety of play and the book learning abilities. For training games, I believe it makes most sense to put a high variety of play and turn down the influence of the learning value and learning strength. It is not important for your training that Fritz learns about in which openings it scores best. This function is only significant when the program is playing against other programs or in serious games against humans.

8 Improve Your Tactics

Botvinnik is working hard at trying to make a computer play chess as well as a human being, so let me teach human beings to analyse with the accuracy of a machine.
ALEXANDER KOTOV, Soviet Grandmaster (1913-81)

The quotation above is from Alexander Kotov's famous book *Think Like a Grandmaster*, in which he described how to calculate variations. Kotov's main point is well-known. When calculating variations one should initially list all candidate moves in the position before examining each line once and once only. This 'machine-like' way of thinking has proved to be a useful way of analysing, yet we cannot learn how to calculate from watching computers. Their 'thought-processes' are simply too different from ours. The main difference is that computers calculate nearly all moves in a position, while a human being only seldom looks at more than 4-5 different initial moves, which are the ones that seem most promising.

However, there are a lot of other possibilities. Several tactics courses available on CD for use within the main database programs and tactical test positions can also be downloaded for free from the Internet. These tests are useful to get acquainted with the various combinative themes, and they can serve as a fun way to train in basic tactics for the average club player. However, often these exercises are solved on the screen, and thus they are not well-suited for learning in-depth calculation. Far too often you find yourself 'testing if that bishop sacrifice on h7 works' without calculating more than a few moves ahead. This happens quite often when solving the exercises on the screen – your calculations simply get too superficial. For serious calculation training it is more useful to find some complicated positions and analyse them for 15 minutes or more on a real board, sorting out the various candidate moves and analysing each in turn such as Kotov described.

One way of training in tactics with the computer is to play out complicated positions against a program. You may find the positions in magazines and databases, and it does not matter if you know which moves were played in the game, because the program will usually deviate at some point, in which case you will have to play on yourself.

I suggest playing out some positions in which one side has a winning advantage. It is a common weakness to have problems with winning won positions, because realizing an advantage often requires exact play and good calculation. In this chapter I have selected some exercises in which one side has a decisive advantage. Precise play is needed to realize the advantage, but still there may be more than one way to win some of the positions. In others you need to find a string of precise moves to win the game. In some of them there is an immediate tactical point, in others you just need to continue the attack.

For the following tests I suggest giving yourself around half an hour to play the rest of the game against the computer. The program does probably not need more than 5-10 minutes for the whole game to come up with a stubborn defence. Depending on your playing strength, you should consider if some kind of 'handicapping' of the program is necessary. If you do not win from the position, then try again, or get some ideas for how to play the position by looking at the solutions on page 153. I believe it will help you to set up the positions on a real board or to use an electronic chess board.

On the ChessBase CD 'Mating against 0-0' you will find some similar examples of attacking positions to play out against a computer program.

Playout Exercises

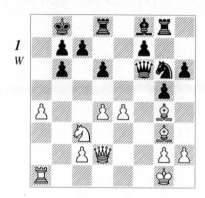

1
W

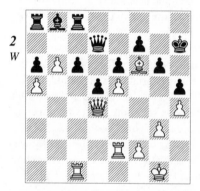

2
W

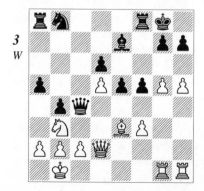

3
W

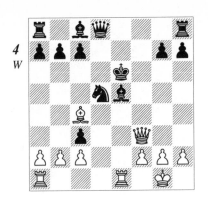

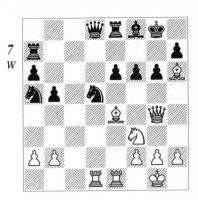

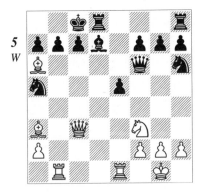

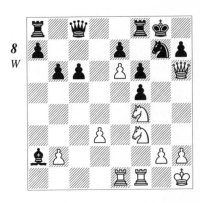

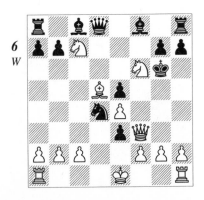

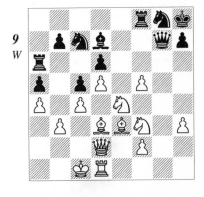

10
W

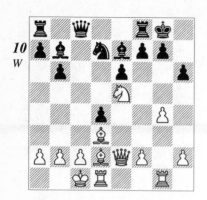

11
W

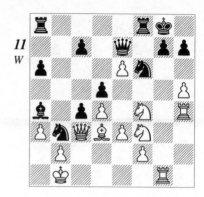

Solutions

1)

W. Steinitz – L. Paulsen
Baden-Baden 1870

24 ♘d5

This is the most precise continuation. 24 a5 is also strong and could transpose, but White chooses to win a tempo with the knight before advancing on the queenside.

24...♕g7 (D)

On 24...♕h8, 25 a5! is obviously also quite strong.

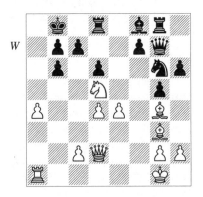

25 a5 f5

A desperate move. 25...♘e7 26 axb6 ♘xd5 (26...cxb6 27 ♘xb6 with a decisive attack) 27 ♖a8+! ♔xa8 28 ♕a5+ mating; if 25...b5 26 a6 b6 27 a7+ ♔b7 White has various ways of winning. One is 28 ♘xc7 ♔xc7 29 ♕c3+ ♔b7 30 ♗c8+! mating.

26 axb6! cxb6 27 ♘xb6 ♘e7

27...fxg4 leads to a quick mate: 28 ♖a8+ ♔c7 29 ♕c3+ ♔xb6 30 ♕a5+ ♔c6 31 d5+ ♔d7 32 ♕xd8#.

28 exf5

28 ♕b4 is the most accurate move according to computer analysis, because it forces mate most quickly.

28...♕f7 29 f6

29 ♖a8+ ♔c7 30 ♕a5 mating, is quicker.

29...♘c6 30 c4 ♘a7 31 ♕a2 ♘b5 32 ♘d5

32 ♕a8+ ♔c7 33 ♕a5 is the quickest way to mate.

32...♘xd5 33 cxd5 ♘xd4 34 ♕a7+ ♔c7 35 ♖c1+ ♘c6 36 ♖xc6# (1-0)

2)

G. Kasparov – Deep Blue
Match (6), Philadelphia 1996

This position is from the last game in the first match between Kasparov and Deep Blue. Kasparov has sacrificed a pawn, but Black's pieces are inactive and completely tied up, and the game is lost. There are many ways to win. Kasparov chose one in which the computer nearly ended up in zugzwang:

41 ♕c5

Blocking the c-pawn leaves Black with very little space and few options.

41...♔h6 42 ♖b2

This is the most elegant, but 42 ♕e7 also wins: 42...♕xe7 43 ♗xe7 ♖e8 44 ♗c5 and the threat of b7 costs Black material.

42...♕b7 43 ♖b4! 1-0

The operator resigned on behalf of the Deep Blue team. Black is losing in all lines; e.g.:

a) 43...♕d7 44 b7.

b) 43...♖e8 44 ♕xc6 ♕xc6 45 ♖xc6 ♔h7 46 b7 ♖a7 47 ♖c8 ♖g8 48 f4 and Black has no sensible moves.

c) 43...♔h7 44 ♕e7 (44 g4, initiating an attack on the black king, is also a strong possibility) 44...♕xe7 45 ♗xe7 ♖e8 (45...♗xe5 46 b7) 46 b7 ♖a7 47 ♗c5 winning.

3)

C. Kongsted – J. Carstensen
Copenhagen 2002

20 g6 f4

Black is trying to block the kingside, but White will do everything to keep it open.

a) 20...h6 is met by 21 ♗xh6!, when 21...gxh6 22 ♕xh6 leads to mate, while 21...a4 allows White several ways to win; e.g., 22 ♗xg7! axb3 (22...♔xg7? 23 h6+) 23 cxb3 ♕a6 24 a4! bxa3 25 h6 (e.g., 25...axb2? 26 h7+ ♔xg7 27 ♕h6+ ♔f6 28 h8♕+ ♖xh8 29 ♕xh8#).

b) 20...a4 21 h6 axb3 22 gxh7+ ♔f7 23 hxg7 is winning for White.

c) 20...♗f6 21 h6!.

21 h6!

A thematic break. The kingside files are opened.

21...hxg6

On 21...fxe3 White plays either 22 ♕g2! or 22 gxh7+ ♔f7 23 hxg7 exd2 24 g8♕+ ♔e8 25 h8♕ which shows a very nice destiny for the two attacking pawns! 21...♗f6 is met by 22 ♕h2! with a strong attack.

22 hxg7 ♔xg7

22...♖c8 23 ♕h2!.

23 ♕g2!

White is still winning after 23 ♕h2, but the text-move is faster, as the black king does not get a chance to escape.

23...♖f6 24 ♕h3

24 ♕h2 is the same.

24...♕xd5

24...♔f7 25 ♕h8!.

25 ♕h8+

25 ♕h7+? is not so clear.

25...♔f7 26 ♖h7+ ♔e6 27 ♕g8+ 1-0

Black loses his queen (27...♔d7 28 ♕xd5).

4)

P. Morphy – NN
New Orleans simultaneous 1858

Here is the first of three Morphy games. In this simultaneous game the American chess champion had already sacrificed a bishop and knight, but the sacrifices did not stop there. White has to continue the active play:

14 ♖xe5+! ♔xe5 15 ♖e1+ ♔d4

If 15...♔d6? then 16 ♕xd5#.

16 ♗xd5 ♖e8

Other options:

a) 16...♖f8 17 ♕xc3+ ♔xd5 18 ♖e5+ ♔d6 19 ♕c5+ ♔d7 20 ♕d5#.

b) 16...♕f6 17 ♖d1+ ♔c5 (17...♔e5 18 ♕e4+ ♔d6 19 ♗xb7+ mating) 18

♕e3+ ♚b4 (18...♚b5 19 a4+! ends with mate as well) 19 a3+ ♚a5 20 ♕c5+ b5 21 a4 c6 22 b4+ ♚a6 23 ♗xc6 with mate to follow.

17 ♕d3+ ♚c5 18 b4+! ♚xb4

Or: 18...♚b6 19 ♕d4+ ♚a6 20 ♕c4+ ♚b6 21 ♕c5+ ♚a6 22 ♕a5#; 18...♚d6 19 ♗xb7#.

19 ♕d4+ ♚a5

Everything leads to mate: 19...♚b5 20 ♖b1+ ♚a5 21 ♕b4+ ♚a6 22 ♕b5#; 19...♚a3 20 ♕xc3+ ♚a4 21 ♕b3+ ♚a5 22 ♕a3+ ♚b6 23 ♖b1#.

20 ♕xc3+ ♚a4 21 ♕b3+ ♚a5 22 ♕a3+ ♚b6 23 ♖b1# (1-0)

5)

P. Morphy – E. Morphy
New Orleans 1850

In this game Morphy was playing his father. He had sacrificed three pawns, but is now regaining material:

16 ♖ec1!

16 ♖xb7? ♘xb7 brings White nothing, and 16 ♕xa5 ♕xa6 is not convincing either, as it is difficult to justify having sacrificed three pawns, when there is no clear attack.

16...♗c6 17 ♕xa5

Now the capture is stronger, because the possibility of Black taking on a6 with the queen is ruled out.

17...bxa6 18 ♕xa6+ ♚d7 19 ♖xc6! ♕f5 20 ♖xc7+! ♚e8

20...♚xc7? 21 ♕b7#.

21 ♕c6+ ♚d7 22 ♖b8

Or simply 22 ♖xd7.

22...♕xc6 23 ♖e7+ ♚f8 24 ♖xd8+ ♕e8 25 ♖dxe8# (1-0)

6)

P. Morphy – A. Anderssen
Match (game 9), Paris 1858

The position is rather messy, as several white pieces are hanging. White focused on the attack and continued strongly:

15 ♕h5+ ♚xf6 16 fxe3!

White opens the f-file and the attack is decisive. An alternative is 16 f4! ♚e7 (or 16...♘xc2+ 17 ♚d1 ♘xa1? 18 ♕g5#) 17 ♕xe5+ ♘e6 18 ♘xe6 winning. White has other possibilities too, but he should not be tempted by 16 ♘e8+? due to 16...♕xe8! 17 ♕xe8 ♗b4+.

16...♘xc2+

16...♕xc7 is more resilient, but loses to 17 ♖f1+ ♘f5 18 ♖xf5+! ♗xf5 19 ♕xf5+ ♚e7 20 ♕e6+ ♚d8 21 0-0-0! ♗d6 22 ♗xb7 ♕xb7 23 ♖xd6+ ♚c7 24 ♖d7+ ♚b8 25 ♕xe5+ ♚c8 26 ♖xb7 ♚xb7 27 ♕g7+, when White's pawn force is overwhelming.

17 ♚e2! 1-0

A possible line is 17...♕xc7 18 ♖hf1+ ♚e7 19 ♖f7+ ♚d6 20 ♖xc7 ♚xc7 21 ♖c1 ♚b6 22 ♖xc2, when White has a material advantage and possibilities of continuing the attack on the black king.

7)

N. Pert – S. Ganguly
British Ch, Torquay 2002

22 ♗xg6! hxg6 23 ♕xg6+

23 ♖xd5 is also possible, but the move-order in the game is more accurate.

23...♗g7

Other moves lose as well: 23...♔h8 24 ♖xd5!, and 23...♖g7 24 ♗xg7 ♗xg7 25 ♖xd5!.

24 ♖xd5! ♕xd5 25 ♕xe8+ ♔h7 26 ♗xg7

26 ♘h4!? is an alternative; for example, 26...♗xh6 27 ♕g6+ ♔h8 28 ♕xh6+ ♔g8 29 ♕xf6.

26...♖xg7

26...♔xg7 can be met with 27 ♘h4, continuing the attack, or simply 27 ♕xe6.

27 ♖e3! *(D)*

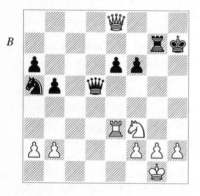

This is the most direct move, covering the f3-knight and setting up new threats.

27...♘c4

If for instance 27...e5 then the attack continues 28 ♘g5+! ♖xg5 29 ♖h3+ ♔g7 30 ♕h8+ ♔f7 31 ♖h7+ ♔g6 32 ♖h6+ ♔f7 33 ♖xf6+ ♔e7 34 ♕f8+ ♔d7 35 ♖f7+ ♕xf7 (35...♔c6 36 ♕c8+ ♔d6 37 ♕c7+ ♔e6 38 ♕e7#) 36 ♕xf7+ and White picks up the rook as well. 27...♕f5 is probably best

because it covers h3, but simply 28 ♕xe6 ♕xe6 29 ♖xe6 wins.

28 ♘g5+ ♖xg5

28...♕xg5 29 ♖h3+ ♕h6 30 ♖xh6+ ♔xh6 31 ♕xe6 is also winning for White.

29 ♕f7+ ♔h6 30 ♕xf6+ ♔h7

30...♖g6 31 ♖h3+.

31 ♕f7+ 1-0

Black resigned in view of 31...♔h6 32 ♖xe6+ ♕xe6 33 ♕xe6+ or 31...♔h8 32 ♖h3+.

8)

M. Hebden – P. Large

British Ch, Torquay 1982

White played...

21 ♖e3

...with the idea of bringing the rook to g3 at some point. Another move with the same idea is 21 ♘d4, when 21...c5 is met by 22 ♖f3! with the idea of ♖g3.

21...♘xe6

On 21...♗xe6, 22 ♘e5! fxe5 23 ♖g3 ♖f7 24 ♘xe6 is the most effective.

22 ♘xe6

22 ♘e5, clearing the third rank for the rook, is another idea.

22...♗xe6 23 ♖xe6!

23 ♘d4 or 23 ♘h4 with the threat of ♖g3+ also wins.

23...♖f7

23...♕xe6 24 ♘g5!.

24 ♖fe1 ♕d7

Or 24...♕f8 25 ♕f4, and ♘h4xf5 is coming.

25 ♘h4 ♖e8 26 ♘xf5 ♕xd3 27 ♘d6! 1-0

9)

I. Manor – Y. Afek
Czerniak memorial, Tel Aviv 1996
21 f6!

Sacrificing a pawn to open lines against the black king and at the same time stopping ...♕a1+ ideas.

21...♘xf6

After 21...♖xf6 22 ♘xf6 ♕xf6 23 ♕b2 White is a pawn up and after a queen exchange the attack continues with the manoeuvre ♗d2-c3+.

22 ♗h6 ♕e7 23 ♕c3!

Obviously, White could just take the rook with 23 ♗xf8 ♕xf8 and be a pawn up, but he reckons that the h6-bishop is more valuable than the rook when attacking, so he keeps it on the board. Now ♗xf8 is threatened because the f6-knight hangs after a recapture.

23...♘ce8 24 ♖e1 ♘g7 25 ♘eg5 ♕d8 26 ♘xh7! ♖a8

26...♘xh7? 27 ♕xg7#, while on 26...♘fh5 comes 27 ♗g6.

27 ♘xf8 ♕xf8 28 ♘h4 1-0

The game is over; e.g., 28...♔g8 29 ♘g6 ♕f7 30 ♖e7.

10)

V. Iordachescu – L. van Wely
Romanian Cht, Eforie Nord 2000
16 g5!

16 ♘g6 is not really convincing and gives no more than a draw after 16...fxg6 17 ♕xe6+ ♖f7 18 ♗xg6 ♕e8 19 ♗xf7+ ♕xf7 20 ♕xd7 ♕xa2 21 ♗xh6 (this is the only move, since, for example, 21 ♗f4? loses to 21...♕b4!)

21...♕a1+ 22 ♔d2 ♕a5+, when 23 ♔c1 ♕a1+ is a perpetual check, while 23 ♔e2 ♕e5+ 24 ♔f1 ♕e4! gives Black good attacking chances: he threatens to take on h6 as well as ...♗a6+.

16...♘xe5

Other options:

a) 16...♗xg5 17 ♗xg5 ♘xe5 (or 17...hxg5 18 ♕h5 ♘f6 19 ♕xg5 ♘e8 20 ♕h4 f5 21 ♘g6 +–) 18 ♕xe5 hxg5 19 ♕xg5 g6 20 ♗xg6 f6 21 ♕h6 +–.

b) 16...hxg5 17 ♕h5 f5 18 ♘g6 ♖e8 19 ♗xg5 ♗xg5+ 20 ♖xg5 followed by doubling on the g-file with a very strong attack.

17 gxh6!

If 17 ♕xe5 then 17...♕c5 offers chances of defending.

17...♘xd3+

Other moves also lose:

a) 17...♗f6 18 hxg7 ♘xd3+ (after 18...♗xg7 White plays 19 ♖xg7+!) 19 ♕xd3 ♖e8 20 ♕h3 is winning for White.

b) 17...♘g6 18 hxg7 and then:

b1) 18...♔xg7 19 ♕e5+! ♗f6 (or 19...♔g8 20 ♗h6 f6 21 ♕h5) 20 ♕h5 ♖h8 21 ♖xg6+ ♔f8 22 ♗h6+ ♔e7 23 ♖xf6 +–.

b2) 18...♖d8 19 ♕h5 ♖d5 20 ♕h6 ♖f5 (trying to stop the attack on the g6-knight) 21 ♖g3 and White threatens to win by ♖h3 and ♕h8+. On 21...♗h4, 22 ♖xg6! seems promising; e.g., 22...fxg6 23 ♕xh4 ♕d8 (23...♖h5 24 ♕e7! and the attack continues) 24 ♕h8+ ♔f7 25 ♗xf5 exf5 26 g8♕+ ♕xg8 27 ♕xd4 and White is a pawn up, Black's king is very unsafe, and the opposite-coloured bishops favour White's attacking chances.

18 ♕xd3 ♖d8

There is nothing better:

a) 18...g5 19 ♗xg5 ♗xg5+ 20 ♖xg5+ ♔h8 21 ♖g7 f5 22 ♕xd4 e5 23 ♕xe5 ♕b8 24 ♖g8+! ♔xg8 25 ♕g7#.

b) 18...g6 19 ♖xg6+ ♔h8 20 ♖g7 f5 21 ♖xe7 +–.

c) 18...♗f6 19 ♖xg7+! ♗xg7 20 ♖g1 +–.

19 ♖xg7+ ♔f8 20 ♖dg1 ♗f6 21 ♖xf7+! 1-0

The game could have concluded 21...♔xf7 22 ♕h7+ ♗g7 23 ♖xg7+ ♔f6 24 ♗f4 and the mate threats of ♖f7# and ♕g6# cannot be stopped.

11)

V. Kovačević – R. Zelčić
Vinkovci 1995

25 h6!

The most direct continuation. Naturally, White also has a clear advantage after 25 ♗c2, but the text-move is stronger.

25...g6

25...cxd3 26 ♖xg7+ ♕xg7 27 hxg7 ♖fc8 28 ♕xd3 is also lost for Black.

26 ♗xg6! ♔h8

26...hxg6 27 ♖xg6+ ♔h8 28 ♖g7 and White wins.

27 ♗f5

27 ♗xh7!, smashing a hole in the black defences, looks even stronger.

After 27...♕xh7+ 28 ♘g6+ ♔g8 29 ♔a2! White will regain material, while the attack rages on; e.g., 29...♖fe8 30 e7! with the threat of ♘f8+.

27...♗e8

27...♖g8 is probably best. In that case White is just two pawns up, and the pawns on h6 and e6 cement White's attacking chances.

28 ♖g7 ♕d6 29 ♖h1

White chooses a slightly slow plan, doubling on the g-file.

29...♖g8 30 ♖hg1 ♖xg7 31 ♖xg7

Or 31 hxg7+ ♔g8 32 ♕c2! with the decisive threat of sacrificing twice on h7 and promoting the pawn.

31...♖b8 32 ♔a2

32 ♘e5, with the threat of ♗xh7! followed by mate with ♘g6+, is the quickest way to a win.

32...♕b6 33 ♘g5

33 ♘e5 and 33 ♘h4 with the idea of ♗xh7 are slightly faster ways of winning.

33...c5

Black is losing anyway, but opening up for the white queen speeds up the end.

34 dxc5 ♘xc5

34...d4 is better but is of course still losing.

35 ♖xh7+ 1-0

Black resigned in view of 35...♔g8 36 ♖h8+! ♔xh8 37 ♕xf6+ ♔g8 38 ♕g7#.

9 Improve Your Endgame Technique

Play the opening like a book, the middlegame like a magician, and the endgame like a machine.
RUDOLF SPIELMANN (1883-1942), Austrian chess master

Despite Spielmann's quote above, the endgame is a part of the game where computers have generally been regarded as fairly weak. As mentioned earlier, there was a match in the mid-1960s between a Soviet and an American program in which the games were adjudicated drawn if they reached the endgame phase. The programmers did not want to display the poor endgame skills of the programs.

Now the situation has changed. The increasing speed of the computer's calculations makes them able to see much deeper in endgames than they used to, and they can no longer be said to be weak endgame players. They can in fact easily find mistakes in many chess endgame books, especially the older ones. Their calculating abilities are especially useful in pawn endgames where they can often calculate very deeply because of the fewer possibilities available. In other endgames their calculation is also of great help for analysis. What they lack in knowledge, they can often compensate for with calculation. Their weaknesses are most obvious in strategic endgames that require good planning, or positions where endgame knowledge is required. As mentioned before, the area of fortresses in the endgame is a dark hole for computers.

Computer analysis of endgame positions has improved very much since the construction of endgame tablebases which enable the programs to play endgames with five or fewer pieces perfectly.

The engines can consult the endgame tablebases during their search even well before the actual five-piece endgame is reached. For instance, in an endgame with ten pieces on the board, the computer can analyse a line which ends with five pieces and then retrieve information from the tablebases. Obviously this makes the assessment of a position much more accurate, and it also helps to cut off unnecessary calculation. As a part of the evaluation output of some programs, it is possible to see when they start hitting the tablebases. When they display e.g. 'tb=41', it means that the program has hit the tablebases 41 times at this point of the search.

A technical explanation of how endgame tablebases are constructed is somewhat beyond the scope of this book. In short, they are made by analysing the game of chess backwards. When constructing a tablebase for king and queen versus king the computer is programmed to find all possible mate positions. From these 'terminal positions' the computer works one step backwards and looks at all positions that could have led to this mate position. In this way it finds all possible mate-in-one positions, then the mates-in-two and so on up to mate-in-ten, which is the maximum for this particular ending.

A 'terminal position' can also be a position in which a pawn is promoted or a piece is captured. In this case the program has to find the information in another endgame tablebase.

A nearly complete set of tablebases, including all endings with three or four pieces and the main endings with five pieces, is available for sale under the name 'Fritz Endgame Turbo' from ChessBase or 'Nalimov Ending Tablebases' from Convekta (Chess Assistant). However, all tablebases, including some of the six-piece endings, can be downloaded from Robert Hyatt's FTP site, and the only thing you need in that case is a fast Internet connection. Currently, Dr Eugene Nalimov is working on constructing all of the six-piece endings, and when this process has

finished, it will markedly improve the endgame analysis of the computer.

Playing Out Endgame Positions

Your chess program can be an excellent partner when studying the endgame, and optimally it should be used in parallel with reading a good chess endgame book. 'Playing out' positions from an endgame book is a rather slow way of reading the book, but your understanding of the positions will be much better. This is the best way to assure that you are not just moving the pieces around when going through an endgame. On the following pages, I will give some examples of how to play out endgame positions against computer programs.

Depending on your level, I can recommend that you start out by playing through some of the simple endgames. These are ♔♕ vs ♔, ♔♖ vs ♔, the more difficult ♔♗♗ vs ♔, and the very challenging ♔♗♘ vs ♔. If you are in doubt about how to play any of these endgames, then consult an endgame book that describes the principles behind them. The Fritz 8 interface includes some training positions with these endgames, amongst other endings like ♔♕ vs ♔♙, ♔♕ vs ♔♖, and ♔♖ vs ♔♘. However, you can also find these positions in most endgame books, along with a description of the principles behind winning or drawing from various positions. Note that sometimes you will have to make the program play without endgame tablebases to have it setting up a realistic defence. (In the Fritz interface this is done by deselecting the 'Use Tablebases' check-off box in the Engine dialogue box – F3).

When you have worked on the basic endings, you can proceed to endings with more pieces on the board. I believe it is very instructive to play out positions of a 'technical' nature, for instance positions in which one side needs to realize a one-pawn advantage. I will use the following well-known Capablanca game to show how to do this.

If you do not know the game already, try to think about how to proceed from the diagram position. Do not give any analysis; just give a suggestion for the best square of each piece.

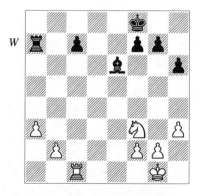

J. Capablanca – V. Ragozin
Moscow 1936

White is a pawn up, and he has to consider how to realize his queenside majority. However, before trying to push his pawns, he should find the best squares for his pieces.

Capablanca wrote about this position that White should prevent the advance of the enemy c-pawn, which would make his own b2-pawn weak. Moreover, his aim was to control the whole board as far as the fifth rank, and this was done by putting the knight on d4, rook on c3, king on e3 and pawns on b4 and f4. After that White will start pushing the queenside pawns.

The Cuban world champion gave no variations, only these verbal comments, and thus this endgame is well-suited for a playing-out exercise. Try to follow Capablanca's plan and win against your computer program from this position. The program does not need more than 5 minutes for the remainder of the game to play a reasonable defence, however you should give yourself some more time, possibly between 15 and 30 minutes for the rest of the game. Weaker players should again consider if some of the handicapping options should be used.

If you do not succeed the first time, play through the moves in the actual game below to see if you can get some new ideas about how to realize White's advantage. Then try once more.

This is what happened in the game:
33 ♘d4 ♖b7 34 b4 ♗d7 35 f4 ♔e7 36 ♔f2 ♖a7 37 ♖c3 ♔d6 38 ♖d3

Everything was proceeding according to plan at this point, but now Capablanca takes time to chase the black king away before continuing his plan.

38...♔e7 39 ♔e3 ♖a4 40 ♖c3 ♔d6 41 ♖d3 ♔e7 42 ♖c3

White repeats the position to gain time and to find the right plan. 'Do not hurry' is a common endgame principle.

42...♔d6 43 ♘e2

White now gets ready to set up a new formation. He will put the king on d4, the rook on e3 and the knight on c3, where it supports the advance of the queenside pawns.

43...g6 44 ♖d3+ ♔e6 45 ♔d4 ♖a6 46 ♖e3+ ♔d6 47 ♘c3

White has reached the desired formation and is now ready to advance his queenside pawns. ...♖xa3 is of course not possible now or on the following moves, because of the discovered check with the knight on e4 or b5.

47...f5 48 b5 ♖a8 49 ♔c4 ♗e6+ 50 ♔b4

The king is now supporting White's pawn advance.

50...c5+ 51 bxc6 ♗g8 52 ♘b5+ ♔xc6 53 ♖d3 g5 54 ♖d6+ ♔b7 55 fxg5 hxg5 56 ♖g6

This picks up a pawn and essentially wins the game.

56...♖f8 57 ♖xg5 f4 58 ♘d4 ♖c8 59 ♖g7+ ♔b6 60 ♖g6+ ♔b7 61 ♘b5 ♖f8 62 ♘d6+ ♔b8 63 h4 1-0

Because of his schematic way of thinking, Capablanca made this look very easy. However, if you have not already played out the position, then it is now your turn to show that you can win the position using the scheme that Capablanca used. Most likely, your program will deviate at some point, and then you have to proceed on your own. Here is the playout between the author and Shredder 7.04:

33 ♘d4 ♗d7 (D)

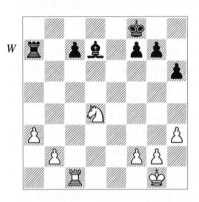

The program immediately deviates, but it does not make so much difference. I just continue according to the scheme.

34 ♖c3 ♔e7 35 b4 ♔d6 36 f4 ♔d5

Shredder is certainly playing very aggressively with its king, trying to spoil my beautiful scheme! However, the king does not have a great future on d5, and it is soon pushed back.

37 ♘e2 ♔d6 38 ♔f2 ♖a8 39 ♖d3+

Chasing the king back.

39...♔e7 40 ♔e3 ♗b5 41 ♖c3 ♖e8

41...♗xe2 42 ♔xe2 is possible, but White should still win.

42 ♘d4 ♗d7

I have now reached Capablanca's formation, and I get ready to prepare an advance of the queenside pawns. Shredder plays quite actively, however, and disturbs me in achieving this goal.

43 ♔d3

43 ♖xc7? is of course not possible due to 43...♔d6+.

43...♔d6 44 ♖c1

To prevent the black rook from entering via e1.

44...♖a8 45 ♖c3 ♖e8 46 ♔d2 ♖e4 47 ♖d3 ♔e7

47...♖xf4 is not possible because of the discovered check 48 ♘e2+.

48 ♘e2

Or 48 ♖e3 straight away.

48...g6 49 ♖e3 ♖xe3 50 ♔xe3

Shredder's active play has only led to a rook exchange, and without the rooks it is much easier for White to advance his queenside pawns. Note that the theme of a rook exchange was never relevant in the real game. The playing-out of the position brings up new aspects of the position.

50...♔e6 51 ♘c3

Supporting the advance of the kingside pawns.

51...♗c6 52 g3 ♗g2 53 h4 f5 54 a4 ♗b7 55 ♔d4 ♗c6 56 b5 ♗h1 57 a5 ♗f3

Now the knight gets ready to go to e5 to put pressure on the kingside, especially g6, while pushing the pawns on the queenside.

58 ♘a4 ♗g2 59 ♘c5+ ♔d6 60 ♘d3 ♗f1 61 a6 c5+ 62 ♘xc5 ♗xb5 63 a7 ♗c6 64 ♘d3 ♗g2 65 ♘e5

The knight arrives on e5 with devastating effect. Black cannot cover his kingside while he is trying to hold back the a-pawn.

65...h5 66 ♘xg6 ♗h1 67 ♘f8 ♔c7 68 ♔e5 ♔b7 69 ♔xf5 1-0

Black is losing all the kingside pawns and, with them, the game.

It is worth noting Capablanca's 'schematic' way of thinking in this game. In endgames of a strategic nature you will get by much easier if you are able to think like this rather than only analysing concrete variations.

Let us take another example of this. Once again, consider for yourself where White's pieces should be located to win the position.

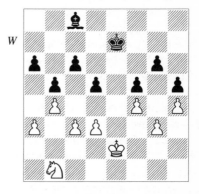

Capablanca said about this position that White wins by bringing his king to d4 and the knight to e5. I will verify this by playing out the position against Shredder 7.04.

1 ♔e3 ♔d6 2 ♔d4 ♗e6 3 ♘d2 ♗c8 4 ♘f3 ♗d7 5 ♘e5 ♗e8

The key position has been reached. White's king and knight are in their optimal positions, and White now goes on to the next stage. He plays a pawn break to push back the black king.

6 c4! dxc4 7 dxc4

A position close to a zugzwang has been reached. If Black's king moves, the white king will enter the position via c5, and the white king enters the black position after 7...bxc4 8 ♘xc4+ ♔c7 9 ♔c5 ♗f7 10 ♘e5 ♗e8 11 a4, which is a zugzwang position. In the game Black just loses a pawn.

7...♗d7 8 ♘xg6 ♗c8 9 ♘e5

Transferring the knight to c5 to paralyse the bishop on c8.

9...♗b7 10 ♘d3 bxc4 11 ♔xc4 ♗c8 12 ♘c5 ♔c7 13 ♔d4 ♔b6 14 ♔e5 a5 15 ♘e6 axb4 16 axb4 c5

This looks desperate, but everything loses. For instance 16...♔b5 is met by 17 ♘d4+ ♔xb4 18 ♘xc6+, when White easily picks up the kingside pawns.

17 bxc5+ 1-0

Obviously, these positions and the following exercises can also be played out with a human training partner. However, I find that a computer program can be a good substitute in these simple, technical games because it usually defends very stubbornly. It does not get tired and depressed by defending, and for this reason you have to stay alert all the time. This is optimally what you have to do against humans as well. If you put the program on the highest level, it will punish nearly any mistake you make, and thus you should be able to find the right way of playing more quickly.

In the following exercises I have chosen games or positions in which one side has a winning advantage that has to be realized by means of good technique. Remember that these exercises could just be the starting point of your studies. You can find many more examples yourself by going through your endgame books and playing out various positions. In the bibliography, I have listed some titles of the endgame books I have used, and the reader can use these books as inspiration.

Playing out positions while reading an endgame book is a very effective way of studying, because it forces the reader to read **actively**, to think about the moves given and to enter into a kind of dialogue with the author. If you are in doubt about how to win or draw, or the moves or annotations given by the author, you can always ask your computer program what it thinks.

I urge the reader to play out the positions once before looking at the solutions given on page 169. If you fail, play through the solution to get some ideas about how to approach the position, and then try again. Do not despair if you do not solve the exercises the first or the second time. The intention is that you play through them until you win, and in this manner you are improving your technique. However, if you do not succeed in winning after four or five times, you should probably consider using one of the handicapping options mentioned in Chapter 5.

Note also that the solutions given are not really solutions, but merely examples of how to win the positions. In all the exercises there are several paths to achieve the same goal, and the 'solutions' are mainly meant for guiding the reader as to which way the advantage might be realized.

Once again I can recommend using a real chess board or an electronic chess board to set up the positions.

2
B

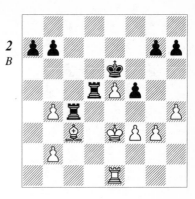

3
B

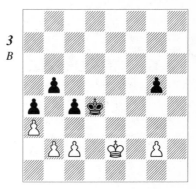

Playout Exercises

1
W

4
W

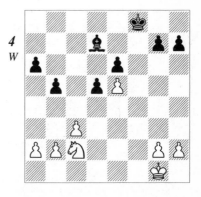

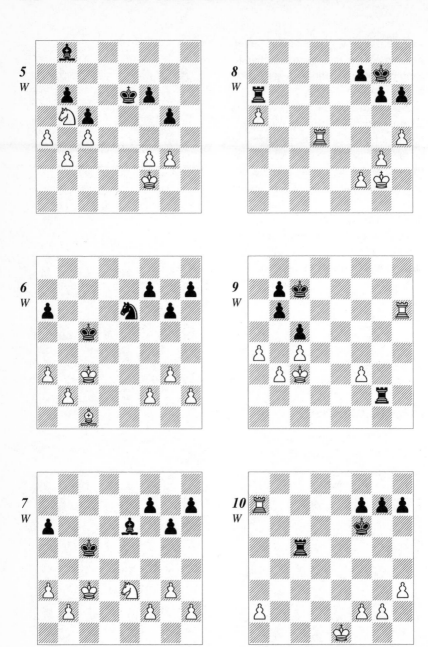

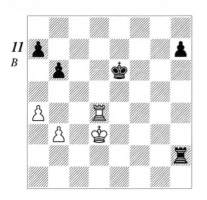

11
B

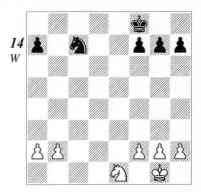

14
W

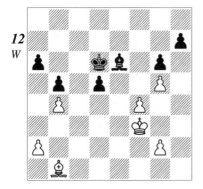

12
W

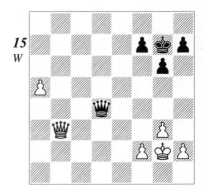

15
W

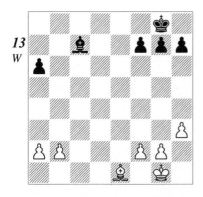

13
W

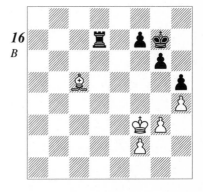

16
B

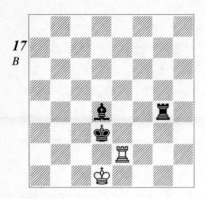

17
B

Solutions

1)

J. Capablanca
Last Lectures

White wins by advancing his king in front of the pawns.

1 ♔d2

One of the pitfalls in this endgame can be seen in the line 1 e4 ♔c7 2 f4 ♔c6 3 ♔e2 ♔d6 4 ♔d3 e6 5 ♔d4? e5+! 6 fxe5+ ♔e6 with a draw.

1...♔d7 2 ♔d3 ♔d6 3 ♔d4 ♔e6 4 ♔e4 ♔d6 5 ♔f5 e6+ 6 ♔f6 ♔d5 7 e3 ♔d6

7...e5 is met by 8 f4 exf4 9 exf4 and White promotes the pawn.

8 f4 ♔d7 9 e4 ♔d6 10 f5 exf5 11 exf5 ♔d7 12 ♔g7

and White wins.

2)

W. Lombardy – R. Fischer
USA Ch, New York 1960/1

Black can exchange pieces to a won pawn endgame with the following combination.

1...♖xc3+! 2 bxc3 ♖xe5+ 3 ♔d2 ♖xe1 4 ♔xe1 ♔d5 5 ♔d2 ♔c4

Black wins because he can create an outside passed pawn on the a-file.

6 h5 b6

White has no chance of stopping the creation of a passed a-pawn. The game is lost.

7 ♔c2 g5 8 h6 f4 9 g4 a5 10 bxa5 bxa5 11 ♔b2 a4 12 ♔a3 ♔xc3 13 ♔xa4 ♔d4 14 ♔b4 ♔e3 0-1

3)

A. Brinckmann – A. Rubinstein
Budapest 1929

1...b4! 2 ♔d2

If 2 axb4, then 2...c3! 3 bxc3+ ♔c4! 4 ♔d2 a3 5 ♔c1 ♔xc3 6 ♔b1 ♔xb4 7 ♔a2 ♔c3 and the outside passed a-pawn once again decides the matter.

2...b3! 3 c3+ ♔e4 4 ♔e2 ♔f4 5 ♔f2 ♔g4 6 ♔f1 ♔g3 7 ♔g1 g4 8 ♔f1 ♔h2

An unusual king manoeuvre.

9 ♔f2 ♔h1 10 ♔g3 ♔g1 11 ♔xg4 ♔xg2 0-1

4)

Y. Averbakh
Bishop vs Knight Endings (1976)

In this position White can penetrate the black position and force a zugzwang. The following is a playout between the author and Shredder 7.04.

1 ♔f2 h6 2 ♔e3 ♔e7 3 ♔d4 ♔d8 4 ♔c5 ♔c7

Now the kings are opposing each other. White's aim is to force Black to run out of moves and to create a zugzwang. When this happens he will be able to penetrate deeper into the black position and win material.

5 ♘d4 ♗c8 6 ♘e2 ♗d7 7 ♘f4

White is planning to threaten the kingside pawns and make them advance until the point where they cannot move any more.

7...g5 8 ♘h5 ♗e8 9 ♘f6 ♗g6 10 ♘g4

Forcing the pawns forward.

10...h5 11 ♘f2 g4

Otherwise ♘h3 would have forced this move. Now White locks the kingside, and Black is slowly running out of possibilities.

12 g3 ♗f5 13 ♘d1

White seeks to create a zugzwang by transferring his knight to the excellent f4-square. If the knight gets to f4, the black bishop is forced to be on f7, covering the weaknesses of e6 and h5, and in that case the zugzwang moves closer.

13...♗b1 14 a3 ♗c2 15 ♘e3 ♗e4

Stopping ♘g2-f4.

16 b4?!

I played this move rather quickly, not noticing that there is a faster way to win the position. Naturally, it would be better to push the pawn only one square in a tempo duel like this. Zugzwang could be forced after 16 b3! ♗g6 (Black has to allow White to play ♘g2-f4, as 16...♗f3 loses to 17 ♘c2 ♗e4 18 ♘d4) 17 ♘g2 ♗e8 18 ♘f4 ♗f7 19 b4!. The knight has reached f4, and Black is in zugzwang. White will win material no matter what Black plays.

16...♗d3 17 ♘g2 ♗g6 18 ♘f4 ♗f7 19 ♘e2

19 h4 straightaway is faster, but in an endgame like this there is no need to hurry.

19...♗g6 20 ♘d4 ♗f7 21 ♘c6 ♗g6 22 ♘d4 ♗f7 23 ♘e2 ♗g6 24 ♘f4 ♗f7

This is just a repetition of the position. A knight cannot lose a tempo. However, now White hits upon the right plan.

25 h4!

Black has to take this pawn as the king and the bishop are forced to remain in their defensive positions.

25...gxh3 26 ♘xh3 ♗g6 27 ♘f4 ♗f7 28 ♔d4

The king is transferred to h4 and the h-pawn falls. If the black king tries to go to the kingside to cover h5, the white knight is transferred to c5 and the a-pawn will be lost.

28...♔b6 29 ♔e3 ♔b7 30 ♔f2 ♔c8 31 ♔g2 ♔d7 32 ♔h3 ♔d8 33 ♔h4 ♔e7 34 ♘xh5 ♗g6 35 ♔g5 ♗c2 36 ♘f4 ♗h7 37 g4 ♔f7 38 ♔h6 ♗g8 39 g5 ♔e7 40 g6 1-0

On 40...♔f8 White can play 41 ♘h5 and the white king penetrates via g7.

5)

T. Petrosian – G. Borisenko
USSR Ch, Moscow 1950

White's plan is to transfer his knight to d5, play g4 to put the pawns on light squares, and then move his king to the queenside, supporting a breakthrough to realize his pawn-majority.

1 ♘c3 ♗c7 2 ♘d5 ♗d8 3 g4 f5 4 ♔e2 ♔e5 5 ♔d3 ♔e6 6 ♘e3 f4

6...fxg4 7 fxg4 ♔e5 8 ♘d5 does not change anything, since the black king cannot approach the white pawn on g4.

7 ♘d5 ♔e5 8 ♔c3 ♔e6 9 ♔d3 ♔e5 10 ♘c3

White decides to put his knight on d3 before playing b4, so as to control c5 better after a pawn exchange.

10...♗f6 11 ♘e4 ♗e7 12 ♔c3 ♔e6 13 ♘f2 ♗f6+ 14 ♔c2 ♔e5 15 ♔d3 ♗d8 16 ♔c3 ♗e7 17 ♘d3+ ♔d6 18 b4 ♗f6+ 19 ♔b3 ♗d4 20 bxc5+ bxc5 21 a5 ♔c6 22 ♔a4 ♗f6 23 a6 ♗e7 24 a7 ♔b7 25 ♔b5 ♔xa7 26 ♘xc5 1-0

6)

J. Speelman
Endgame Preparation (1981)

After two closed positions with a superior knight, I have chosen a ♗ vs ♘ endgame in an open position. With pawns on both sides the bishop is much stronger than the knight as it can use its long range. Once again I have picked Shredder for the thankless task of defending with the black pieces.

1 ♗e3+ ♔b5 2 b3 ♘g7 3 a4+ ♔c6 4 ♔c4 ♘e8 5 ♗c5 ♘c7 6 b4 f6 7 ♗d4 f5 8 ♗e5

Forcing Black to retreat, as a pawn endgame a pawn down would be lost immediately.

8...♘a8 9 b5+ axb5+ 10 axb5+ ♔b7 11 ♔c5 ♘b6 12 h4 ♘d7+ 13 ♔d6 ♘b6 14 ♔e6

Black cannot watch the passed b-pawn and the kingside at the same time.

14...♘c8 15 ♗d4 ♔c7 16 ♔f6 ♔d6 17 b6 ♔c6 18 ♔g7 f4 19 ♔xh7 1-0

White easily picks up the kingside pawns.

7)

J. Speelman
Endgame Preparation (1981)

With the knight, White has to fight a bit more, but the extra pawn counts in the end. Shredder plays Black again.

1 a4 a5?!

A slightly inaccurate move, as it forces Black's king into a passive position.

2 b3 ♔b6 3 ♘c4+ ♔a6 4 f4 f6 5 b4 axb4+ 6 ♔xb4 ♗d5 7 ♘d6 ♗c6 8 a5 h6 9 ♘f7 h5 10 h4 ♗e4 11 ♘d6 ♗c6 12 ♘c4 (D)

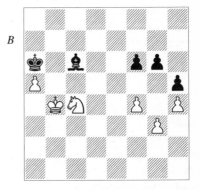

The knight should go to c5 to push the a-pawn further on the queenside.

12...♔b7 13 ♘b2 ♗h1 14 ♘d3 ♗g2 15 ♘c5+ ♔c6 16 ♔c4 ♗f1+ 17 ♔d4 ♗h3 18 a6 ♔b6 19 ♔d5

Once again it is difficult for Black to fight against the passed a-pawn and the threat of the king getting nearer to the kingside pawns.

19...♗g4 20 ♔d6 f5 21 ♘d7+

White gives up the a-pawn but as a result picks up the weak black kingside pawns.

21...♖xa6 22 ♘f8 ♔b7 23 ♘xg6 ♔c8 24 ♔e6 ♔d8 25 ♘e7 ♔e8 26 ♘xf5 1-0

White wins.

8)

A. Alekhine – J. Capablanca
World Ch match (game 34),
Buenos Aires 1927

1 ♖a4!

The rook belongs behind the passed pawn.

1...♔f6 2 ♔f3 ♔e5 3 ♔e3 h5 4 ♔d3 ♔d5 5 ♔c3 ♔c5 6 ♖a2!

Forcing Black to take a decision about where to put his king.

6...♔b5

6...♖a7 7 a6 is no help to Black, and if 6...♔d5 7 ♔b4 ♔c6 8 f4, Black is slowly pushed back.

7 ♔b3 ♔c5 8 ♔c3 ♔b5 9 ♔d4! ♖d6+

9...♔b4 is met by 10 ♖a1! ♔b3 11 ♔c5 winning, and 9...♖xa5 10 ♖xa5+ ♔xa5 11 ♔e5 is of course just a lost pawn endgame for Black.

10 ♔e5 ♖e6+ 11 ♔f4 ♔a6

Black now tries to block the pawn with his king instead of the rook. 11...f6 loses to 12 a6! ♖e8 (or 12...♖xa6 13 ♖xa6 ♔xa6 14 ♔e4, winning the pawn endgame) 13 a7 ♖a8 14 f3 ♔b4 15 g4 ♔b3 16 ♖a6 hxg4 17 fxg4 ♔b4 18 h5

♔b5 19 ♖a1 gxh5 20 gxh5 with an easy win.

12 ♔g5 ♖e5+ 13 ♔h6 ♖f5 14 f4

14 ♔g7 ♖f3 15 ♔g8 ♖f6 16 f4 is another option.

14...♖c5 15 ♖a3 ♖c7

If 15...♖f5 then 16 ♔g7 with zugzwang.

16 ♔g7 ♖d7 17 f5 gxf5 18 ♔h6 f4 19 gxf4 ♖d5 20 ♔g7 ♖f5 21 ♖a4 ♔b5 22 ♖e4 ♔a6

If 22...♔xa5? then 23 ♖e5+.

23 ♔h6 ♖xa5

If 23...♔a7 then 24 ♖e5 ♖xf4 25 ♔g5 ♖a4 26 ♖f5 ♔a6 27 ♔xh5 ♖d4 28 ♖xf7 ♔xa5 29 ♔g5 winning.

24 ♖e5 ♖a1 25 ♔xh5 ♖g1 26 ♔g5 ♖h1 27 ♖f5 ♔b6 28 ♖xf7 ♔c6 29 ♖e7 1-0

9)

A. Beliavsky – M. Gurevich
Groningen 1992

First of all, White has to find the right location for his pieces, and e3 is the optimal square for the rook. From here it covers both b3 and f3. The king should go to e4 to support the advance of the f-pawn.

1 ♖e6! ♖f2 2 ♖e3!

An excellent square for the rook. The next step is to activate the king.

2...♔d7 3 ♔d3 ♔d6 4 ♔e4 ♔e6 5 f4 ♖h2 6 ♖g3 ♖e2+

6...♔f6 is slightly more stubborn. In that case White could proceed 7 ♖d3 ♖e2+ 8 ♔f3 ♖h2 9 ♔g4 ♖g2+ 10 ♖g3 ♖f2 11 ♖h3 ♔g6 12 f5+ ♔g7 (after 12...♖xf5 13 ♖h6+ ♔g7 14 ♔xf5

Kxh6 15 Ke6 White also wins) 13 Rd3 Rb2 14 Rd7+ Kf8 15 Rxb7 Rxb3 16 a5 and White wins.

7 Kd3 Rf2 8 Ke3 Rh2 9 Rg6+ Kf5 10 Rxb6 Rh3+ 11 Kd2 Kxf4 12 Rxb7

Having won two queenside pawns, the rest should be a matter of technique, but it takes some time to realize the advantage.

12...Ke5 13 Rb6

Cutting off the king.

13...Rh2+ 14 Kc3 Rh3+ 15 Kb2 Rh2+ 16 Ka3 Rh1 17 Rg6

Transferring the rook to a2 to support the a-pawn. In the following it is possible that White does not find the fastest way, but he wins in the end.

17...Rf1 18 Rg2 Kd6 19 a5 Ra1+ 20 Ra2 Rh1 21 Rd2+ Kc6 22 Kb2 Rh8 23 Rg2 Ra8 24 Rg6+ Kc7 25 a6 Rc8 26 Ka3 Kb8 27 Ka4 Ka7 28 Ka5 Rb8 29 Rg7+ Ka8 30 Rb7 Rc8 31 Rb6 Ka7 32 Kb5 Rh8 33 Rc6 Rh3 34 Rc7+ Ka8 35 Ka4 Rh5 36 Rd7 Rh8 37 Rc7 Rh5 38 Ka5 Rh3 39 Rb7 Rh6 40 Rb6 1-0

Black resigned in view of 40...Rh3 41 Rb5 Ka7 42 Ka4 Rh5 (42...Kxa6 43 Rxc5) 43 b4 Kxa6 44 Rxc5.

10)

A. Karpov – R. Knaak
Baden-Baden 1992

This exercise is not so easy if you do not discover the basic idea. White sees that his rook is not well placed in front of the pawn, and he seeks to find a better set-up. Karpov's idea is to arrange his pieces in the following manner: Ra3, Kd2, Kc3 and a3, and get ready to push the a-pawn on the queenside. If you did not succeed in winning the game yourself before reading the solution, you should try again using this idea.

1 Ra3!

Just pushing the pawn with 1 a4 Rc2 2 a5 Ra2 gives Black the better rook position. 1 Kd2 does not deal with White's problem of having his rook placed in front of his own pawn.

1...g5

1...Rc2 was chosen by Shredder when I played out this position. This can be met by 2 Rf3+!, and the play-out game continued 2...Kg6 3 a3! Ra2 4 Kd1 (now the king walks to b1 to ensure that the a-pawn can march onwards) 4...f6 5 Kc1 Re2 6 Kb1 Kf7 7 a4 Re4 8 Ra3! (White's rook manoeuvre has made it possible for him to position the rook behind the pawn) 8...Re1+ 9 Kb2 Re2+ 10 Kc3 Rxf2 (White loses a pawn, but his a-pawn is dangerous enough to win the game) 11 a5 Re2 12 a6 Re8 13 Kc4 g5 14 Kc5 Re5+ 15 Kd4 Re8 16 a7 Ra8 17 Kc5 Kg6 18 Kc6 h5 19 Kb7 Rd8 20 a8Q Rxa8 21 Rxa8, winning for White.

2 Kd2 Kg6 3 Kc3 Ra5 4 a3

Excellent play by Karpov. White has now reached the desired set-up and gets ready to push his a-pawn with the help of the king.

4...h5 5 Kc2 Ra8 6 Kb3 Rb8+ 7 Ka2 Ra8 8 Kc4

Slowly preparing the advance of the a-pawn.

8...f5

Black tries to get counterplay on the kingside. If 8...♖e8, then 9 ♖b4 ♖e2+ 10 ♖b2 ♖e4 11 ♔b3 is winning.

9 a4 ♔f6 10 ♖a3 ♔e5 11 ♖c5+ ♔e4 12 a5 h4 13 ♔a4 ♔f4 14 ♖c4+

White prevents Black's counterplay before proceeding.

14...♔e5 15 ♖b4 ♔d5 16 ♖b5+ ♔e4 17 ♖b6 ♔f4 18 a6 g4 19 ♔a5 g3

19...gxh3 20 ♖b4+ ♔e5 21 gxh3 wins for White.

20 ♖b4+ ♔e5 21 f3 f4 22 ♖e4+ ♔f5 23 ♖e2 ♔f6 24 ♔b6 ♖b8+ 25 ♔c7 ♖f8

25...♖b1 26 ♖a2 ♖c1+ 27 ♔b6 ♖b1+ 28 ♔a5 ♖b8 29 a7 ♖a8 30 ♔b6 and White wins.

26 a7 ♖f7+ 27 ♔b6 ♖f8 28 ♔b7 ♖f7+ 29 ♔a6 ♖f8 30 ♖b2 1-0

11)

J. van der Wiel – Y. Seirawan
Haninge 1990

1...♖h5!

This contains the same idea as in the game Karpov-Knaak above: Black re-routes his rook to a better position behind his passed h-pawn. He intends to play ...♖d5-d7, followed by ...h5 and ...♖h7. 1...h5 gives White the possibility of activating his rook by ♖d8-a8, or ♖d8-h8 putting it behind the passed pawn.

2 ♖g4 ♔f7 3 b4

If 3 ♖f4+, Black can continue his plan like this: 3...♔g6 4 ♖f8 ♖d5+! 5 ♔e4 ♖d7! (Black is preparing to back up his passed pawn with ...h5 and

...♖h7) 6 ♖f1 h5 7 ♖h1 ♖h7 8 ♔f4 ♔f6 9 b4 h4 10 ♖h3 (White cannot win the pawn with 10 ♔g4, since he will lose any pawn endgame that may arise) 10...♖h6! (the position is getting closer to a zugzwang, because White is running out of reasonable moves) 11 a5 b5 12 ♖c3 h3 13 ♖c6+ ♔g7 14 ♖c7+ (the pawn endgame after 14 ♖xh6 ♔xh6 15 ♔g3 ♔g5 16 ♔xh3 ♔f4 is lost for White) 14...♔f8 15 ♖c1 ♔e7 16 ♔e5 ♖h5+ 17 ♔e4 h2 18 ♖h1 ♔d6 19 a6 ♖h4+ 20 ♔f3 ♔d5 21 ♔g3 ♖h6 22 ♔f4 ♔c4 and Black wins.

3...♔e5 4 ♔d4 ♖e6 5 ♔d5 h5 6 ♖h4 ♖h6!

Black has succeeded in putting his rook behind the passed pawn, and now wins the endgame by slowly pushing the white king back.

7 ♔e5 ♔g6 8 ♔f4 ♔f6 9 ♔g3 ♔e5 10 ♔h3 a6 11 ♖c4 ♔d5 12 ♖c8 ♖c6 13 ♖a8

If 13 ♖h8 then 13...♔c4 and the queenside pawns fall.

13...b5 14 axb5 axb5 15 ♖a1 ♖c4 0-1

After 16 ♖b1 ♖d4 17 ♔g3 ♔c4 18 ♔f3 ♔c3 Black wins the b-pawn and the game.

12)

A. Karpov – V. Hort
Budapest 1973

In bishop endings the theme of zugzwang is also of relevance. In the game there followed:

1 ♔e3 ♗g4 2 ♗d3 ♗e6 3 ♔d4 ♗g4 4 ♗c2

White now aims for a position in which the white bishop is on f3, while the black bishop is on e6 with Black to move. In that situation Black has to play ...♗f7 or ...♗g8, when White can reply ♗g4, threatening to enter the black position and win a pawn with ♗c8xa6.

4...♗e6 5 ♗b3

Another possibility is 5 ♗d1 ♗c8 6 ♗f3 ♗e6 7 a3, which also achieves the desired position. White always has the extra tempo of a2-a3, and this makes his task easier.

5...♗f7 6 ♗d1 ♗e6 7 ♗f3

White has reached his goal.

7...♗f7 8 ♗g4 1-0

White wins without big problems. A possible continuation is 8...♗g8 9 a3 ♗f7 10 ♗c8 ♔c6 11 ♔e5 and White penetrates the black position. (However, White should watch out for the last little trap 11 ♗xa6? ♗e6, which threatens to shut in the bishop and win it with ...♔b6.)

13)

Y. Averbakh
Bishop Endings (1977)

Another simple technical position in which White wins by creating a passed pawn on the queenside. When Black is preoccupied by stopping the pawn, the white king shifts to the kingside. Shredder 7.04 had the black pieces in this playout.

1 ♔f1 ♔f8 2 ♔e2 g6 3 ♔d3 ♔e7 4 ♔c4 ♔e6 5 b4 ♗b6 6 a4 ♔d6 7 f3 f5 8 ♗g3+ ♔c6 9 ♗e5

White puts his pieces on optimal squares before pushing the b-pawn. The bishop is transferred to d4 before pushing the b-pawn.

9...♗d8 10 ♗d4 ♗g5 11 b5+ ♔b7

After 11...axb5+ 12 axb5+ ♔b7 the white king can still go to the kingside and pick up pawns.

12 ♔d5 ♗d2

Shredder finds a way to win the b-pawn, but in the meantime White's king harasses the kingside.

13 ♔e6 f4 14 ♔f6 axb5 15 axb5 ♗e3 16 ♗e5 ♔b6 17 ♔g7 h5 18 ♔xg6 h4 19 ♔g5 ♗f2 20 ♗xf4 ♔xb5 21 ♔g4 ♔c6 22 ♗g5 1-0

The rest is easy.

14)

Y. Averbakh, V. Chekhover
Knight Endings (1977)

With knights on the board, the winning strategy is similar to the one with bishops. White centralizes his king, prepares to advance his queenside pawns, and finally creates a passed pawn. The many possible knight manoeuvres may be slightly confusing, so one has to take care and be aware of the opponent's possibilities. In this example the black pieces were once again played by Shredder.

1 ♔f1 ♘d5 2 ♔e2 ♔e7 3 a3

Limiting the scope of the black knight by denying it the b4-square.

3...♔d6 4 ♔d3 h5 5 g3

Covering the f4-square and getting ready to activate the knight.

5...f6 6 ♘c2 ♘e7 7 b4 g5 8 f3

Otherwise ...g4 might be annoying.

8...g4 9 f4 ♔e6 10 ♘e3 ♘c8 11 a4 ♘d6 12 ♔d4 ♔d7 13 ♔d5 ♘c8 14 a5 ♘d6 15 f5 ♘e8 16 b5 ♘d6 17 b6 axb6 18 axb6 ♘e8 19 ♘c4

The black knight gets still fewer squares.

19...♘g7 20 ♘d6 1-0

There are no sensible moves left. If 20...h4 then 21 gxh4 ♘h5 22 ♘b5, and Black loses more material.

15)

J. Speelman

Endgame Preparation (1981)

In this queen endgame White wins by cutting out any possibility of checking with the black queen. The following line is given by Speelman:

1 ♕b7! h5 2 a6

The a-pawn wins.

2...h4 3 a7 ♕g4 4 h3 ♕d4 5 a8♕

16)

J. Speelman

Endgame Preparation (1981)

Jonathan Speelman gives the winning strategy for Black:

1) Black drives White's pieces back so as to get his own king to e2 and his rook to f3.

2) After this he advances ...f5-f4.

3) The rook moves from f3 gaining a tempo on the bishop, after which ...f3 is played, to be followed by ...♖xf2.

Speelman gives the following analysis:

1...♔f6 2 ♔f4 ♖d5 3 ♗a7 ♖f5+ 4 ♔e4 ♔e6 5 ♗e3 ♖a5 6 ♔f4 ♖b5 7

♗a7 ♖f5+ 8 ♔e4 ♖a5 9 ♗e3 ♖a4+ 10 ♔f3 ♔f5 11 ♗b6 ♖a3+ 12 ♔g2 ♔e4 13 ♗c5 ♖a6 14 ♗e3 ♔d3 15 ♔f1 ♖a1+ 16 ♔g2 ♔e2 17 ♗c5 ♖b1 18 ♗e3 ♖b3 19 ♗d4 ♖f3

First stage completed.

20 ♗c5 f5 21 ♗b6 f4

Second stage completed.

22 ♗a7

22 gxf4 ♖xf4 23 ♔g3 ♖g4+ 24 ♔h3 ♔f3 followed by ...♖g2xf2 wins.

22...♖a3 23 ♗c5 f3+ 24 ♔h2 ♖a1 25 ♗e3 ♖f1 26 ♗d4 ♖xf2+!

Third stage completed, and Black wins.

However, when I played this position out with Fritz 8 as White, things went slightly differently.

1...♔f6 2 ♔e4 ♔e6 3 ♗d4 ♖b7

In this specific position 3...f5+ 4 ♔e3 f4+! 5 gxf4 ♔f5 is an interesting idea that also leads to a won position for Black.

4 f3?!

In his notes to this position Speelman did not mention what to do if White starts pushing the pawns, so now I am on my own. It soon becomes clear, however, that moving the pawns creates an opening that will help Black when attacking the white pawns later on. Black continues by pushing back the white pieces.

4...♖b4 5 ♔e3 ♔d5 6 ♗g7 ♔e6 7 ♗d4 ♔f5 8 ♗c3 ♖b3 9 ♔d3

The move f3 has made White's position much more unstable, because the bishop does not have any safe place to rest any longer (in the previous line it had e3). Moreover, the white pawns are easier to hit for the black rook when the pawn itself is on f3. The pawn does not cover g3 any longer, and on f3 it cannot be covered by the bishop.

9...♖a3 10 ♔c4 f6 11 ♔b4

White had to go all the way to b4 with his king to get rid of the annoying rook.

11...♖a8 12 g4+

Trying to exchange some pawns, but Black wins anyway. On any other move the white kingside pawns would have been easy targets because of the off-side position of the white king.

12...hxg4 13 fxg4+ ♔xg4 14 ♗xf6 ♖f8 15 ♗e7 ♖h8 16 ♔c4 ♖xh4 17 ♔d4

17 ♗xh4 ♔xh4 is of course lost for White.

17...g5 18 ♔e3 ♖h2 19 ♗d8 ♖g2 20 ♗b6 ♔h3 21 ♔e4 g4 22 ♔d3 ♖b2 0-1

17)
Ni Hua – Ye Jiangchuan
Tan Chin Nam Cup, Shanghai 2001

This kind of position has been known by theory since the days of Philidor more than 200 years ago. Black can win because the white king is on the edge of the board.

This exercise is rather difficult to solve if you do not know the winning idea. You should play through the following moves and try it several times against your program. It takes some time to master this ending, but when

you get the main idea I can recommend trying out some more positions with ♔+♖+♗ vs ♔+♖ to be sure that you can apply your knowledge to other positions as well. To get some variation in the defence you can play this position against the program with and without tablebases.

1...♖g1+ 2 ♖e1 ♖g2 3 ♖e7

On 3 ♖e6 comes 3...♖d2+ 4 ♔e1 (4 ♔c1 is met by 4...♖a2) 4...♖b2 5 ♔f1 ♖f2+ 6 ♔e1 ♖f5 (threatening ...♗c3+ and ...♖f1+) 7 ♖d6 ♖g5 and Black wins.

3...♖h2!

Forcing the rook to the eighth rank, where it will be in a worse position.

4 ♖e8 ♖b2 5 ♖c8

5 ♔c1 is met by 5...♖a2 6 ♖b8 ♖g2 7 ♔b1 ♖g1+ 8 ♔a2 ♖a1+ 9 ♔b3 ♖b1+ winning the rook.

5...♗b6!

This is the key move. Now it is clear why Black wanted the white rook to be on the eighth rank. If the white rook were on the seventh rank, White would have an annoying check on d7.

6 ♔c1 ♖b5

Threatening ...♗e3+ and ...♖b1+.

7 ♔d1 ♖f5 8 ♖e8

8 ♔c1 is met by 8...♗d4 mating; for instance, 9 ♔b1 ♖a5.

8...♗a5 9 ♔c1 ♗c3

9...♖b5 is a quicker way to mate due to the threat of ...♗d2+ and ...♖b1#, but Black wins anyway.

10 ♖d8+ ♗d4 0-1

The game is over, because of 11 ♔b1 ♖a5 mating.

10 Playing Chess on the Internet

No matter how hard we tried to involve television – we failed. The Internet completely changes the disposition. The Net restores the interconnection between chess professionals and a huge chess audience.
GARRY KASPAROV, World Champion 1985-2000

The Internet has opened up a lot of new possibilities for chess-players. We now have chess clubs that are open 24 hours a day, 7 days a week, and with chess-players from many different countries. We can watch grandmasters play live or follow the games of the world elite while analysing their games with a computer program.

The largest and best-known chess server is the **Internet Chess Club** (**ICC**), which is a pay service (but free for GMs and IMs if they make their name public). Every week it has online relays of international chess tournaments, and it is the server that has the most titled players. Thus ICC is the best choice if you are a strong player.

However, there are several free alternatives. One is the **Free Internet Chess Server** (**FICS**), which is a good service and the largest of the free chess servers. A newer alternative is **World Chess Network**, which also has some titled players and is well-known for 'banter chess', which is games between grandmasters that are commenting upon the games while they play. Additionally, I have listed some more alternative chess servers in the bookmark section of the book.

Also chess-playing programs like Fritz and Chessmaster now have chess servers connected to them. At present the Chessmaster server at Ubi.com is not so much visited, but the ChessBase server at Playchess.com is getting more popular and it may become a serious competitor to ICC as the main place to play online chess in some years.

Playing on the chess servers is a good way of keeping oneself in form and mentally prepared for a game or a tournament. If you have not played chess for some months, it is a good training opportunity to log in and play 5-10 blitz games for two or three evenings some days before taking part in a tournament or playing an important game. Playing blitz training games helps you to calculate a bit faster, your play becomes more stable, and your tournament results will be better.

I believe that online blitz games can also help you when working on your opening repertoire. On most chess servers it is possible to 'log' your games, and after having played 10 blitz games one evening, you can make some quick checks against your database to see how your opening play could be improved. Naturally, you can also analyse logged games with a computer engine, but blitz games are rarely interesting enough for longer analysis. Another interesting use of logged online games is to run statistics on your openings. For instance, after playing some hundred blitz games, you can merge all your white games into one, to see in which openings your score is not good enough. By doing this, it is easy to identify the lines that are the most troublesome and the variations in which you could benefit from doing some more work.

On ICC games can be logged by checking the function on or off in the 'Game' menu. This creates a file with your games in PGN (Portable Game Notation) format, which can be read by all chess programs. Chess Assistant has ICC incorporated as a part of the program, so if you own Chess Assistant, handling the online games is quite easy. With Chess Assistant you get a one-month free membership of ICC, but if you want to continue after that you have to pay.

A Few Search Tips for ICC

I am going to skip most of the basic information about how ICC works, as this information can be found in the help files available on the Internet.

Instead I will give a few tips on how to search for information on the server. In general, the 'help' and 'info' commands are useful ways to learn how the interface works.

If you know that you are going to play a serious tournament against a player who has a handle on ICC, you will be able to get a little additional information about him from the games he played on the server. Naturally, blitz games are not as important as the 'serious' games you can find in the main databases, and you should not necessarily expect your opponent to play the same lines he did in some online games. However, you may still be able to figure out something about your opponent. He could have been testing some opening improvement in a blitz game – you never know.

If you know the name of his handle, it makes your task easier. Otherwise you have to ask a 'search robot'. This is done by typing, for instance, 'tell searchbot name dreev' in the main console, if you want to find out under which accounts Alexei Dreev has played on ICC. I find that Dreev has used the two accounts 'Dreev' and 'Igrok'.

The search robot has more than 20,000 names in the database. However, some people choose to stay anonymous on ICC, and in that case you have no way of finding the name of their account. For more information about how to use the search robot, type 'finger searchbot'.

You can find a player's latest games by using the 'history' command; for instance, 'history dreev' gives me the last twenty games played by Alexei Dreev on the ICC server. However, Dreev has played more than a thousand games on ICC. Some of those can be seen by using the 'search' command, which gives access to an ICC one million+ database with games mostly including titled players. All games with GMs, IMs or WGMs are added to the database, except for bullet games (two minutes or less for the whole game), and also games in which both players are rated 2300 or higher and the time control is longer than 3 minutes for the whole game are included.

When typing 'search Dreev' in the main console, I get a search result of 904 games. Moreover, I can add other parameters to the search. For instance, 'search dreev eco=c1" gives me 28 games with Dreev and the ECO codes C10 to C19. The search by opening is useful if you want to check if your opponent has any games in the database with a specific opening. There are other good search possibilities, which you can learn more about by typing 'help search'.

In general I can recommend testing the demo-version from the various servers to see which one suits you best and to find out if you are ready to pay for one of the services. ICC has a free trial period of one week.

11 Computer Chess in the Future

The reality in 2001 is that a palmtop computer equipped with a 0.13 micron CMOS chess chip would have a decent chance to beat him [Garry Kasparov]. If you want to get fancy, you can even fit the entire machine into a cola can. It would be one very expensive can, but it can be done.
FENG-HSIUNG HSU, creator of Deep Blue

The advances of chess-playing computer programs have more than anything else been fuelled by the speedy developments in the hardware industry. Without the fast processors of today the chess programs would not be anywhere near their current strength.

In 1965 Intel co-founder Gordon Moore observed an exponential growth in the number of transistors per integrated circuit and predicted that this trend would continue. Since then there has been a doubling of transistors around every second year, and this has later been known as 'Moore's Law'.

The doubling of the computer power means that there has also been a huge increase in the speed with which a computer can analyse chess positions. In 2003 the fastest processors commercially available are around 3 GHz, and Gordon Moore has recently stated

that he expects his 'law' to roll on for another decade. What will happen at that time is unclear. Some have implied that there may be a slowdown because the industry will start reaching the physical limits to what degree a transistor size can be shrunk. Moreover, there are exponential increases in the costs as each reduction takes place, and this may seriously reduce the speed of the development. Other experts believe that nanotechnology will be able to continue Moore's Law for as far as 30 years. No matter what, it seems unlikely that the computer industry will suddenly hit a wall in the near future.

Following Moore's Law for another 10 years means that in 2013 there will be five doublings of the computer power, which leads to processors of a speed around 100 GHz. Fantasizing about where we may be in 2030 is obviously clear speculation. However, if Moore's Law continues until that time, computers may be about ten thousand times faster than the ones we have today. Naturally, it is at present far beyond human comprehension what we could do with computers with so much power, and it is impossible to say how such an amazing speed could be transformed into Elo points.

Some experts have suggested that increased search depth has diminishing returns, i.e. going from ply 6 to 7 gives a higher Elo increase than going from ply 13 to 14. Moreover, the chess tree has an exponential nature that makes it very time-consuming to analyse a chess position one level deeper. This can most easily be explained by the old story where you put a grain of rice on the first square, two on the second, four on the third and so on. When you get to the second half of the chess board, each successive doubling is enormous. Likewise, going from ply 3 to 4 is not very time-consuming, but from ply 13 to 14 can take a lot of time, and the time grows exponentially with each ply. A computer around 1,000 times faster than the fastest computer of today may be able to go around 5 plies deeper than now. This should make the chess programs very hard to beat in practical tournament chess for nearly anyone, but it will not solve some of the main problems for computer programs on an overall level. Major concepts in chess such as positional planning and fortress draws will still be troublesome even when computers are searching five plies deeper. Naturally, computers will play better positional chess if they search deeper, but there may still be positions in which they would play nonsense moves, because of the problems connected to lack of long-term planning. In Chapter 3 (page 43) we saw an example of Fritz searching several billion positions without understanding anything about the fortress position it was analysing. I am convinced that analysing trillions of positions instead of billions would not change anything significantly as long as the program does not understand what it is seeing. Thus software improvements are necessary to make the program play well in all areas of the game. If the problems with fortress draws and positional planning are not solved, the programs may hit an Elo wall, or at least experience a marked slowdown compared to the current development in strength. If these holes in their knowledge persist, strong players will still be able to set up fortresses and draw against the programs in some games.

So what will happen if (or when) the programs gain several hundred more Elo points and will be able to beat the human world champion convincingly in a match?

Not very much I guess. As I have mentioned before, computers are already way beyond most of the chess-playing population, and they can easily find tactical mistakes in games at all levels. I believe, however, that we are still very far from the day when computers can master all areas of chess better than humans. Winning a match against the human world champion may be possible sometime during the next 10 years, because of the fact that computers are difficult opponents in practical tournament play. They are seldom affected of problems like time trouble, and exterior and psychological factors, such as nerves or tiredness, are of course only relevant for humans. For this reason, computers have a huge advantage in over-the-board chess.

Theoretically however, it is very likely that there will be areas of the game which will cause problems for the programs for many years to come. Thus I believe that future development in chess will see humans and computers working together to achieve greater insights into chess.

The cooperation between man and machine has also been the main issue in this book. I believe the synthesis of human knowledge, intuition and creativity combined with computer calculation and accuracy is an excellent blend for chess analysis. It is important to perceive the whole issue as a question of man and machine **working together** rather than a fight between the two.

I hope that this book will help chess-players to understand how to benefit from the possibilities that computers offer. One of the challenges for the programmers is to develop better software, focusing not only on the strength of the engines, but also on improving the chess software's capabilities to explain and instruct. The strength of the programs has reached a sufficient level. What we need now is software that improves the possibilities in our chess training and helps us to understand the game better.

Finally, I would like to emphasize that the whole discussion of computers in chess is mostly of interest if it can be used for a better understanding of games where two humans are playing against each other. Thus, when you have read this book, I recommend you join your local chess club – if you are not already a member.

Good luck with your chess training!

Bookmarks on the Internet

Commercial Chess Database Programs

ChessBase
www.chessbase.com

Chess Assistant
www.chessassistant.com

Chess Academy
www.chessacademy.com

BookUp
www.bookup.com

Free Database Programs

Scid (Shane's Chess Information Database)
http://scid.sourceforge.net

ChessBase Light
www.chessbase.com/download/cblight

Chess Assistant Light (and other demo-versions from Chess Assistant)
www.convekta.com/downloads.asp

Chess News Websites

The Week In Chess
www.chesscenter.com/twic/twic.html

Chess Café
www.chesscafe.com

WorldChessRating.com
www.worldchessrating.com

FIDE
www.fideonline.com
Homepage of the international chess federation with ratings and some news.

Chess Program Reviews
www.chessreviews.com
Robert Pawlak's site with reviews of chess software.

Commercial Chess Programs

Lokasoft
www.lokasoft.com/uk
Lokasoft sells the ChessPartner interface and the engines Chess Tiger and Deep Sjeng amongst others.

ChessBase
www.chessbase.com
ChessBase sells the engines Fritz, Hiarcs, Shredder, Junior, Nimzo and many more.

Chessmaster
www.chessmaster.com
The Chessmaster program, sold by Ubisoft.

Free Chess Programs

Arena Chess GUI
www.playwitharena.com
Arena is an attractive graphical user interface for use with most engines. This site also has engines for downloads and close to 200 links to various chess engines.

Timm Mann's chess pages
www.tim-mann.org/chess.html
A site with information about the Winboard interface and links to 175 chess engines, of which most are free.

Homepage for chess engines
http://wbec-ridderkerk.nl
More free chess engines.

Free engines for use in ChessBase programs
www.chessbase.com/download/index.asp?cat=Engines
www.chessbase.com/download/index.asp?cat=UCI-Engines
Includes engines such as List, Crafty and Sjeng for use within ChessBase and the Fritz interface.
Other downloads from ChessBase can be found at www.chessbase.com/download

Tutorial Programs

Chess Mentor
www.chess.com

Electronic Chess Boards

DGT Projects
www.dgtprojects.com
Homepage of the Dutch company DGT Projects, with drivers for the DGT electronic chess board

Shahcom
www.ruschess.com/Shahcom/Shahcom.html

Novag
www.novag.com

Free Tactical Test Positions

http://webplaza.pt.lu/ckaber
www.mailchess.de/engl/indexe.html

Internet Chess Clubs

ICC (Internet Chess Club)
www.chessclub.com

World Chess Network
www.worldchessnetwork.com

Chess.net
www.chess.net

Free Internet Chess Server
www.freechess.org

Chess Programming

Ed Schröder's pages about Rebel
http://members.home.nl/matador/chess840.htm

The Computer-Chess Club discussion forum
www.talkchess.com

Description of the program Dark Thought
http://supertech.lcs.mit.edu/~heinz/dt/

Bruce Moreland's (author of Ferret) programming page
www.seanet.com/~brucemo/topics/topics.htm

Games Download

ChessBase's online database
www.chesslive.de
Currently includes 2.5 million games

The Week in Chess games download
www.chesscenter.com/twic/twicp.html
Weekly updated games section with thousands of games from the best tournaments all over the world

University of Pittsburgh
www.pitt.edu/~schach/
The University of Pittsburgh's chess archives with lots of games for download

Chesslab
www.chesslab.com
A searchable online game database

Ftp Sites

Robert Hyatt's site
ftp://ftp.cis.uab.edu/pub/hyatt
The site contains the program Crafty, endgame tablebases and much more.

Dann Corbit's site
ftp://cap.connx.com
Contains huge game databases, CAP (the computer analysis project) data, test suites for computer programs, tons of chess engines, etc.

Internet Newsgroups

rec.games.chess.computer
rec.games.chess.analysis
rec.games.chess.misc

Bibliography

About Computer Chess

M.M. Botvinnik: *Computers, Chess, and Long-Range Planning*, English Universities Press, 1970

M.M. Botvinnik: *Computers in Chess: Solving Inexact Search Problems*, Springer-Verlag, 1984

M. Crowther, *Chess on the Net*, Everyman, 2001

P. W. Frey, *Chess Skill in Man and Machine*, Springer-Verlag, 1977

T.D. Harding, *The Chess Computer Book*, Pergamon Press, 1981

F. Hsu, *Behind Deep Blue*, Princeton University Press, 2002

J. Kaplan, *How to Get the Most from Your Chess Computer*, R.H.M. Press, 1980

D. Levy, *The Chess Computer Handbook*, Batsford, 1984

D. Levy, *Computer Chess Compendium*, Batsford, 1988

D. Levy and M. Newborn, *How Computers Play Chess*, Computer Science Press, 1991

M. Newborn, *Kasparov versus Deep Blue: Computer Chess Comes of Age*, Springer-Verlag, 1997

M. Newborn, *Computer Chess*, Academic Press, 1975

M. Newborn, *Deep Blue: An Artificial Intelligence Milestone*, Springer-Verlag, 2003

R. J. Pawlak, *Chess Software Sourcebook*, Treehaus Books, 2000

About Chess in General

A. Beliavsky and A. Mikhalchishin, *Winning Endgame Technique*, Batsford, 1995

G. Burgess, *The Mammoth Book of Chess*, Robinson, 1997

J. R. Capablanca, *Capablancas schackskola*, Prisma, 1969

I. Chernev, *Capablanca's Best Chess Endings*, Dover, 1978

P. Dürrfeld, *12 skakmyter*, Information, 2000

M. Dvoretsky, *School of Chess Excellence 1 – Endgame Analysis*, Edition Olms, 2001

M. Dvoretsky and A. Yusupov, *Training for the Tournament Player*, Batsford, 1993

M. Dvoretsky and A. Yusupov, *Opening Preparation*, Batsford, 1994

J. Gizycki, *Den store skakbog*, Stig Jensens Forlag, 1965

I. Linder, *Das Schachgenie Capablanca*, Sportverlag Berlin, 1987

J. Nunn, *Secrets of Practical Chess*, Gambit, 1998

J. Nunn, G. Burgess, J. Emms and J. Gallagher, *Nunn's Chess Openings*, Everyman/Gambit, 1999

J. Nunn, *Secrets of Rook Endings* (2nd edition), Gambit, 1999

S. Pedersen, *The Gambit Guide to the Benko Gambit*, Gambit, 1999

T. Rosenlund, *Politikens lærebog i skak (med afsnit om computerskak)*, Politiken, 1999

M. Schereschewski, *Strategie der Schachendspiele*, Sportverlag Berlin, 1985

J. Speelman, *Endgame Preparation*, Batsford, 1981

J. Aagaard, *Excelling at Chess*, Everyman, 2001

ChessBase Magazine issues 58, 82, 89 and 91.

Index

Games

When a player's name appears in bold, that player had White. Otherwise the first-named player had White.

Human vs Human

Computer vs Computer

Human vs Computer

Computers